Violence Elsewhere 1

Studies in German Literature, Linguistics, and Culture

Violence Elsewhere 1

Imagining Distant Violence in Germany 1945–2001

Edited by
Clare Bielby and Mererid Puw Davies

CAMDEN HOUSE
Rochester, New York

Copyright © 2024 by the Editors and Contributors

The eBook edition of this book is available under the Open Access Licence CC BY-NC-ND. This book, including the Open Access edition, is funded by University College London.

Some rights reserved. Without limiting the rights under copyright reserved above, any part of this book may be reproduced, stored in or introduced into a retrieval system, or transmitted, in any form or by any means (electronic, mechanical, photocopying, recording or otherwise)

First published 2024 by Camden House

Camden House is an imprint of Boydell & Brewer Inc.
668 Mt. Hope Avenue, Rochester, NY 14620, USA
and of Boydell & Brewer Limited
PO Box 9, Woodbridge, Suffolk IP12 3DF, UK
www.boydellandbrewer.com

ISBN-13: 978-1-64014-114-8 (hardcover);
978-1-64014-216-9 (paperback)

Library of Congress Cataloging-in-Publication Data

CIP data is available from the Library of Congress.

The publisher has no responsibility for the continued existence or accuracy of URLs for external or third-party internet websites referred to in this book, and does not guarantee that any content on such websites is, or will remain, accurate or appropriate.

Contents

List of Illustrations — vii

Acknowledgments — ix

Introduction — 1
   Clare Bielby and Mererid Puw Davies

1: Projecting Violence Elsewhere: Remembering Conflict-Related Sexual Violence in Cold War Germany — 18
   Katherine Stone

2: Watching Violence Elsewhere: Louis Malle's *Viva Maria!* in 1960s West Germany — 38
   Mererid Puw Davies

3: Images as Weapons: DEFA, Studio H&S, and the Global Cold War — 60
   Seán Allan

4: *KriegsErklärung* (Declaration of War): Volker Braun's Cold War Camera — 81
   J. J. Long

5: The Vietnam Veteran in Anna Seghers's *Steinzeit* (Stone Age, 1975) — 104
   Ernest Schonfield

6: "So It Has to Be Said: Hammer and Sickle Here, Hammer and Sickle There": Heynowski-Scheumann's *Die Angkar* (1981) and the Problem of *Khmer Rouge* Violence for the GDR — 127
   Martin Brady

7: Narrating Violent Agency Elsewhere in Inge Viett's *Nie war ich furchtloser* (Never Was I More Fearless, 1996) — 149
   Clare Bielby

8: Problematizing Political Violence in the Federal Republic of Germany: A Hauntological Analysis of the NSU Terror and a Hyper-Exceptionalized "9/11"   174
Katharina Karcher and Evelien Geerts

Selected Bibliography   197

Notes on the Contributors   209

Index   213

Illustrations

3.1 *Piloten im Pyjama* (Pilots in Pajamas, Studio H&S, 1967) 73

3.2 *Piloten im Pyjama* (Studio H&S, 1968) 74

3.3 *Fünf Patronenhülsen* (Five Cartridges, Frank Beyer, 1960) 75

4.1 "Die New Yorker Börse" (The New York Stock Exchange) 89

4.2 "Kreativität" (Creativity) 92

4.3 "Flakstellung in einem Dorf bei Thai Nguyen" (Flak Installation in a Village near Thai Nguyen) 94

4.4 "Die Straße" (The Street) 100

4.5 "Im Freistaat Bayern" (In the Free State of Bavaria) 102

6.1 Shedding light on "and" (Jean-Luc Godard, Anne-Marie Miéville, *Ici et ailleurs*, 1976) 136

6.2 Shedding light on "and" (Jean-Luc Godard, Anne-Marie Miéville, *Ici et ailleurs*, 1976) 136

6.3 Constructing meaning (Heynowski-Scheumann, *Die Angkar*, 1981) 143

6.4 Chinese propaganda in American cans (Heynowski-Scheumann, *Die Angkar*, 1981) 143

Acknowledgments

THIS COLLECTED VOLUME of essays emerged from a research project titled "Violence Elsewhere: Imagining Violence outside Germany since 1945," which we co-led from the Centre for Women's Studies (CWS) at the University of York and the School of European Languages, Cultures and Society-Centre for Multidisciplinary Intercultural Inquiry (SELCS-CMII) at University College London (UCL).

Neither the project, nor this volume showcasing some of its work, could have come into being without generous funding from 2018 to 2021 from the Deutscher Akademischer Austauchdienst/German Academic Exchange Service through its "Promoting German Studies" program. We thank the German Academic Exchange Service very warmly, and Katie James, in particular, for her collegial support throughout the project's lifetime.

At the University of York, we wish to acknowledge material and administrative support from CWS, the Department of English and Related Literature, and the Professional Services teams at the Humanities Research Centre and Research Grants Operations. At UCL, we express our thanks to the Institute for Advanced Studies for hosting and supporting our events and the Professional Services team at SELCS-CMII for its support.

We wish to thank Volker Braun for his very kind permission to reproduce poems and images from his work *KriegsErklärung* (Declaration of War), which is discussed in chapter 4.

We are also grateful to our colleagues at York and UCL more broadly for their continued interest in, and support in many practical and moral forms for, the work of the "Violence Elsewhere" project and for this publication.

We are indebted to all at Camden House, and most especially to Jim Walker for his wise guidance and editorial counsel throughout the development and publication of this volume. We wish also to acknowledge the anonymous peer reviewers who advised on the manuscript.

Especially warm thanks are due to the Core Group of scholars who animated and sustained "Violence Elsewhere," as well as the publication of this book: Katharina Karcher, Susanne Knittel, Birga Meyer, Katherine Stone, and Lizzie Stewart.

In particular, we would like to highlight the many contributions of the project's two project coordinators, Francesca Lewis and Kathrin

Wunderlich. They not only furthered its research in key ways through discussions and events but also conceptualized, designed, developed, and maintained its online presence in the form of its website, blog, bibliography, and other resources. We also thank Sarah Colvin for her support early on in the project's development.

In addition, we are grateful to Francesca Lewis for the project artwork from which the design of this volume's cover evolved, and to Beckie Rutherford for compiling its index.

We also wish here to thank the authors of the chapters in this volume for their gracious and patient collaboration.

Finally, we wish to express our appreciation to the scholars, artists, and activists who participated in the "Violence Elsewhere" project at various times and in many ways: at its events and seminars, in discussions of many kinds beyond them, and in the development of this volume. We are grateful for all their work and ideas, which enriched and deepened it.

Introduction

Clare Bielby and Mererid Puw Davies

EVERY VIOLENT ENCOUNTER is complex, and so too is its representation. Owing, however, to Germany's history of extreme violence and war in the twentieth century, imagining and depicting violence in postwar Germany has been fraught and challenging in distinctive, acute ways. As a result, it can be difficult to locate and explore critically the significance of violence in and for the postwar German states. And yet, this inquiry matters, as we look back at a century of violence in many forms from a time in which it has by no means been laid to rest. A nuanced understanding of what violence is in its many manifestations, and of how that violence resonates through time in ways which are sometimes overwhelming, sometimes subliminal, allows a better understanding of an often difficult present. In turn, such insight allows us to reflect more broadly on relationships between violence, history, culture, community, and the creation of identities.

This book makes the case that thinking about violence elsewhere in the German context can provide a new, productive lens through which to view this issue.[1] By violence elsewhere, we mean constructions of violence taking place in distant, imagined, or temporally distinct times and places. As the chapters in this volume demonstrate, critical analysis of such constructions allows us better to examine ideas about violence in, around, and in relation to postwar Germany itself. Violence elsewhere, as the volume argues of the period 1945–2001, has offered a stage where violence could become imaginable and representable for what could loosely be termed the German imaginary. Moreover, because, as literary critic Arlene A. Teraoka puts it, "discourse about others" is

---

1 This volume emerges from a research project titled "Violence Elsewhere: Imagining Violence outside Germany since 1945." The project, based at University College London and the University of York and funded by the Deutscher Akademischer Austauschdienst (German Academic Exchange Service), ran from 2018 to 2021. For further details, including the project team and events, see the project website, updated April 21, 2022, https://sites.google.com/york.ac.uk/violence-elsewhere/home.

"self-referential,"[2] representations of violence elsewhere are simultaneously images of Germany itself. Thus, such representations reveal something about otherwise submerged or deeply encoded meanings and functions of violence in German cultures.

In pursuit of this inquiry, the case studies that follow consider a range of forms, texts, and genres; for instance, film, photography, narrative fiction, poetry, theory, autobiography, political and legal texts, journalism, speeches, and ephemera, as well as wider public discourses. Engagement with this varied corpus shows that close, often symptomatic analysis of texts of all kinds can be remarkably revealing about the (competing or contradictory) impulses and outlooks of a culture. To this end, our volume draws on perspectives from cultural, literary, film, visual, and gender studies and introduces theoretical approaches to the topic of violence elsewhere that may be transferable between disciplines and beyond German studies.

Scholarly conversations on violence are rightly expansive, ranging from conceptualizations of "normative violence," through "discursive violence," to "structural" and "slow" violence, among other ideas.[3] The chapters in this volume, however, for the most part concentrate on those notions of violence that perhaps come most quickly to mind for many: that is, on physical acts that do bodily harm in immediate ways.[4] They also focus, albeit not exclusively, on what tends to be understood as

---

2   Arlene A. Teraoka, *East, West, and Others: The Third World in Postwar German Literature* (Lincoln: University of Nebraska Press, 1996), 1.

3   On "normative violence," see Judith Butler, "Preface (1999)," in *Gender Trouble: Feminism and the Subversion of Identity*, 10th Anniversary Edition (London: Routledge, 1999), vii–xxvi; on "discursive violence," see Krystal A. Smalls, "Fighting Words: Anti-Blackness and Discursive Violence in an American High School," *Journal of Linguistic Anthropology* 28, no. 3 (2018): 356–83; on "structural violence," see Johan Galtung, "Violence, Peace, and Peace Research," *Journal of Peace Research* 6, no. 3 (1969): 167–91; on "slow violence," see Rob Nixon, *Slow Violence and the Environmentalism of the Poor* (Cambridge, MA: Harvard University Press, 2011). There also exist myriad conceptualizations of violence in other terms; for example, Boaventura de Sousa Santos's notion of "epistemicide" in *Epistemologies of the South: Justice against Epistemicide* (Boulder, CO: Paradigm, 2014).

4   See Nixon, *Slow Violence*, on how questions of temporality shape what tends to be understood as violence. With reference to what is recognized as *physical* violence, feminist scholarship on sexual violence has demonstrated the long-term physical and psychic harm of sexual violence and harassment, beyond the immediate act of rape or other kinds of sexual assault. In addition, feminist affect studies, with its attention to, for instance, fear and shame and to what these affects/emotions "do" to bodies, is particularly well equipped to problematize what counts as physical violence from a feminist perspective.

political violence.[5] Thus, key forms of violence under discussion here include terrorism, state violence, wars and revolutions and their aftermaths, and conflict-related sexual violence (CRSV).

Likewise, the chapters turn frequently to what might be considered self-evident: geographical ideas of elsewhere. They focus primarily on events in, or works about, other countries, as they could be imagined, represented, or debated in Germany. The works and representations in question stage violence taking place, for example, in Latin America, Vietnam, Cambodia, the USA, and the Middle East. And since during the Cold War period, the geopolitical elsewhere for inhabitants of both German states included the "other" Germany, this remarkable circumstance is addressed here also. Furthermore, the chapters consider violence that is elsewhere in other ways, whether it is from another time or from a fictional world. They think at times too about different spaces, like other kinds of subjects or subjectivities, as elsewhere.

Yet even as we think about other places and eras, we wish to interrogate reductive notions of here and there, then and now, or home and elsewhere. In his study *Foreign Front: Third World Politics in Sixties West Germany*, historian Quinn Slobodian has observed that there are political and ethical dangers in mobilizing categories of "self" and "other" (or in our terms "here" and "elsewhere," "then" and "now") to investigate "how cultural self-understanding is constructed." "The perverse legacy of [Edward] Said's Orientalism," argues Slobodian, "has been that modern European historians pay attention to 'the East' primarily as a mirror with which to see the West more clearly. When applied to the 1960s, the actual agency of individuals in the Third World, and Third World individuals in West Germany, can vanish as they become shadows of Germans themselves on geographically far-flung cave walls."[6] Reading Slobodian's work at a crucial point in our project's development proved instructive, compelling us to think more searchingly about the place of the "other" within it and to look beyond binary notions of "here" and "elsewhere."

The chapters that follow share an interest in what our subtitle identifies as "Germany." They explore selected emblematic works and cultural and political moments from the Federal Republic of Germany (FRG; West Germany), the Democratic Republic of Germany (GDR; East Germany), or both; some reflect on unified Germany after 1990. Yet we recognize that these terms of engagement are (deceptively) difficult.

---

5   On troubling what counts as "political violence," see Clare Bielby, "Gendering the Perpetrator; Gendering Perpetrator Studies," in *The Routledge International Handbook of Perpetrator Studies*, ed. Susanne C. Knittel and Zachary J. Goldberg (London: Routledge, 2020), 155–68, here 164.

6   Quinn Slobodian, *Foreign Front: Third World Politics in Sixties West Germany* (Durham, NC: Duke University Press, 2012), 10, 11.

The cultures of the different Germanies under discussion demand differentiated reflection, as do their commonalities, including their shared pasts and futures. In addition, this volume aims to widen understandings of what is, or could be, German. It notes the complexity and diversity of German identity, both within and outside the country, drawing in, for instance, experiences of people with diverse cultural or international backgrounds. It examines too the ways in which German subjects have engaged with transnational movements and connected or identified with ideas, people, places, even objects (from) elsewhere. In so doing, they were able to "[imagine] themselves into the world" in different ways.[7] At times, the studies in this book highlight intimate connections between Germany and (supposedly) elsewhere, in ways that relativize or collapse the apparently essential distinctions between them. Simultaneously, work toward this volume has involved reflection on ways in which people, works, impulses, and discourses originating outside Germany can circulate within it, and so be of it.

In other words, one objective of this collection is to open up a more inclusive understanding of what "Germany" or "German" can mean in a global world, and thereby to contribute to a growing body of scholarship that seeks to expand understandings of German studies.[8] Or, put more theoretically, we wish to use our book's starting premise, as expressed in its title, at the same time as a prompt to reflect on the ways in which subjectivities, discourses, languages, cultures, and artifacts can be limited by assigning to them static or essential national or cultural identities. In fact, they can be plural and constantly crisscross and change one another.

The temporal focus of the volume (1945–2001) reflects the widely held view that the events of September 11, 2001, marked a historical caesura, after which certain forms of violence appeared transnationally mobile in new, spectacular ways. As Rob Nixon argues with reference to what he terms "slow violence," September 11 had a powerful impact on what would from then onward be recognizable as violence and what would not: "The fiery spectacle of the collapsing towers was burned into the [US] national psyche as *the* definitive image of violence, setting back by years attempts to rally public sentiment against climate change, a threat that is incremental, exponential, and far less sensationally visible."[9]

---

7 Timothy S. Brown, "'1968' East and West: Divided Germany as a Case Study in Transnational History," *American Historical Review* 114, no. 1 (February 2009): 69–96, here 70.

8 See, for example, Rebecca Braun and Benedict Schofield, eds., *Transnational German Studies* (Liverpool: Liverpool University Press, 2020). See also the network H-Transnational German Studies, updated July 20, 2023, https://networks.h-net.org/h-tgs.

9 Nixon, *Slow Violence*, 13.

The same is true of European countries. Nonetheless, while we retain this understanding of the significance of September 11, 2001, in broad terms, as the final chapter of this volume argues, the terrorist attacks on that date, simultaneously yet indirectly, facilitated the perpetuation of certain understandings of violence in the FRG, rather than changing them. The idea of September 11 as a crucial turning point is therefore not straightforward: complex continuities run through the year 2001 and beyond.

* * *

This volume collects eight chapters on the theme of violence elsewhere as it appears in mostly, but not exclusively, German-language sources, from the immediate postwar period to 2001. The chapters appear in broadly chronological order and identify especially revealing representations of violence elsewhere that also have wider significance.

In the first chapter, Katherine Stone makes the case for the importance of literature as an especially productive medium through which to understand the complexity of violence elsewhere. She asks, inter alia, "how the elsewhere functioned as a memory-political paradigm" in the FRG and GDR in the early years of their existence. To this end, Stone compares memories of CRSV in two novels from East and West Germany that depict the Second World War and its aftermath. These works are *Zwischen Nacht und Morgen* (Between Night and Morning, 1955) by East German Otto Gotsche and *Berlin* (1954) by FRG-based Theodor Plievier. In the former, US personnel perpetrate sexual violence; in the latter, Soviet soldiers do so.

Stone identifies East and West Germany and their Cold War allies, the USSR and US, respectively, as elsewhere to one another and shows how competing narratives about all of these states were furthered by stories about CRSV. This argument demonstrates how imagery of sexual violence against women and girls can be instrumentalized to shore up political discourse. The chapter thus highlights the need to think critically about such commonplaces and the ways in which they can diminish the importance of sexual violence itself, consigning those who suffer it to what is theorized as an emotional and narrative elsewhere. Yet at the same time, Stone argues that such imagery in literature can "[complicate] the binary logic that underpinned Cold War narratives about war and occupation" and other ideas about elsewhere. In addition, her focus on CRSV highlights the importance of reframing war in ways that spotlight sexual abuse in war (and postwar) zones as well as more widely discussed forms of military action. Moreover, this emphasis draws attention to links between CRSV and other kinds of sexual violence, so that the chapter rethinks wartime violence itself from a more comprehensive perspective.

Chapter 2, by Mererid Puw Davies, explores the West German reception of Louis Malle's 1965 musical-comedy film, *Viva Maria!*, which starred Brigitte Bardot and Jeanne Moreau. This film is set in the early twentieth century in a fictional Latin American country. It follows a troupe of European cabaret artistes, including Bardot's and Moreau's characters: singers and dancers who are both called Maria, accidentally invent the striptease, and go on to lead a successful revolution against a cruel landowner and a corrupt dictatorship. For West German viewers, this French-Italian coproduction made in Mexico, with French dialogue and a multinational cast, offered a vision of a different world. And while Malle later said he did not mean his film to be a serious revolutionary blueprint, it seems that some West German antiauthoritarians excitedly read it as such. This chapter considers, with reference to a 1968 essay by West Berlin activist Bernd Rabehl, why this might be so, and multiple ways in which the film resonated with antiauthoritarian theory. Rabehl identified the film as an allegory of a revolution that unites anarchist and orthodox Marxist thought, just as antiauthoritarians such as he sought to do. His essay also highlights the film's appeal to his internationalist interest in anticolonial revolution in the Global South, as well as the so-called subjective factors of politics, which demanded sexual and political liberation. This chapter therefore draws out the importance of violence elsewhere for antiauthoritarian politics in the 1960s: that is to say, as a model that was easily idealized.

The chapter, however, points also to severe contradictions in the West German reception of Malle's film and offers a different, more feminist account of its subversive potential. It goes on to consider a memoir of the filming process by a cast member, Gregor von Rezzori. This diary suggests that Malle's imagined Mexico was, for von Rezzori, simultaneously an uncanny landscape haunted by Europe's wartime past—above all, Germany's. Von Rezzori describes also the violent, accidental death of a young local extra during the shoot, of which the film's diegesis can make no mention. Read in this light, *Viva Maria!* is itself as ambiguous as its West German reception.

In its third chapter, the volume turns back to GDR culture. Here, Seán Allan presents violence elsewhere in films by documentarists Walter Heynowski and Gerhard Scheumann, who founded the high-profile East German production company Studio H&S. While traditionally this studio's films have been disregarded in criticism as blunt propaganda tools, Allan argues that in fact, they reward study as formally distinctive modernist works. He begins by showing that images of direct violence were rare in GDR film and television drama. The state's political interests meant, however, that violence did have a place in feature films depicting historical conflicts like the Spanish Civil War and in documentaries on contemporary post- or anticolonial struggles, like Studio H&S's cycle of films about the Vietnam conflict made between 1966 and 1984. The chapter goes on to examine more closely the "infamous" film *Piloten im Pyjama* (Pilots in Pajamas, 1967), which consists of a series of interviews with US pilots captured in the Democratic Republic of Vietnam (DRV; North Vietnam) and held under conditions that were in defiance of the Geneva Convention, which offers protections to prisoners of war.

This film suggests that the pilots have been dehumanized by their capitalist socialization. In formal terms, its striking stylizations mean that it can be understood as a cinematic "Lehrstück" (learning play) in the tradition of Bertolt Brecht, which seeks to "disrupt conventional modes of viewing" and offer "a stark corrective" to more familiar imagery of extreme violence in Vietnam. Allan concludes by reflecting on the ways Studio H&S's Vietnam films implicitly undermine any overly simple notion of violence elsewhere by linking their material to Cold War politics close to home in divided Germany.

Following on in terms of both theme and context, J. J. Long explores the use of images from news media in GDR poet Volker Braun's *KriegsErklärung* (Declaration of War, 1967) in chapter 4. The short poems in this collection comment critically on the ways in which media frame the Vietnam War through photography and so can be read as a successor to the "photo-epigrams" of Brecht's *Kriegsfibel* (War Primer, 1955). Consequently, Long embeds Braun's undertaking in twentieth-century Marxist theorizations of the photographic image and its uses in capitalism, notably those of Brecht and Walter Benjamin.

Long goes on to provide close readings of a series of photographs and poems from *KriegsErklärung* that critique what Braun sees as the intimate relationship between the Vietnam War and US interests. In these respects, Braun's poems conform to official GDR positions on Vietnam. The next part of the argument, however, demonstrates that the poems are also open to alternative, less conventional readings, in particular with reference to gender politics. On the one hand, the poems offer highly traditional images of women; on the other, their more nuanced images of men problematize a classic military masculinity. Long concludes that the poems are self-reflexive in numerous senses, registering as they do conditions in divided Germany, and in commenting on some traditional European expectations about gender. Significantly too, the chapter argues that the poems offer "an interrogation and critique" of the representational forms in which "violence elsewhere is mediated to the audience 'at home.'"

Further analysis of the Vietnam conflict and violence elsewhere in East German literature is provided by Ernest Schonfield in chapter 5, as he investigates Anna Seghers's late novella *Steinzeit* (Stone Age, 1975). In this work, a fictional Vietnam veteran from the US, Gary, has hijacked a plane, successfully obtained a ransom as a result, and goes on the run in

Colombia, where his childhood mother tongue, Spanish, allows him to forge a series of new identities. None of these new lives, however, is one in which he can feel at home, and his flight through various lifestyles and communities continues until it contributes to his untimely death.

Schonfield argues here that Seghers's novella is characterized by a subtle narrative technique that "places cognitive gaps at the center of the reading experience" and so invites readers to piece together Gary's backstory and experience via a series of ellipses and omissions. The novella implies that he may be suffering from post-traumatic stress disorder (PTSD), a condition that came to be diagnosed formally for the the first time as a result of studies on Vietnam veterans in the 1970s. While that specific term and diagnosis were not used in the GDR at the time Seghers wrote her story, Schonfield nonetheless demonstrates that her protagonist displays symptoms that resonate with that disorder, and hence with depictions of traumatized veterans in US popular culture too. He goes on to explore Gary's relationships with other men and masculinity, suggesting that the novella makes space for a critique of a harmful, violent masculinity. In conclusion, the chapter illuminates ways in which *Steinzeit* may reflect back on the context in which Seghers herself was writing and hence, how "this story of 'violence elsewhere' speaks to the fears and concerns of Seghers and her East German readers."

Chapter 6 continues discussion of visual culture in the GDR and its representation of East Asian conflicts. Here, Martin Brady considers the work of Studio H&S in the 1980s. He investigates the studio's documentary trilogy about the "Killing Fields" of Cambodia (1980–1983); in particular, the second of these films, *Die Angkar* (The Angkar [Organization], 1981). This trilogy, with its highly critical perspective on China, was made during a time of rapid change in GDR policy regarding that country. Among other concerns, the chapter tracks the impact of those political shifts on the films, as well as on the work of Studio H&S itself, which effectively came to an end as a result.

Brady explores Studio H&S's theoretical and aesthetic positions and its distinctive rhetorical style, which he terms "modernist blatancy," as it is exemplified by the filmmakers' series of sixteen documentaries on the era's "paradigmatic distant war" in Vietnam. Indeed, this series can be understood as a model for Studio H&S's modes of debating violence elsewhere more generally. The chapter proceeds to look in depth at *Die Angkar* and pinpoints the problem posed for Studio H&S by the Khmer Rouge's use of revered symbols of Marxism-Leninism, the hammer and sickle. As such, it explores difficult questions in GDR identity with reference to a distant other. *Die Angkar* works extensively, too, with repeated comparisons with the crimes of National Socialist Germany to offer a complex account of "political oppression both elsewhere and at home."

Clare Bielby, in chapter 7, brings discussion of violence elsewhere back to the Cold War FRG and takes up the theme of left-wing activists' vivid interest in liberation struggles outside Europe. Such ideas about violence elsewhere played a life-changing role for Inge Viett, a former member, from 1972, of the terrorist group Bewegung 2. Juni (Movement 2nd June) and, briefly, the Rote Armee Fraktion (Red Army Faction [RAF]). To make this case, Bielby provides a close analysis of Viett's autobiography, *Nie war ich furchtloser* (Never Was I More Fearless, 1996).

Bielby argues that the domestic political culture of the time made little or no space for militant women's agency. Consequently, as Viett recounts her search for a viable model of revolutionary subjectivity, she draws on ideas about Germany's pre-Nazi revolutionary past and on encounters with male "Third-World" fighters. By contrast, living women do not figure as meaningful role models for her; her sense of identification is not with contemporary women but with the long-dead Rosa Luxemburg. Importantly too, Viett imagines a previous owner of her gun, a Yugoslavian woman partisan of the Second World War, to whom she feels she is linked by this significant object. In sum, Bielby argues that in a context in which there was little discursive space to imagine women's revolutionary agency, the notion of "violent agency elsewhere was particularly generative and necessary for the woman militant" of Viett's time.

In the eighth chapter, Katharina Karcher and Evelien Geerts coauthor a hauntological analysis of political discourse about violence elsewhere as an affect-laden phenomenon around the turn of the twenty-first century in Germany. They present the aftermath of murders committed by the neo-Nazi terror group the Nationalsozialistischer Untergrund (National Socialist Underground [NSU]) in 2000–2001, which were part of a longer series of murders claiming ten victims altogether. This topic is explored through vignettes about the murdered and the bereaved and critical theoretical "musings" or "snippets," as well as exploration of legal and cultural obstacles to identifying the NSU killings as political violence. For years, the NSU murders were thought to have been committed by criminal gangs originating outside Germany and were therefore regarded, and exoticized, as violence from a supposed elsewhere, which was not a priority for the German authorities. Furthermore, the contemporaneous "hyper-exceptional" terrorist attacks in the US of September 11, 2001, served to obscure awareness in Germany of this different kind of terrorism as it unfolded at home. Karcher and Geerts make the case for a "critical (new) materialist hauntological perspective" for understanding the NSU case. Their theoretical approach seeks to make space for the troubling affect of the murders and for a complex understanding of historical processes. This methodology, as modeled by the chapter in practice, opens up new formal and stylistic possibilities for writing about history too.

In exploring the very end of the historical period covered by this book, chapter 8 simultaneously offers an opportunity to think back on it in a questioning mood. As noted above, September 11, 2001, is commonly seen as a historical caesura that ushered in a new phase in world politics as well as in thinking about global violence. Indeed, this perception played a part in the design of this volume, as it explores constructions of violence elsewhere up to 2001. Here, however, Karcher and Geerts problematize the idea of that date as a watershed, for the NSU murders began in 2000 and ended only in 2007. Moreover, they argue that in the FRG, September 11 "reinforced a pre-existing tendency among the white German majority to forget about victims of far-right violence." Thus, this chapter invites ongoing critical contemplation not only of potentially limiting historical meanings ascribed to September 11, 2001 but, in part through its methodological approach, of the very notion of history as a uniform, linear process.

* * *

Important as the essays collected here are individually, this volume is, in addition, more than the sum of its parts. Taken together, its chapters offer scope for comparative reflection, especially where they form evident thematic clusters and connections. Chapter 1 lays the ground for what follows by analyzing foundational narratives of memory for both German states under discussion in later chapters. Chapters 3, 4, 5, and 6 reflect on GDR representations of conflicts in East Asia. As such, they form a tightly linked, mutually informative group, and some share an interest also in (post-)Brechtian theory and practice. On a different note, chapters 2 and 7 offer interrelated accounts of the intense ways in which West German activists of the 1960s and 1970s responded to liberation struggles around the world, in fantasy and in praxis. They also foreground the gendered character of those scenes. In so doing, they link especially strongly to chapters 1, on CRSV; 4, on GDR poems and photographs about Vietnam and their gendered politics; and 6, on masculinity and PTSD in relation to violent conflict elsewhere. And the political contexts of chapter 7, on the autobiography of a left-wing woman terrorist in West Germany, helped lay the ground for the legal definitions of terrorism in postunification Germany that are in turn problematized in chapter 8.

Gradually emerging as these contributions did from a long-running, diverse series of engagements and conversations with scholars, artists, and activists, certain (often unexpected) concentrations in the volume are striking. In stylistic terms, for instance, at the center of this volume there is focus on a cohesive tradition of often polemical, and often visual, modernism from the GDR. The chapters in question draw out its cultural history and identify in it key affordances for representing violence elsewhere.

By extension, this sequence of chapters on GDR modernism(s) highlights the importance of thinking more broadly and comparatively about the forms in which violence elsewhere can be imagined. Key genres and narrative modes discussed across this volume range from the documentary to life writing to realist fiction, as well as comedy and the surreal; it is productive to consider how each is mobilized and what distinct light it can shed on the field.

In thematic terms, there is a critical mass of studies on the FRG and GDR prior to unification in 1990. Beyond reflecting the fact that Germany was divided for most of the period covered by the volume, that emphasis holds open the possibility that during the Cold War era, violence elsewhere may have had particular, compelling contours related to awareness of a paradoxically German elsewhere that had been generated violently and was both foreign and proximate.

Within this volume, women writers and artists—namely, Seghers, Viett, and *Viva Maria!*'s Bardot and Moreau—as well as other, lower-profile women collaborating on that and other films under consideration, for instance, are in a minority as producers of culture; those from other minoritized backgrounds, in terms, for example, of nationality, culture, or ethnicity, are rarer still. This imbalance is in part due to the volume's temporal focus, for the work of women and artists of diverse backgrounds did not dominate the postwar canon in Germany to 2001 and thus became less accessible to posterity. This circumstance is also related to the book's topical focus. The instances of violence elsewhere examined are, for the most part, conventionally recognizable manifestations of direct violence, notably political violence, and their aftermaths. This stress is bound up with the fact that our exploration of violence elsewhere has a key point of origin in Germany's twentieth-century history of violence, most prominently the First and Second World Wars and the genocidal regime of the "Third Reich," paradigmatic examples of political violence understood in the straightforward sense. As a result, an emphasis has evolved here on the "'high' politics of 'political' violence."[10] In German contexts in the period in question, works and representations in that specific sphere are arguably most prominently associated with cultural producers who are white men. Thus, the studies collected here offer privileged vantage on certain canonical perspectives that have been especially influential or

---

10 Bielby, "Gendering the Perpetrator," 156. Bielby is referencing Laura Sjoberg and Sandra Via, who state that "high politics refers to the traditional sites of power in global politics, such as state governments and international organizations, as opposed to the 'low' politics of everyday life with which most feminist work is concerned." See Laura Sjoberg and Sandra Via, "Introduction," in *Gender, War, and Militarism: Feminist Perspectives*, ed. Laura Sjoberg and Sandra Via (Santa Barbara, CA: Praeger, 2010), 1–13, here 13.

representative in thinking about violence elsewhere, understood in this way, in the second half of the twentieth century.

These studies often draw the gaze especially toward perpetrators of violence. They thus reflect and contribute to the recent international turn to interdisciplinary perpetrator studies[11] whose roots can be traced back in part to trends in historiography of the National Socialist period, which came to particular prominence from the 1990s.[12] This field is interested, among other things, in understanding what moves individuals and collectives to commit violence and how it affects them in turn. The work of this volume points, then, to current interest in the place of perpetrators in the wider German postwar imaginary. At the same time, and in tandem with the field of perpetrator studies more broadly, it complicates simplistic notions of perpetratorhood as a monolithic position.[13] In the case of Seghers's fictional protagonist, for instance, the perpetrator of violence has also been subject, or witness, to extreme violence himself in ways that have lasting legacies, not least at the level of trauma.[14]

All the more important, then, are the volume's considerations of the victims and survivors of violence.[15] Stone's chapter, for example, draws attention to the manner in which the victims and survivors of CRSV were, in a sense, made victim a second time through the discursive appropriation of their experiences that had "material consequences." And the closing chapter foregrounds the victims and the bereaved of the NSU terror attacks and argues for the importance of finding new ways, in scholarship

---

11   The Perpetrator Studies Network, based at the University of Utrecht, was launched in 2015. Two years later, the first issue of the *Journal of Perpetrator Research* was published, followed in 2020 by the publication of Knittel and Goldberg's *The Routledge International Handbook of Perpetrator Studies*. See also Clare Bielby and Jeffrey Stevenson Murer, eds., *Perpetrating Selves: Doing Violence, Performing Identity* (Basingstoke, Hampshire, UK: Palgrave Macmillan, 2018).

12   While the publication of Christopher Browning's *Ordinary Men: Reserve Police Battalion 101 and the Final Solution in Poland* (1992; London: HarperCollins, 2001) is considered a key text in the historiographical turn to the study of National Socialist perpetrators, other studies on the perpetrators of National Socialism preexist that text.

13   See, for example, Bielby and Murer, "Perpetrating Selves: An Introduction," in *Perpetrating Selves*, 1–13.

14   For a fascinating reflection on perpetrator trauma, see Ruth Glynn, "Writing the Terrorist Self: The Unspeakable Alterity of Italy's Female Perpetrators," *Feminist Review* 92 (2009): 1–18.

15   Feminist scholarship in particular has drawn attention to the risks inherent in essentializing and reifying identity categories through use of terms such as "victim." According to Miranda Alison, "Narrating women who have suffered violent or abusive events in war as victims . . . is disempowering, inaccurate, and constitutes further victimization." Miranda Alison, *Women and Political Violence: Female Combatants in Ethno-National Conflict* (London: Routledge, 2009), 119.

and other kinds of discourse, of commemorating and giving voice to them and their agency.

A variety of "elsewheres" is discussed in the chapters that follow, from the "other Germanies" and their Cold War allies, depicted in realist novels of the immediate postwar period, to the past, or to the patently fictional world of Malle's escapist cinema. Nonetheless, it is striking that in the chapters on the Cold War years, there is a focus on the Global South, or Third World, as wide regions of the world were then often known in Europe. Most evidently, this theme registers the impact of complex, often violent decolonizing processes and postcolonial politics around the world. The chapters collected here demonstrate how wide-ranging contemporary interest was in such global affairs, focusing as they do on conflicts, real and imagined, from around the decolonizing world, from Cambodia to a fictional Latin American state.

Emblematic among these examples is the era's "paradigmatic distant war" in Vietnam, as Brady puts it. Especially in the context of then-vivid memories of the Second World War in the two Germanies in the 1960s and 1970s, the Vietnam conflict was elevated by many to a symbolic benchmark for right and wrong.[16] As such, it took on a synecdochal quality for the world order after 1945 in that it seemed to embody, in extreme and violent form, the essential positions and contradictions of Cold War politics and ethics. In addition, it could be understood as the apotheosis of technological modernity itself, as Critical Theory would put it.[17] Expressed another way, the Vietnam War was genuinely global, in ways that could seem new, and conducted using the very latest technology. Moreover, awareness of the conflict and its impact worldwide was fostered powerfully by modern media and their ability to bring images of distant violence home. It is no coincidence that the discourses about this conflict, as they are explored in this book, are tightly linked with distinctive modernist, Brechtian aesthetics that exploit the essentially modern possibilities of technologically reproducible, documentary art forms. Neither is it unexpected that the difficult positionality of the witness to distant violence comes to the fore in West German antiwar discourse about Vietnam, for the war underlined the fact that in global modernity, everyone's interests are intertwined. Indeed, in more general terms, the era's conflicts in the Global South involved the interests of the Global North in plural, visible ways. Therefore, they prompted an awareness for many Germans of the complex interconnectedness of "here" and "elsewhere."[18]

16 Cf. Mererid Puw Davies, *Poetic Writing and the Vietnam War in West Germany: On Fire* (London: UCL Press, 2023), 3.
17 Davies, *Poetic Writing*, 106–7.
18 Cf. Davies, *Poetic Writing*, 106–7.

A further issue that runs centrally through this volume is gender. At one level, this thematization is no doubt linked to our own interests as feminist scholars. But at another, it suggests that both the gendering of dicourses about violence and the violence that may be involved in thinking about gender itself[19] reward study. On one hand, violence, perpetration, and victimhood often seem to be conventionally gendered here, with chapters exploring scenarios in which men perpetrate violence, and women and girls are victims. On the other hand, women come to the fore as perpetrators too, albeit of startlingly contrasting kinds, in the cases of Malle's film *Viva Maria!* and Viett's memoir. And at times, men also appear as victims. Moreover, ideas of place, home, nation, and "elsewhere" are often traditionally imagined in gendered terms as feminine.[20] Thus, a number of this volume's authors, explicitly or implicitly, shed light on the complex ways in which representations of violence, "here," "there," and gender can inflect one another. They also demonstrate how feminist theoretical approaches to the topic of violence elsewhere may be particularly generative.

This volume's opening chapter, Stone's analysis of literary representations of sexual violence committed by Allied troops in Germany around the end of the Second World War, coins both a verb and a theoretical concept. It uses the term "narrative elsewhering" to denote ways in which CRSV is presented in literature; that is to say, in allegorizing terms that draw attention away from its correspondences with women's lived experience. On one level, CRSV lends itself to this sort of portrayal because of complex connections between the feminine and allegory[21] and between the feminine and conflict in particular. On another, it can be argued that the deflection of disturbing preoccupations onto different, more distant spaces and agents makes them speakable, albeit in relativizing terms that detract from their horror. Paradoxically, then, as Stone argues, this figurative process involves calling something to mind by "direct[ing] attention *elsewhere*." In the novels she explores, CRSV is simultaneously evoked yet (partly) erased or blurred by the ways in which the perspectives and experiences of the victims and survivors themselves tend to be replaced by those of male bystanders and witnesses. Stone concludes that "'elsewhering' thus becomes an eloquent label for the ethical problems inherent in metaphorical constructions of the significance of sexual violence." The

19 See Butler, "Preface (1999)."
20 See, for example, Nira Yuval-Davis, *Gender & Nation* (Thousand Oaks, CA.: Sage, 1997). On gender and nation in the German context, see Patricia Herminghouse and Magda Mueller, "Introduction: Looking for Germania," in *Gender and Germanness: Cultural Productions of Nation*, ed. Patricia Herminghouse and Magda Mueller (Providence, RI: Berghahn, 1997), 1–16.
21 Marina Warner, *Monuments and Maidens: The Allegory of the Female Form* (1985; London: Vintage, 1996).

same may be said of the portrayal of further kinds of violence, which may invite expression through (gendered) displacement and "elsewhering."

In this volume, Stone's chapter is an exception in thematizing primarily the Second World War years in Germany and their immediate aftermath. In doing so, it demonstrates that those earlier years had a significant formative impact on the cultural history of later times. One implication here is that in a further instance of "elsewhering," Germany's recent wartime past inhabits the works explored throughout, alongside their manifest subject matter, albeit in more latent ways. As such, in identifying "elsewhering" as a discursive mode of the times, and "violence elsewhere" as a significant trope in German culture of the postwar period, these studies contribute to memory culture and its theorization. They broach prospects for further examination of the interrelationships of violence past and present, and (apparently) far and near, in the cultural imaginary of the second half of the twentieth century.

* * *

Such insights invite reflection on potential future directions for scholarship interested in "violence elsewhere" across disciplines, including and beyond German studies. In formal terms for instance, taking our authors' case study of (visual) modernism from the GDR as a model, there are prospects for reflecting further on the potentials of various different types of narrative, genre, and style for thinking about elsewhere.

There is scope, too, to widen the kinds of violence under discussion, beyond this volume's emphasis on direct physical acts of what tends to be understood as political violence. Indeed, the very construction of political violence itself is not self-evident. As Bielby observes, the feminist maxim "the personal is political" urges us to "continuously interrogate the gendered politics of representation at stake when we use terms such as 'political violence.' . . . We need to ask whose interests and experiences we are representing and privileging when we apply these terms and knowledges."[22] Thus, Laura Sjoberg comments, for instance, that terrorism "is often represented as the product of the fears and problems of a small (often masculine) elite part of the population. Feminists have also argued that domestic violence is a means of inculcating fear so as to coerce compliance, a common definition of terrorism."[23] And as Liz Kelly asks in relation to sexual violence against women, "When is a war a war, and

---

22 Bielby, "Gendering the Perpetrator," 164.
23 Laura Sjoberg, "Conclusion: The Study of Women, Gender, and Terrorism," in *Women, Gender, and Terrorism*, ed. Laura Sjoberg and Caron E. Gentry (Athens: University of Georgia Press, 2011), 227–39, here 236–37.

what constitutes peace from the perspective of women?"[24] Likewise, as Tarak Barkawi demonstrates, constructions of war need to be called into question from a decolonizing perspective.[25] Such considerations could flow productively into future accounts of violence elsewhere.

Other forms of (political) violence to which further study of violence elsewhere could reach include "slow violence," defined by Nixon as "a violence that occurs gradually and out of sight, a violence of delayed destruction that is dispersed across time and space, an attritional violence that is typically not viewed as violence at all."[26] While Nixon is writing here about environmental violence, the term "slow violence" can be applied, also, to the impacts of domestic and psychological violence, with its long-lasting, incremental, often bodily harms, which are sometimes (almost) imperceptible to an unquestioning gaze.[27] Equally, engagement with discursive or epistemological violence—that is, the harm enacted by written or spoken language and by ways of knowing or organizing knowledge that can do tangible bodily harm—would merit examination.

Important, too, is the question opened up by the present volume of how more-readily accepted manifestations of (political) violence elsewhere articulate with examples of violence in these wider senses. Simultaneously, we ask: How far can we expand the meaning of violence—for example, with regard to the notion of violent language—before it loses its conceptual edge?[28] This kind of development to consider different kinds of violence can make room for a wider range of cultural productions. Future studies concentrating, for instance, on sexual or domestic violence in times of (so-called) peace or on discursive/epistemological violence or racism would likely investigate more works authored by women and cultural producers of color in timely ways.

Finally, with reference to the idea of elsewhere, there is scope to incorporate understandings of it beyond the geographical, which proves to predominate in this volume, to, for example, the temporal elsewhere or the elsewhere of fictional, even science-fictional and speculative, worlds. And in light of Slobodian's critique of mobilizations of "self" and "other"

---

24 Liz Kelly, "Wars against Women: Sexual Violence, Sexual Politics and the Militarized State," in *States of Conflict: Gender, Violence and Resistance*, ed. Susie Jacobs et al. (London: Zed Books, 2000), 45–65, here 47.

25 Tarak Barkawi, "Decolonizing War," *European Journal of International Security* 1, part 2 (2016): 199–214.

26 Nixon, *Slow Violence*, 2.

27 Nixon briefly discusses the "slow violence" of domestic abuse in his text, but this aspect is not elaborated. Nixon, *Slow Violence*, 16.

28 With reference to feminist approaches to violence and how widely that term can usefully be applied, see Lisa Price, "Defining Violence," in *Feminist Frameworks: Building Theory on Violence against Women* (Halifax, NS, Canada: Fernwood, 2005), 11–23.

and the importance of what he has called the "the tension between abstract identification and embodied collaboration,"²⁹ we hold out the hope that future scholarship can engage with representations of elsewhere alongside the agency of those subjects associated with it in sustained, dialogical ways.

---

29 Slobodian, *Foreign Front*, 13.

1: Projecting Violence Elsewhere: Remembering Conflict-Related Sexual Violence in Cold War Germany

Katherine Stone

VIOLENCE ELSEWHERE WAS ever-present on the ideological terrain of the Cold War. Both Germanies keenly observed proxy conflicts in other divided nations such as Korea (1950–53) and Vietnam (1955–75).[1] Media reports of bombing, rape, and civilian suffering imbued this distant violence with dynamic immediacy, recalling recent German experiences of war and occupation during World War II.[2] Against this backdrop, the present chapter investigates how the elsewhere functioned as a memory-political paradigm in the first decade of the Federal Republic of Germany (FRG) and German Democratic Republic (GDR). In particular, it asks which memories of German wartime suffering were exploited in each state to highlight the cruelty of the Soviet Union and US as occupiers and allies. In what ways did evocations of violence in historical and geographical elsewheres therefore bolster Cold War discourses about ideological otherness? And how did narratives linking violence with these elsewheres illuminate debates about German identity in the present?

My discussion focuses on memories of conflict-related sexual violence (CRSV), which were particularly fraught after 1945. Historians agree that several hundred thousand German women were likely assaulted by Allied soldiers as World War II ended. The stigma attached to sexual violence compounded the ethical and political challenges that burden discussions of German suffering more generally. Notably, the Cold War set the tone for the emergent memory cultures of the FRG and GDR. Their

---

1 See Hannes Mosler, "South Korea's April Revolution through the Lens of West Germany," *Korea Journal* 60, no. 3 (2020): 118–150; Wilfried Mausbach, "America's Vietnam in Germany—Germany in America's Vietnam," in *Changing the World, Changing Oneself: Political Protest and Collective Identities in West Germany and the US in the 1960s and 1970s*, ed. Belinda Davis et al. (New York: Berghahn, 2010), 41–64.

2 See Christina Schwenkel, *Building Socialism: The Afterlife of East German Architecture in Urban Vietnam* (Durham, NC: Duke University Press, 2020), 97.

oppositional memory regimes determined which memories of violence became politically expedient, and which acquired an air of unspeakability. Thus, the GDR's position as Soviet satellite state made discussions of (sexual) violence committed by the Red Army taboo, while US and British bombing campaigns became propaganda staples. The formula was reversed in the FRG, which was defined by a desire to forge positive relations with the West. Accordingly, public memory emphasized Soviet brutality toward prisoners of war and toward civilians fleeing or expelled from the former eastern territories. Against the background of such political maneuvering around memory, Elisabeth Krimmer evokes a discursive context in which discourse about rape was consistently "detached from individual suffering and made to perform the work of ideology."[3] As this chapter will show, however, this context also made memories of CRSV particularly explosive as they complicated the binary logic that underpinned Cold War narratives about war and occupation.

To begin, I elaborate on the politicization of these memories, unfolding the discursive contexts in which CRSV became embedded in an assemblage of spatial and temporal elsewheres—from the closing stages of World War II and the Korean War to the activities of foreign troops in both Germanies. Having established the propagandistic value of CRSV, I turn to fiction. Literature is a valuable tool for deconstructing the prejudices and anxieties that inform constructions like the elsewhere. The dense symbolic networks through which novels are constructed make it possible to untangle assumptions about sexual violence and ideological others that are often naturalized in other discursive realms. Furthermore, the extended plots of novels generate excess and ambiguity, which have the potential to destabilize the deliberate projections of violence elsewhere found in the abbreviated forms of political propaganda analyzed in the first section of this chapter.

My case studies are *Zwischen Nacht und Morgen* (Between Night and Morning, 1955) by East German author Otto Gotsche (1904–85) and *Berlin* (1954; *Berlin*, 1956) by Theodor Plievier (1892–1955), who settled in West Germany from the GDR in 1947.[4] Each author was widely

---

3   Elisabeth Krimmer, *German Women's Life Writing and the Holocaust: Complicity and Gender in the Second World War* (Cambridge: Cambridge University Press, 2018), 118. See also Birgit Dahlke, "'Frau komm': Vergewaltigungen 1945; Zur Geschichte eines Diskurses," in *LiteraturGesellschaft DDR: Kanonkämpfe und ihre Geschichte(n)*, ed. Birgit Dahlke, Martina Langermann, and Thomas Taterka (Stuttgart: Metzler, 2000), 275–311; Bill Niven, *Representations of Flight and Expulsion in East German Prose Works* (Rochester, NY: Camden House, 2014).

4   Otto Gotsche, *Zwischen Nacht und Morgen* (Berlin: Verlag Kultur und Fortschritt, 1959); Theodor Plievier, *Berlin* (Cologne: Kiepenhauer und Witsch, 2018). Further page references follow in the text.

read in his time. Gotsche published eleven novels, alongside literary criticism, travelogues, and historical texts. In the GDR, *Zwischen Nacht und Morgen* was serialized on the Berliner Rundfunk I radio station and listed on school syllabi.[5] Plievier was equally prolific, with ten novels to his name. The trilogy comprising *Stalingrad* (1945), *Moskau* (1952), and *Berlin* consolidated his reputation as one of twentieth-century Germany's most commercially successful and internationally recognized authors of war literature.

Zwischen Nacht und Morgen and *Berlin* contain some of the most extensive depictions of CRSV in the first postwar decade. Both feature perpetrators from the "ideological elsewhere," a term I use to describe discursive practices that emphasize ideological difference by associating Cold War adversaries with distant times and places. As one of the most pervasive tropes for imagining risks to the security and reproduction of the nation, sexual violence is an apt frame for examining such constructions. In propaganda and reality, conflicts are all too often "played out over the feminine body: over the feminine space of the nation—battlefields, farmlands and homes—and over actual female bodies."[6] Moreover, sexual violence transcends war and peace. Connecting the exceptional cruelty of conflict zones to everyday forms of violence, CRSV is particularly suggestive of broader cultures of criminality and morality, not to mention gender politics. My readings of these novels ultimately ask what happens when violence is made to speak to the values of the ideological elsewhere. In other words, to what extent do these political allegories enact a form of narrative elsewhering that directs attention away from victims and toward broader political concerns?

Memory and Propaganda

Images of sexualized violence permeated the lurid propaganda of the "Third Reich." When Soviet forces briefly occupied the East Prussian village of Nemmersdorf in October 1944, for instance, a Wehrmacht propaganda company produced grisly photographic evidence of atrocities, including rape. Such propaganda is widely credited with impelling millions of Germans to flee westward in 1944 and 1945 and partially

---

5   Konrad Dussel, "Rundfunk in der Bundesrepublik und in der DDR: Überlegungen zum systematischen Vergleich," in *Zwischen Pop und Propaganda: Radio in der DDR*, ed. Christoph Classen and Klaus Arnold (Berlin: C. H. Links, 2004), 301–22, here 318.
    6   Julie Mostov, "Sexing the Nation/Desexing the Body: Politics of National Identity in the former Yugoslavia," in *Gender Ironies of Nationalism: Sexing the Nation*, ed. Tamar Mayer (London: Routledge, 2000), 89–112, here 91.

explains why the cultural memory of wartime rape revolves around the Red Army. Even before the war concluded, propagandists had cultivated the idea that US, French, and British troops were "das weitaus kleinere Übel" (by far the lesser evil).[7] Available records about actual encounters between German civilians and occupation soldiers support this narrative.

In addition, Miriam Gebhardt identifies Cold War frameworks as one reason why assaults by Western Allies received relatively little attention until recently.[8] As political tensions escalated, selective memories of CRSV—as well as bombing, flight, and expulsion—offered emotive anchors for the propaganda of each German state. Consider a 1951 propaganda poster circulated by the West German Volksbund für Frieden und Freiheit e.V. (People's League for Peace and Freedom [VFF]). The caption warns about the consequences of socialism taking root in the FRG. The specter of future invasion is evoked by the illustration, which depicts a Soviet soldier reaching for a frightened woman.[9] The poster is annotated with the words "Frau komm" (Come here, woman), which historical accounts show frequently portended rape by Red Army troops. As Júlia Garraio argues, such propaganda exploited women's experiences "to bear witness to Soviet brutality and to indicate that the right course for the new Germany, the good Germany, lay with the Western Allies."[10]

The poster counts on a long history of anti-Russian prejudices to convince observers of the need to protect the "Abendland" (occident). This term accumulated political cogency after the Russian Revolution (1917) and World War I (1914–18), events that foreshadowed the dangers

---

7   Waltraud Wende, "Beschützer kritisiert man nicht—oder vielleicht doch? Zum Bild Amerikas in der westdeutschen Publizistik der späten 40er und 50er Jahre," in *Modernisierung als Amerikanisierung? Entwicklungslinien der westdeutschen Kultur 1945–1960*, ed. Lars Koch (Bielefeld: Transcript, 2007), 63–89, here 70. Unless otherwise noted, all translations are the author's own.

8   Miriam Gebhardt, *Als die Soldaten kamen: Die Vergewaltigung deutscher Frauen am Ende des Zweiten Weltkriegs* (Munich: Pantheon, 2016), 9. For another recent study of US perpetrators, see Ruth Lawlor, "Contested Crimes: Race, Gender, and Nation in Histories of GI Sexual Violence, World War II," *Journal of Military History* 84 (2020): 541–69.

9   Volksbund für Frieden und Freiheit, "'Frau komm . . . ohne mich,'" October 17, 1951, W110/2: Plakatsammlung II/1945–1952, no. 0192, Landesarchiv Baden-Württemburg, https://www.deutsche-digitale-bibliothek.de/item/UBLAMOPVP3MLPWU3VQ7XO2BVJQ3GOC2J.

10 Júlia Garraio, "Hordes of Rapists: The Instrumentalization of Sexual Violence in German Cold War Anti-Communist Discourses," trans. João Paulo Moreira, *RCCS Annual Review* 5 (2013): 46–63, here 61.

associated with liberalism, individualism, secularism, and modern nationalism.[11] As Paul Hanebrink explains, Western European commentators

> projected their fears and fantasies about the decline of the West onto a stylized (and geographically imprecise) East that embodied a brutal and primitive vitality alien to the more refined, but also more fragile, Europe. One version of this fantasy resurrected ancient histories of invasions from the East by Tatars, Mongols, or Islam, casting Europe's fight against Bolshevism as the latest "clash of civilizations." Still another cast Russia as Europe's eastern "other," and understood Bolshevism as the inevitable product of a barbarous place inhabited by a variety of uncivilized races. Another cast Jews as the quintessentially "Eastern" (read: un-European) people.[12]

The ideological elsewhere of Bolshevism was thus constructed in palimpsestic fashion. Long histories of violence were superimposed on notions of actual and allegorical distance. After the Holocaust, antisemitism no longer (openly) defined discourses about the dangers of Bolshevism and Soviet expansionism; references to the "Asiatic" elsewhere lingered, however.[13] Indeed, in the VFF poster, the soldier's narrow eyes, swarthy complexion, angular face, and prominent jaw encourage a racist physiognomic reading that conjures up the specter of "Asiatic Bolshevism." As historian Elisabeth Heineman has demonstrated, moreover, in West German political discourse references to "Asian atrocities" were frequently used as a euphemism for "rape," thereby emphasizing the national and racialized dimensions of CRSV. The rhetorical currency of violence against women did not, however, translate into substantial political recognition of or support for survivors.[14]

This lack of recognition was mirrored in the Soviet zone of occupation, and later in the GDR, where the history of rape by Soviet soldiers was a political inconvenience that jeopardized the socialist project. In the early years of occupation, the Soviet military administration's reluctance to address "excesses" by its troops was not reflected in the wider population. The problem of rape was a subtext in debates among doctors and

---

11 Rosario Forlenza, "The Politics of the Abendland: Christian Democracy and the Idea of Europe after the Second World War," *Contemporary European History* 26, no. 2 (2017): 261–86, here 265.

12 Paul Hanebrink, *A Specter Haunting Europe: The Myth of Judeo-Bolshevism* (Cambridge, MA: Harvard University Press, 2018), 40–41.

13 Hanebrink, *A Specter Haunting Europe*, 207.

14 Elizabeth Heineman, "The Hour of the Woman: Memories of Germany's 'Crisis Years' and West German National Identity," *American Historical Review* 101, no. 2 (1996): 354–95, here 373.

local health officials about abortion, for instance.¹⁵ Additionally, political commentators and local leaders of the socialist parties attributed recruitment issues and the electoral disappointments of 1946 to women's anger about the behavior of Red Army soldiers, which had been clear to campaigners on the streets.¹⁶ Into the 1950s, however, complaints about the violence and criminality of Red Army soldiers, both in 1945 and into the period of occupation, were increasingly construed as detrimental to Soviet-German relations and as playing into the hands of the GDR's bellicose enemies. As a result, open allusions to sexual violence perpetrated by the Red Army were increasingly rare.¹⁷

Until the official end of West German occupation in 1955, GDR newspapers did, however, frequently report on sexual attacks on civilians perpetrated by US soldiers on the other side of the internal border. These ranged from brief news reports with titles such as "Amerikanische Schule" (American School), "Amis vergewaltigen und überfallen" (Americans Rape and Raid), "Deutsche Mädchen sind kein Freiwild" (German Girls Are Not Fair Game) to longer features under headlines including "Die Kult der Brutalität" (The Cult of Brutality) and "Wildwest in Koblenz" (Wild West in Koblenz).¹⁸ One weekend crime report published in the *Berliner Zeitung* in March 1952 described various attacks in West Berlin by US soldiers, who are compared to "gangsters."¹⁹ The headline, which runs "Chikagoer Sonntag in Westberlin" (Chicago Sunday in West Berlin), relies on established "imaginative geographies" to consolidate the moral boundaries between Western capitalism and Eastern

---

15 Atina Grossmann, *Jews, Germans, and Allies: Close Encounters in Occupied Germany* (Princeton, NJ: Princeton University Press, 2009), 58–59.

16 Norman Naimark, *The Russians in Germany: A History of the Soviet Zone of Occupation 1945–1949* (Cambridge, MA: Belknap Press of Harvard University Press, 1995), 119–29.

17 Regina Mühlhäuser, "Vergewaltigungen in Deutschland 1945: Nationaler Opferdiskurs und individuelles Erinnern betroffener Frauen," in *Nachkrieg in Deutschland*, ed. Klaus Naumann (Hamburg: Hamburger Edition, 2001), 384–408, here 385.

18 "Amerikanische Schule," *Neues Deutschland*, September 22, 1946, 2; "Amerikanische Ausschreitungen," *Berliner Zeitung*, September 27, 1949, 6; "Amis vergewaltigen und überfallen," *Neues Deutschland*, April 26, 1951, 2; "Deutsche Mädchen sind kein Freiwild," *Neue Zeit*, May 14, 1952, 5; V. J. Jerome, "Die Kult der Brutalität," *Neues Deutschland*, December 14, 1949, 3; "Wildwest in Koblenz," *Die Frau von heute*, July 6, 1956, 3

19 "Chikagoer Sonntag in Westberlin," *Berliner Zeitung*, March 18, 1952, 6. On the continuities between GDR and National Socialist critiques of US culture, see Uta Poiger, *Jazz, Rock, and Rebels: Cold War Politics and American Culture in a Divided Germany* (Berkeley: University of California Press, 2000), 45.

Communism.[20] This mention of Chicago, a notorious hotbed of organized crime, implies that the FRG is ridden with crime and corruption. It attributes the violence of American soldiers to a fundamentally immoral and violent cultural framework. While West Germany appealed to the ideal of the "Abendland" to construct itself as the home of freedom, peace, and humanity, then, the GDR claimed the same values for itself.

The Korean War presented countless opportunities for the GDR state to reinforce this utopian narrative. In June 1950, financed and supported by the Soviet Union, Kim Il Sung's Communist government invaded South Korea, triggering a counterattack backed by United Nations forces under US general Douglas McArthur. GDR propaganda offered a different interpretation of events, depicting South Korea as a puppet state that had instigated the conflict at the behest of the US.[21] More broadly, the East German press interwove different elsewheres to depict US expansionism as a violent threat—not only to Korea but to both Germanies. One April 1951 article, published in the state organ *Neues Deutschland* (*ND*) and titled "USA-Imperialisten wollen das koreanische Volk ausrotten" (US Imperialists Want to Exterminate the Korean People), describes rape and torture by US soldiers. It hardly appears coincidental that this almost full-page report appears alongside a shorter piece about sexual assaults by US soldiers on women in Bamberg.[22] In February 1952, another report linked attacks on Germans in Baden-Württemberg to the arrival of US soldiers from South Korea. An ironic reference to these troops as "Kulturverteidiger" (preservers of culture) alludes to the Truman Doctrine, which construed US foreign policy as a defense of Western values.[23] President Harry S. Truman's famous address before Congress on March 12, 1947, described US culture in opposition to a "way of life" that "relies upon terror and oppression."[24] The *ND* article

---

20 Elizabeth Edwards, "The Colonial Archival Imaginaire at Home," *Social Anthropology* 24, no. 1 (2016): 152–66, here 57.

21 Burghard Ciesla, "Korea als Generalprobe? Wahrnehmungen und Wirkungen des Koreakrieges in der DDR," in *Korea—ein vergessener Krieg? Der militärische Konflikt auf der koreanischen Halbinsel 1950–1953 im internationalen Kontext*, ed. Bernd Bonwetsch and Matthias Uhl (Oldenburg: Oldenbourg Wissenschaftsverlag, 2012), 103–14, here 104.

22 "USA-Imperialisten wollen das koreanische Volk ausrotten" and "Blutige Zwischenfälle in Bayern," *Neues Deutschland*, April 18, 1951, 5.

23 See Dianne Kirby, *Religion and the Cold War* (Basingstoke, Hampshire, UK: Palgrave Macmillan, 2003), 4.

24 Harry S. Truman, "Truman Doctrine: President Harry S. Truman's Address before a Joint Session of Congress," March 12, 1947, https://avalon.law.yale.edu/20th_century/trudoc.asp.

reverses this characterization, instead portraying the ideological elsewhere of the US as fundamentally violent.[25]

These brief examples illuminate the knotting of spatial and temporal elsewheres that frequently overlaid stories about CRSV in the Cold War German context. In all cases, the focus is on the act of violence, the perpetrator, and the political system that he represents. These thin, allegorical narratives only selectively acknowledge the complex reality of CRSV as it is experienced by survivors. In what follows, I use literary examples to dig deeper into the ambivalences that defined representations of CRSV in this period.

Otto Gotsche's *Zwischen Nacht und Morgen* (1959)

It would be remiss to examine the relationship between literature and politics in the 1950s without considering Gotsche, one of the architects of GDR cultural policy. From his youth, Gotsche was a committed member of the Kommunistische Partei Deutschlands (Communist Party of Germany) and was arrested several times for his political engagement. In 1939, he founded the Antifaschistische Arbeitergruppe Mitteldeutschlands (Central German Antifascist Workers' Group [AAM]). From 1947 until 1949, Gotsche was involved in the postwar reconstruction of Saxony-Anhalt and served as state minister for the interior. His subsequent move to Berlin inaugurated a period of close collaboration with Walter Ulbricht, for whom he served as official adviser until 1960. Gotsche's advocacy for official cultural policy goes some way toward explaining why his writings were largely ignored in the West and after unification.[26]

Zwischen Nacht und Morgen fictionalizes the activities of the AAM. This prototypical account of antifascist resistance begins in January 1945 when Ernst Haring receives a telephone call from Herta Pohlenz, a secretary and ally at the hydrogenation plant where he is a foreman.[27] She warns Haring that the Gestapo has arrived to interrogate him about the circulation of anti-Nazi pamphlets. The first half of the novel details his escape and underground resistance work. Haring's feelings of impotence

---

25 "Eine schmachvolle Landtagssitzung in Württemberg-Baden," *Neues Deutschland*, February 6, 1952, 3.

26 See Thomas Beutelschmidt, "'Die Fahne von Kriwoj Rog': Materialien zur Adaptionsgeschichte eines Kanontextes der frühen DDR-Literatur," in *Realitätskonstruktion: Faschismus und Antifaschismus in Literaturverfilmungen des DDR-Fernsehens*, ed. Thomas Beutelschmidt and Rüdiger Steinlein (Leipzig: Leipziger Universitätsverlag, 2004), 53–100, here 61.

27 In my discussion of *Zwischen Nacht und Morgen* and *Berlin*, I introduce characters by their full names, when these are provided within the novels. In my subsequent analysis, however, I revert to the naming conventions established within the narratives themselves.

about having failed to undermine National Socialism shape the novel's second half, which begins with the arrival of the US Army. Appointed to leadership roles in local government, Haring's comrades grasp the opportunity to rebuild Germany along socialist lines. They increasingly clash with the US military administration, however. The novel's conclusion augurs a new political utopia as Soviet control is established in line with the Yalta agreements.

Zwischen Nacht und Morgen is narrated in the third person, with internal focalizations through members of the AAM. These are the narrative role models with whom readers are meant to empathize and from whom they ought to learn, according to Socialist Realism. This aesthetic doctrine imagined art as a vital tool in the development of socialist personalities. Although Gotsche only offers fleeting insights into the thoughts and feelings of female characters, the novel exploits the symbolic power of their experiences. Indeed, violence against women bookends the first night of occupation. Haring has sought out one of his collaborators, Kurt Seyffarth, to discuss arrangements for the postwar period. Seyffarth's unnamed wife tearfully bursts into the room to announce the arrival of US troops. Other women barricade themselves inside their houses out of fear. This terror is soon justified: "Im Dorf überstieg der Hilferuf einer Frau gellend das Donnern der fernen Geschütze. Es mußte ganz in der Nähe sein, am Straßenende. Trunkener Lärm erstickte die Stimme" (195; In the village, a woman's shrill cry for help eclipsed the thundering of distant artillery. It had to be very close, at the end of the road. Drunken noise suffocated her voice). The focus on what can be heard, rather than what is seen, invites contemporary readers to piece together events using their own memories. The next morning, as Haring observes battered and disheveled women seeking refuge, he surmises, "Sehr schwer wird alles sein, noch schwerer, als wir gedacht haben" (196; Everything is going to be very difficult, worse than we thought). This commentary positions violence against women in a metonymic chain linking US occupation with hardship and the postwar struggles of the AAM.

The rest of the novel foregrounds the group's efforts to undo the damage wrought by National Socialism and the arrival of the US Army, prevent the disassembly of German factories, and effect sociopolitical reform. Minimizing attacks and plunder by the occupiers becomes a priority. Haring is deeply affected by the extent of rape. As he explains to his colleagues in the town administration, this violence demonstrates "was [die Soldaten] unter amerikanischer Lebensweise verstehen" (251; what the American way of life means to [the soldiers]). At the local health department, he converses with a woman who glosses over her own experience of repeated rape. Instead, she focuses on her teenage daughter, who is awaiting transportation to the hospital owing to internal bleeding: "Zuletzt hat einer von den Soldaten die Faust hineingestoßen ..." (251;

In the end, one of the soldiers stuck his fist in . . .). The ellipsis encourages the reader to dwell on this perverse image. The lack of explicit emotional markers in the mother's speech stands out against the rest of this passage, which uses expressive adjectives to emphasize Haring's shock and dismay. We read, for instance, that "der Redeschwall der Mutter fiel schmerzend über ihn her" (251; the mother's torrent of words cascaded painfully on him). This construction downplays the mother's agency and subjectivity and foregrounds Haring's emotional pain, exemplifying Gotsche's tendency to exile women to an emotional elsewhere by foregrounding male responses to rape.

In fact, female victims primarily serve to attest to the brutality of US soldiers. Their anonymity and prompt disappearance from the novel reflect a patriarchal literary tradition that has "disfigured" sexual violence.[28] Lynn Higgins and Brenda Silver use this term to evoke representations that abstract from the actual physical and emotional experiences of women, either because texts treat rape as a trope or plot device, or because they privilege male perspectives. In *Zwischen Nacht und Morgen*, for example, most female figures are reduced to their violation, becoming "unnarratable," to borrow the terminology of literary theorist Gerald Prince.[29] Their stories remain hypothetical and inchoate within the fictional world. Robyn Warhol divides the unnarratable into the paranarratable (literary convention delays narration), the antinarratable (taboo bars narration), supranarratable (something exceeds the expressive capacity of language), and subnarratable (anything deemed insignificant).[30] We might add the allegorical to this taxonomy: what makes some things unnarratable is a narrative practice that directs attention *elsewhere*; here, to men affected by rape and to the culture of which this violence is deemed representative.

A blatant example of such narrative elsewhering follows an attack on the family of the ironmonger, referred to only by his surname, Lenthe. Toward the end of the novel—that is, once peace has ostensibly returned—their leisurely stroll through the countryside is interrupted by US soldiers, who go out of their way to terrorize them. The assailants overpower Lenthe and smear car oil in his eyes. When his vision clears, the disheveled appearance of his unnamed adult daughters implies that they have been sexually assaulted. The narrative barely dwells on the image of

---

28 Lynn Higgins and Brenda Silver, "Introduction: Rereading Rape," in *Rape and Representation*, ed. Lynn Higgins and Brenda Silver (New York: Columbia University Press, 1991), 1–14, here 4.

29 Gerald Prince, *Narrative as Theme: Studies in French Fiction* (Lincoln: University of Nebraska Press, 1992), 28.

30 Robyn Warhol-Down, "'What Might Have Been Is Not What Is': Dickens's Narrative Refusals," *Dickens Studies Annual* 41 (2010), 45–59, here 48.

the sobbing young women and instead directs attention to their incensed father, who rushes off to demand an audience with the mayor. As Lenthe processes the attack, he recollects a conversation with an American lieutenant who had warned him that the town would sink into "östliche Barbarei" (430, oriental barbarism) if local Communists were not kept in check. The attack on Lenthe's daughters elicits the question: Which culture is civilized, and which is barbaric?

Gotsche's answer turns on the issue of sexual morality. In an earlier episode, Haring observes US soldiers taunting, molesting, and intimidating young women waiting to register with the new authorities. Their treatment prompts Haring to ask himself, "Konnte man mit diesen Leuten überhaupt zusammenarbeiten? Wie die Plantagenbesitzer in den Südstaaten auf ihren Sklavenmärkten schätzten sie Männer und Frauen ab.... Wert und körperliche Vorzüge bestimmten die Entscheidungen" (292; Was there any way of working with these people? They appraise men and women just like plantation owners in the Southern states at their slave markets.... Value and physical assets guide their decisions). These reflections universalize the harassment experienced by the town's women to draw conclusions about the treatment of the population as a whole ("Männer und Frauen" [men and women]) and the slaveholder mentality of white American soldiers. Such metonymic slippage characterizes the practice of narrative elsewhering in this novel. Gotsche's inference that the sexual objectification of women in US culture is an extension of the exploitative logics of slavery and capitalism is no doubt reductionist and problematic.[31] The analogy stems from classical Marxist texts about the relationship between patriarchy, the accumulation of private property, and class oppression. To quote Friedrich Engels's famous description of the transition from matriarchal to patriarchal forms of socioeconomic organization: "Der Mann ergriff das Steuer auch im Hause, die Frau wurde entwürdigt, geknechtet, Sklavin seiner Lust und bloßes Werkzeug der Kinderzeugung" (Man took control in the home too, woman was debased, enslaved, a slave of his lust, and mere reproductive tool).[32] GDR

---

31 On the relationship between capitalism, slavery, and racism in GDR interpretations of US history, see Daisy Weßel, *Bild und Gegenbild: Die USA in der Belletristik der SBZ und der DDR (bis 1987)* (Wiesbaden: Springer, 1989), chapter 2. Analogies between slavery and women's oppression have been roundly criticized, particularly since the advent of US Black Feminism (see bell hooks, *Ain't I a Woman: Black Women and Feminism* [1981; New York: Routledge, 2015], 126). There remains limited engagement with the legacy of such ideas in the German sphere, however.

32 Friedrich Engels, *Marx-Engels Werke*, vol. 21 (Berlin: Dietz, 1973), 61. On the evolution of this idea in Germany, see Petra Schmackpfeffer, *Frauenbewegung und Prostitution: Über das Verhältnis der alten und neuen deutschen Frauenbewegung zur Prostitution* (Oldenburg: BIS Verlag, 1999).

propaganda developed this idea in its attacks on American culture's obsession with nudity and pornography, which was seen to exemplify objectifying attitudes to women and a shallow, carnal approach to sexuality. Conversely, socialism promoted gender equality, as well as reciprocal (heterosexual) love and sexual relations.[33]

These ideas suffuse *Zwischen Nacht und Morgen*, which emphasizes the misogyny, dissolution, and lechery of US soldiers. When Herta Pohlenz visits Major Fishman, the local commandant, he assumes that she is making a social call and pours her a drink. She is repulsed by his lewd gaze: "So schätzten Männer seiner Art käufliche Ware ab" (433; That's how men like him appraise goods for purchase). When Haring's secretary explains that she is on official business, she is dismissed. After she leaves Fishman's office, her difficulties continue. The guard forces her into the watch room, where jeering soldiers attempt to ply her with food and drink, ignoring her energetic requests to leave. One soldier forces her behind a screen, but she manages to escape. The harassment does not end here: sentries posted in the marketplace catcall as she passes. This concatenation of debasements implies that objectifying attitudes toward women are a defining characteristic of US masculinity.

Zwischen Nacht und Morgen closes with the sight of vehicles bearing the hopeful symbol of the hammer and sickle. This ending sequesters negative experiences of occupation in a temporal elsewhere—the period of US occupation—and adds a secondary layer to the GDR's founding mythology: the Soviets had liberated (East) Germany not only from Nazism but also from the US occupiers.[34] Nevertheless, the novel contains some allusions to a less utopian reality. Haring and his colleagues discuss the fact that local industry magnates are spreading panic among the workers by using the workers' fear of the Russians as a pretext for relocating their factories. The AAM publishes its own counterpropaganda:

VERHINDERT, DASS UNSER LAND ZUR VERBRANNTEN
    ERDE WIRD!
LASST EUCH NICHT LÄNGER AUSPLÜNDERN UND
    BERAUBEN!
NICHT FLIEHEN—HIER MÜSSEN UND WOLLEN WIR
    LEBEN! (411)

[PREVENT OUR COUNTRY BECOMING SCORCHED EARTH! DO NOT ALLOW YOURSELVES TO BE LOOTED

---

33 Ingrid Sharp, "The Sexual Unification of Germany," *Journal of the History of Sexuality* 13, no. 3 (2004): 348–65, here 349. See also Josie McLellan, *Love in the Time of Communism: Intimacy and Sexuality in the GDR* (Cambridge: Cambridge University Press, 2011), 174.

34 See also Weßel, *Bild und Gegenbild*, 141–44.

AND ROBBED ANY LONGER! DO NOT FLEE—WE HAVE TO AND WANT TO LIVE HERE!]

This petition cites the Nazi policy of "scorched earth," which saw retreating armies destroy infrastructure and communities in a bid to sabotage the Red Army.[35] Haring's appeal thus implies parallels between the US and National Socialism.

The population's wariness of the Red Army and its instinct to flee is a subtext of this passage. The presentation of such fears as hearsay exemplifies the "disnarrated." Prince coined this term to describe events that do not occur in a given narrative but that are evoked "in a negative or hypothetical sense."[36] In this instance, the disnarrated betrays a source of narrative and political tension: the behavior of the Red Army. As Warhol elaborates, the disnarrated is where "the 'repressed' of the text returns, not quite not-there."[37] It is almost more telling than what is explicitly censored, because how and why the "repressed" is brought back under control discloses something central about the internal workings of a text and about its ideological premises. Here the immorality of the US occupiers stands out against the background of disnarrated Soviet violence. Such oppositional constructions suggest the extent to which the utopian narrative of socialism presupposed an ideological elsewhere from which it could dissociate itself.[38] Gotsche uses disnarration in these examples to repudiate claims about Soviet brutality both within and beyond the diegesis. Yet the excess of inscription—Red Army violence is at first evoked, then denied or reimagined as a problem of the elsewhere—accommodates a variety of potentially contradictory readings. Ultimately, Gotsche's attempts to manage the memory of CRSV cannot control reader association. Above all, the ending of *Zwischen Nacht und Morgen* leaves the reader free to fill in the disnarrated future of Soviet occupation with more personal, and potentially dystopian, memories.

Theodor Plievier's *Berlin* (1954)

On the surface, Plievier and Gotsche have much in common. Both joined the Bund proletarisch-revolutionärer Schriftsteller (Association of Proletarian-Revolutionary Authors) during the Weimar Republic, and

---

35 See Alan Kramer, "From Great War to Fascist Warfare," in *Fascist Warfare, 1922–1945: Aggression, Occupation, Annihilation*, ed. Miguel Alonso, Alan Kramer, and Javier Rodrigo (Cham, Switzerland: Palgrave Macmillan, 2019), 25–50, here 29.
36 Prince, *Narrative as Theme*, 30.
37 Warhol-Down, "'What Might Have Been,'" 58.
38 See also Edwards, "The Colonial Archival Imaginaire at Home," 60.

both were blacklisted after Adolf Hitler's accession. Plievier's antiwar novels and anarchist politics led the Nazi Party to revoke his citizenship in 1934. He spent most of the next decade in the Soviet Union. Upon returning to Thuringia in 1945, Plievier presided over the Kulturbund zur demokratischen Erneuerung Deutschlands (Cultural Association for the Democratic Renewal of Germany). He grew increasingly wary of Stalinist tendencies in the politics of occupation, however, and defected during a lecture tour of West Germany in 1947.

As Hans-Harald Müller underscores, the anti-Communist tone of *Berlin* does not represent a political volte-face for Plievier because "er nie Kommunist war" (he was never a Communist). Rather it is consonant with an anarchist perspective inflected by Christian values.[39] The novel indeed presents the recent past through a redemptive lens, using historical events and imagined mentalities to reconstruct a cycle of national hubris, nemesis, and possible salvation.[40] It develops the documentary technique synonymous with *Stalingrad*, which reworked letters, diaries, and interviews with German combatants on the Eastern Front. *Berlin* is likewise meticulously researched, with excerpts from military records, parliamentary discussions, and Plievier's own interviews with historical figures.

Although there are no protagonists as such in this kaleidoscopic text, which covers the eight years between the fall of Berlin and the East German workers' uprising, the first and final parts primarily accompany Colonel Zecke, a senior Wehrmacht officer who is initially waiting out the end of the war as a quartermaster in Prague. In April 1945, he is pulled into the vortex of the collapsing front, having received orders to lead a course at the military academy in Berlin. The omniscient narrator intertwines Zecke's westward journey with scenes that introduce new characters, from civilians and common soldiers to members of the military and political elite. Through fly-on-the-wall episodes in Hitler's bunker and Joseph Goebbels's propaganda ministry, the second section of *Berlin* probes the ignorance, fanaticism, and authoritarianism of the German population. The final three parts reconstruct the Soviet military administration's attempts to consolidate its position in the postwar power struggle, increasing authoritarianism in the Soviet zone, and the growing disillusionment of committed socialists.

The extent to which Plievier utilizes CRSV to construct the Soviet Union as an ideological elsewhere becomes apparent at the start of a series of episodes depicting the confrontation between Berlin's inhabitants and the Red Army in 1945. Although Plievier otherwise makes scant use of intrusive structural devices, here he employs decontextualized quotations as flash-forwards to generate suspense:

---

39 Hans-Harald Müller, "Nachwort," in Plievier, *Berlin*, 741–66, here 742.
40 Müller, "Nachwort," 761.

"Frau, komm," hieß es.
"Und du, dumme Ziege, mach die Brosche ab!" hieß es.
"Wo bleibt die Armee Wenck?" hieß es. . . . (201)

["Come, woman," they said.
"And you, silly cow, take off your brooch," they said.
"Where is Wenck's Army?" they said. . . .]

The first proleptic quotation uses a byword for the rape of German women by Soviet soldiers to situate the forthcoming action, which will take place in an air-raid shelter. Some of the occupants retain hope that General Wenck, recently appointed commander of the Twelfth Army, will turn back the Red Army. Overwhelmingly, however, the inhabitants are pragmatic about defeat. They berate a fanatical member of the Reich Labor Service for not removing a brooch identifying her as a party loyalist. The inhabitants beseech her to join the other young women in serving coffee and cigarettes to placate the arriving soldiers. This effort fails. As soldiers pour into the cellar, "Koffer wurden durchwühlt, Sachen umhergeschleudert. Frauen schrien, schrien . . ." (214; Suitcases were ransacked, things tossed aside. Women screamed, screamed . . .). This juxtaposition suggests that the women are treated as possessions to be looted. Further dehumanizing descriptions of the women as "ein hingeworfenes entstelltes Bündel" (a deformed, discarded bundle) or "wimmernde Bedrängnis" (whimpering affliction) erase their individuality and mute the subjective impact of violence. As in Gotsche's novel, *Berlin* foregrounds the emotional impact of sexualized violence on male witnesses who struggle to compute and assign meaning to what they have seen. Here, Plievier uses free indirect speech to foreground the perspective of the cobbler known as Haderer, especially his feelings of impotence at having failed to protect the women. "Schwarzer Sonntag in Weißensee" (215; Black Sunday in Weißensee), he thinks as he exits the cellar. Haderer's stream of consciousness continues to flow as he recalls another "Schwarzer Sonntag": the January 1905 massacre in St. Petersburg. Historians have identified these events as one of the triggers for the First Russian Revolution and the emergence of Bolshevism "as a distinct political movement."[41] This historical allusion thus embeds the ideological elsewhere of the Soviet Union in a tradition of state violence, one that casts doubt on the moral achievements of revolutionary Marxism.

In such examples of narrative elsewhering, Plievier directs readerly attention away from CRSV and its victims: first, by privileging male perspectives, and second, through narrative commentaries that evoke

---

41 Abraham Ascher, *The Revolution of 1905: A Short History* (Stanford, CA: Stanford University Press, 2004), x.

ideological elsewheres. Victims even remain unnarrated in passages designed to educe the scale of violence against women during the Battle of Berlin. Halfway through the novel's second section, we follow Dr. Linth, who is called to an air-raid shelter to help the laboring Frau Halen. Marauding soldiers soon enter in search of female company, picking out the pregnant woman. This scene ends after Dr. Linth has convinced the soldiers to spare Frau Halen (we later discover that she suffers a postpartum attack). The words "dieser Russenbesuch war nicht der erste und auch nicht der letzte" (320; this Russian visit was not the first and nor was it the last) initiate a lengthy montage of similar scenes, each of which transitions soon after the moment of violence. By focusing on the immediate corporeal consequences of rape, these allegorical snapshots magnify the brutality of war. The montage ultimately serves to condense Soviet attitudes toward women: "Frauen, Schnaps, Uhren waren die am meisten begehrten Dinge; auch Frauen waren Dinge, erleidende oder sich sträubende, stumme und manchmal schreiende Objekte" (320; women, schnapps, watches were the most coveted items; women were things too, suffering or resisting, silent and sometimes screaming objects). Such narrative commentaries debunk the notion that misogyny, the commodification of women, and brutality in sexual relations were the preserve of capitalist societies.[42] By leaving the psychological aftermath of rape unnarrated, however, Plievier ultimately objectifies his female characters on the level of diegesis.

The practice of narrative elsewhering that defines representations of CRSV in *Berlin* is especially apparent in the passages concerning Dolores Linth, the wife of the doctor, and one of the only women to function as narrative focalizer. Her name—etymologically linked to the Latin for pain and sorrow—underlines her metonymic function as a representative of the suffering nation. Her plight begins when she is abducted by a Soviet tank commander, who holds her hostage during his several-day journey across the besieged capital. The narrative capitalizes on the contrast between Dolores Linth's initial sensory overload, heightened by the darkness of the tank, and her eventual numbness. While her stupefaction is plausibly a traumatic response to multiple violations, the narration dedicates less space to reconstructing her feelings than to chronicling the final stages of the Battle of Berlin.

The celebrations that accompany the end of fighting allow Dolores Linth to escape. Climbing out of the tank, she sees that "Himmel und Erde waren verändert. Die Zeit stimmte nicht mehr. Der Breitengrad hatte sich verschoben. Die Welt war aus den Fugen. Der Zeiger der

---

42 McLellan, *Love in the Time of Communism*, 174. See also Roger Markwick and Euridice Charon Cardona, *Soviet Women on the Frontline in the Second World War* (Basingstoke, Hampshire, UK: Palgrave Macmillan, 2012), 201.

Weltuhr stand auf Untergang" (343; Heaven and Earth were changed. Time was out of sync. The line of latitude had shifted. The world had been thrown out of joint. The hand of the world clock pointed to downfall). This spatiotemporal disarray crystallizes in the hallucinatory image of a historical and cultural elsewhere. Shortly before she collapses and disappears from the narrative, Dolores Linth sees the Tower of Nanjing superimposed on the German capital, the River Spree merging with the Yangtze. A horrific vision of defiled and mutilated female bodies is overlaid with dizzying allusions to conflicts from the invasion of ancient China by "barbarian" tribes to the Taiping Rebellion (1850–64). This episode typifies the extent to which Plievier exploits the symbolic potential of spatial and temporal elsewheres to emphasize the shock of war and brutality of the Red Army.

This imagery recalls the way that Nazi propaganda combined orientalist, antisemitic, and anti-Bolshevist tropes in its constructions of the "Other."[43] Plievier's relation to such ideological traditions is complex. Elsewhere in the novel, he denounces Germany for forsaking the values of the "Abendland" (occident) during the "Third Reich." A passage imagining May 1945 as Germany's hour of reckoning explicitly links the barbarity of occupation to the nation's failings: "Die Stunde war da, und ihr Geruch war der von Leichen aus geöffneten U-Bahn-Schächten, ihr Schrei war der vergewaltigter Frauen, ihr Inhalt war Selbstentäußerung, war Abkehr vom Abendland" (The hour had come, and its odor was that of bodies from exposed subway stations, its cry was that of raped women, its content was self-renunciation, it was a rejection of the occident, 428). Such quotations illuminate the metonymic logic underpinning representations of CRSV in *Berlin*, which often equate women with the nation.

This allegorical treatment of rape ultimately displaces victims into emotional elsewheres. In fact, CRSV is virtually absent in the final two sections of the novel, which focus on Germany's political and spiritual recovery. The fourth segment transports readers to Thuringia. The focal character is Dr Rudolf Paul, a lawyer and anti-Nazi campaigner who became Minister-President in 1946. Paul's interzonal contacts and maverick approach to state politics increasingly brought him into conflict with the Soviet administration, and he fled to West Berlin in 1947.[44] Fictionalizing these historical events allows Plievier to subvert utopian narratives presenting the Soviet zone as liberated from authoritarian, fascist rule. Most of the brief references to CRSV in this part take the form

---

[43] See Caroline Rupprecht, *Asian Fusion: New Encounters in the Asian-German Avant-Garde* (Oxford: Peter Lang, 2020), 5.

[44] Harald Hurwitz, Ursula Böhme, and Andreas Malycha, *Die Stalinisierung der SED: Zum Verlust von Freiräumen und sozialdemokratischer Identität in den Vorständen 1946–1949* (Opladen: Westdeutscher Verlag, 1997), 256.

of political asides. For instance, we read that Dr Paul continues to gather statistics on rapes and other attacks by Red Army soldiers, even though official propaganda blames such violence on German saboteurs in Soviet uniforms (487). The novel also alludes to the notion that these attacks cost the Sozialistische Einheitspartei Deutschlands (Socialist Unity Party of Germany, SED) dearly during the first postwar elections (674–75).[45] Women's subjective responses to CRSV, however, come to epitomize the unnarrated. Part 4 of *Berlin* briefly revisits two of the women tended to by Dr. Linth: Lisa and Anneliese Aachern, the wife and teenage daughter of Wing Commander Helmuth Aachern. Having escaped imprisonment in 1945, Helmuth Aachern lives under a false identity as Dr. Paul's chauffeur. When he visits his family in the US zone for the first time at the end of 1945, he learns of their rape and is alienated by their frankness and apathy. As he tries to make sense of their changed demeanor, Aachern dwells not on the actual violence done to his family but on the fact that "die Vergewaltigung einer ganzen Stadt, Mord, Totschlag, einsames Hungersterben—nichts wurde hier ernst genommen" (511; the rape of an entire city, murder, manslaughter, solitary starvation—nothing was being taken seriously here). He is particularly perturbed by Anneliese's disillusionment, not to mention the fact that she works late into the night at a US military store and is courting a Black GI officer.

Neither the potential trauma of his wife and daughter—nor the choices that they have made to secure some form of subsistence amid the ruins—feature explicitly in Helmuth Aachern's internal monologue or subsequent conversations about the US sector. Instead, he reflects on the demise of Christian culture, comparing Berlin to Shanghai (521). In such moments, the instability of the elsewhere as a conceptual metaphor becomes apparent. In fact, Plievier uses orientalist tropes to associate both the Soviet Union and the United States with the elsewhere. This mutability suggests Plievier's deep skepticism about the potential of either occupation government to foment Germany's moral and spiritual recovery.

The final pages of *Berlin* return Zecke to the German capital after a prolonged, Kafkaesque period of internment in a prisoner-of-war camp. Here, Plievier again draws on the symbolic cogency of female suffering to emphasize the desolate mood as Zecke surveys the ruins of West Berlin. He glimpses a "schwergeprüfte Kriegersfrau" (738; long-suffering warrior's wife), who reminds him of women from his former life: his wife and daughter, whose fate is unknown to the protagonist and the reader, as well as Frau Halen and Frau Pullitzer, both of whom fall victim to rape. Zecke compares the unknown woman's face to a painted lantern, "und in der sich öffnenden Nebenstraße flackerten noch andere bemalte

---

45 See also Grossmann, *Jews, Germans, and Allies*, 65, and Naimark, *The Russians in Germany*, 328–39.

Laternen. Das gab es. Das große Evangelium und schuldlos Schuldige
... Mittelalterliche Schatten am Rande des Atomzeitalters. Und Berlin ist
aufgerissen, ein wüster Krater . . ." (738; and in the side streets opening
out in front of him, yet more painted lanterns flickered. That was it. The
Great Gospel and guiltless guilt . . . medieval shadows on the edge of the
atomic age. And Berlin is torn open, a desolate crater). This image of a
fault line running through the capital imagines the here and the elsewhere
as a form of dualism.

Berlin concludes with Zecke in a public house, listening as other
patrons discuss the workers' uprising over the border as though it were
unrelated to their lives. An intertext from the "Parable of the Rich Fool"
suggests Plievier's attitude to this politics of dissociation. The eponymous figure acquires more grain than he can store and chooses to hoard
rather than share the goods. God reprimands him with the words: "This
very night your life will be demanded from you. Then who will get
what you have prepared for yourself?" (Luke 12:20). Plievier reimag-
ines the West as the rich fool, co-responsible for the creation of a more
democratic, moral Germany and world order. This conclusion reflects
Plievier's resistance to any "anti-Stellung" (anti-attitude) and recognition that black-and-white ideological positions are limited in their ability
to resolve the major issues plaguing Cold War society.[46] Plievier dedicates several hundred pages to male figures' cogitations on these matters. Tellingly, however, women's safety and equality appear merely as
political inconveniences in these reflections and not as problems deserv-
ing extended consideration.

Complicating the Elsewhere

Revisiting *Zwischen Nacht und Morgen* and *Berlin* is doubly rewarding.
Both are rich with insights into the occupation of Germany, the military administration, and how they were remembered at the time. As representative texts of Cold War culture, they illuminate the centrality of
spatial and temporal elsewheres to the oppositional discourses through
which each Germany shored up its self-perception as morally superior.
These utopian constructions functioned in part by jettisoning the violent legacy of dictatorship and war onto the ideological other. The treatment of women anchors such narratives; indeed, the perpetrators of
CRSV personify the ideological elsewhere in the texts that I have analyzed. Projecting responsibility for CRSV onto the ideological elsewhere
did not simply make this sensitive history speakable: it became politically
eloquent. In *Zwischen Nacht und Morgen* and *Berlin,* explicit narrative
commentaries encourage audiences to read sexual violence allegorically;

---

46 Müller, "Nachwort," 755–56.

that is, as the expression of an antithetical political and moral system, on the one hand, and as a metonym for the spiritual and physical danger of invasion, on the other.

There is much to work be done on understanding the extent to which consumers of propaganda, literary and otherwise, during the Cold War did indeed adopt or resist the subject positions constructed for them by authors. On the level of close reading, however, my literary analyses suggest that no matter how insistently Gotsche and Plievier appeal to the elsewhere to reframe and therefore temper the volatile memory of CRSV, they cannot expunge the potentially disruptive dimensions of this history. This is the problem with allegory, which Mieke Bal describes as "a mode of reading that isolates the event from its own history in order to place it within a different one." Her definition foregrounds the agency and disposition of readers whose imaginations might travel elsewhere than intended by the author. To contemporary audiences with direct or indirect experience of CRSV, any reference to assault by occupation soldiers risked activating memories that undermined sanctioned political scripts. As Bal puts it, "allegory can never replace the 'literally' real."[47] Thus, if the elsewhere functioned as a container for difficult memories of CRSV during the Cold War, it was surely a porous and mercurial one.

Ultimately, the analytical prism of the elsewhere elucidates the ambivalence that characterized Cold War memories of CRSV. While it was politically acceptable, and indeed expedient, to engage with CRSV occurring on the stage of the ideological elsewhere, this engagement did not necessarily foment empathy or solidarity. My close readings demonstrate that victims and survivors are repeatedly displaced into emotional elsewheres. Their stories often start and end with the act of violence in a way that produces radically foreshortened accounts of the reality of rape. Emotion does, however, stick to male witnesses who interpret the violence as a sign of the values of the elsewhere. "Elsewhering" thus becomes an eloquent label for the ethical problems inherent in metaphorical constructions of the significance of sexual violence, which deflect attention from the "vehicle" (the raped woman; the act of rape) toward the "tenor" (here: the ideological elsewhere). Outside of fiction, such discursive elsewhering had material consequences. For while East and West German politicians readily appropriated women's experiences of CRSV for propaganda purposes, they had limited appetite to address its lasting repercussions for survivors and their families.[48]

---

47   Mieke Bal, *Double Exposures: The Practice of Cultural Analysis* (New York: Routledge, 1996), 227.
48   See Heineman, "The Hour of the Woman," 372.

2: Watching Violence Elsewhere: Louis Malle's *Viva Maria!* in 1960s West Germany

Mererid Puw Davies[1]

Introduction

IN 1965, FRENCH DIRECTOR Louis Malle made the picturesque musical-comedy film *Viva Maria!* It told the story of a successful revolution in a fictional turn-of-the-twentieth-century Latin American country, starred Brigitte Bardot and Jeanne Moreau, and was a box-office hit in Europe.[2] More surprisingly, *Viva Maria!* has a remarkable place in the political history of the Federal Republic of Germany (FRG; West Germany).[3] Malle later stated that his apparently frothy, big-budget film was not intended as a genuine revolutionary allegory.[4] Nonetheless, in the mid-to-late 1960s, *Viva Maria!* became a cult film for the FRG's antiauthoritarian movement

---

1   I thank Clare Bielby and Annie Ring for perceptive readings of this chapter.
2   *Viva Maria!*, directed by Louis Malle (France and Italy, 1965). *Viva Maria!* was more successful in Europe than in the US. Nathan C. Southern with Jacques Weissberger, *The Films of Louis Malle: A Critical Analysis* (Jefferson, NC: McFarland, 2006), 100, 387; Timothy Schele, "Cowboy and Alien: The Bardot Westerns," *Studies in French Cinema* 19, no. 2 (2019): 108–9. Further page references to both these works follow in the text. In France the film spawned a 1965 comic strip by Julio Ribera in the newspaper *France Soir*. Bas Schuddeboom, "Julio Ribera," last updated August 27, 2021, https://www.lambiek.net/artists/r/ribera_j.htm. It was, however, banned in Spain owing to its portrayal of the Catholic Church. "Viva Maria verboten," *Rhein-Ems Zeitung*, February 22, 1967. Bardot and Moreau were both nominated for Best Foreign Actress at the 1967 British Film Awards; Moreau won. On the film's sparse reception in scholarship, see, e.g. Schele, "Cowboy and Alien."
3   For concision, reference here to the FRG includes West Berlin.
4   Southern, *The Films of Louis Malle*, 96. According to Volker Schlöndorff, *Viva Maria!* cost two million dollars, half as much as comparable US productions. Volker Schlöndorff, "Zauberlehrling in Mexiko: Die Geschichte des Films 'Viva Maria,'" *Die Zeit*, July 8, 1966, Literature Section, 25.

and was seen as a revolutionary blueprint.[5] Prominent West Berlin activist Rudi Dutschke, not otherwise an avid cinemagoer, saw Malle's film at least four times. Indeed, as he and his internationalist comrades increasingly attended to contemporary anti- or postcolonial struggles worldwide, they named themselves the "Viva Maria Group."[6] Historian Timothy S. Brown writes of that group's place in the organization most closely associated with protest, the Sozialistischer Deutscher Studentenbund (Socialist German Student Federation [SDS]): "Meant to function as a vanguard within the SDS, the ['Viva Maria Group'] helped to effect a theoretical reorientation for the West German student movement and ... [channeled] further transnational connections."[7] That small, informal group thus became a significant influence on wider antiauthoritarian thought.[8]

Brown goes on to link the reception of Malle's "lighthearted revolutionary sex romp" (78) to the arson attack perpetrated in Frankfurt am Main in April 1968 by Andreas Baader and Gudrun Ensslin (81). This action is remembered as a precursor to the activities of the terrorist Rote Armee Fraktion (Red Army Faction [RAF]), which Baader and Ensslin cofounded along with others (81). Indeed, journalist and author Klaus-Rainer Röhl wrote polemically in 1974 of the terrorist underground's genesis, "Am Anfang ... stand ein Film" (In the beginning ... was a film): *Viva Maria!*[9] Such associations between *Viva Maria!* and political violence cast a long shadow. In 2001, for instance, West German

---

5   Antiauthoritarian reception was not limited to the FRG. In the Netherlands, a group of Provos, a movement that influenced West German protesters, called its pet chicken "Viva Maria!" Hans Tuynmann, *Ich bin ein Provo: Das permanente Happening*, trans. Helmut Homeyer (Darmstadt: Joseph Melzer, 1967).
6   Gretchen Dutschke, *Wir hatten ein barbarisches, schönes Leben: Rudi Dutschke. Eine Biographie* (Cologne: Kiepenheuer & Witsch, 1996), 78–79; Ulrich Chaussy, *Die drei Leben des Rudi Dutschke*, 2nd ed. (Munich: Pendo, 1993), 151–56.
7   Timothy S. Brown, "'1968' East and West: Divided Germany as a Case Study in Transnational History," *American Historical Review* 114, no. 1 (February 2009): 69–96, here 77. Further page references follow in the text.
8   See, e.g., Werner Balsen and Karl Rössel, *Hoch die internationale Solidarität: Zur Geschichte der Dritte Welt-Bewegung in der Bundesrepublik* (Cologne: Kölner Volksblatt, 1985); Ingo Juchler, *Rebellische Subjektivität und Internationalismus* (Marburg: Verlag Arbeiterbewegung und Geschichtswissenschaft, 1989) and *Die Studentenbewegungen in den Vereinigten Staaten und der Bundesrepublik Deutschland der sechziger Jahre: Eine Untersuchung hinsichtlich ihrer Beeinflussung durch Befreiungsbewegungen und -theorien aus der Dritten Welt* (Berlin: Duncker & Humblot, 1996); Quinn Slobodian, *Foreign Front: Third World Politics in Sixties West Germany* (Durham, NC: Duke University Press, 2012).
9   Klaus Rainer Röhl, *Fünf Finger sind keine Faust: Eine Abrechnung* (1974), quoted in Julian Preece, "Reinscribing the German Autumn: Heinrich Breloer's *Todesspiel* and the Two Clusters of 'Terrorist' Films," *German Monitor* 70

filmmaker Volker Schlöndorff recalled a late consequence of his role as its assistant director. In the 1970s, the right-wing press suspected him of terrorist sympathies, sensationally describing an "illegal arsenal discovered in director's home" by police. In fact, that raid had found a gun—a souvenir from filming *Viva Maria!* on location in Mexico.[10]

Brown identifies *Viva Maria!* as an emblematic instance of the 1960s' "active reception" (78) of internationally circulating discourses. Such reception, he argues, is key to analyzing "1968" in West Germany and globally. It demonstrates "how intimately '1968' was linked to the creation of globalizing imagined communities . . . across national boundaries" (69). Understanding this dynamic requires consideration of "transnational influences, analysing their mode of transmission and exploring how they articulated with local concerns, goals, traditions and histories." Likewise, it demands examination of ways in which "local actors imagined themselves into the world, creating alternative cognitive maps that corresponded to a new type of politics" (70). This chapter seeks to show how these processes, and the dream of a global imagined community and politics, can be tracked in the extraordinary West German reception of *Viva Maria!*

The chapter argues, too, that critical analysis is required of related texts that, like *Viva Maria!*, flowed into the "active reception" Brown describes. Such interpretation is crucial because the complexity of such texts highlights the era's multilayered, at times contradictory responses to the film, an understanding of which is important inter alia for a symptomatic analysis of the protest movements themselves. These points are illustrated by West German director Helke Sander's feature film *Der subjektive Faktor* (The Subjective Factor, 1981), a richly detailed account of West Berlin antiauthoritarianism from around 1967. In a scene set in the SDS offices, a poster for *Viva Maria!* is prominently displayed. Evident contrasts are set up between the poster, which features Bardot and Moreau in glamorous stage costumes posing with a machine gun, and Sander's protagonist, Anni, who is, as usual, dressed for practicality. Anni is delivering a critical text on women's issues for the SDS newsletter, and the men staffing the office react patronizingly. Therefore, as Clare Bielby argues, the poster's triumphant women are at odds with the SDS's patriarchal sexual politics and so underline the ambivalent position of

---

(2008): 213–29, here 214 (ellipsis in original). Röhl was formerly married to RAF cofounder Ulrike Meinhof.

10 Gary Crowdus and Richard Porton, "Coming to Terms with the German Past: An Interview with Volker Schlöndorff," *Cinéaste* 26, no. 2 (2001): 18–23, here 22.

women in antiauthoritarianism.[11] That is, while the movement portrayed by Sander appreciates fantasies of powerful women like *Viva Maria!*'s heroines, it fails fully to recognize Anni's political agency. Yet simultaneously, Sander's scene suggests that around 1968, women and feminism had explosive potential.

This chapter starts from the canonical recognition that *Viva Maria!* was a touchstone for antiauthoritarians in West Germany and elsewhere. It explores that antiauthoritarian reception through a high-profile essay by Dutschke's collaborator Bernd Rabehl, which claims to pinpoint the film's revolutionary message. The chapter shows through close readings how *Viva Maria!* maps with Rabehl's revolutionary interests; namely, tricontinentalism and ideas about the so-called subjective factors of politics. This chapter suggests also that Rabehl's essay reflects, more discreetly, the contemporary idea, derived from Critical Theory, that art and culture were revolutionary zones. Here too, correspondences can be found in Malle's film.

The chapter goes on, however, to identify paradoxes and contradictions in such antiauthoritarian readings of *Viva Maria!* The film deals, for instance, in negative stereotypes of Latin Americans and conventionally sexualized images of women. And yet, the chapter argues too that it might make space for an alternative reading of its spectacle, at least with reference to the representation of women. Subsequently, the chapter examines a memoir published by a cast member: actor and writer Gregor von Rezzori. His *Die Toten auf Ihre Plätze! Ein Filmtagebuch* (Corpses, Places! Diary of a Film, 1966) covers over almost two hundred pages the film's six-month shoot in Mexico in 1965.[12] Von Rezzori's expansive, dreamlike Mexican landscapes offer a difficult, equivocal view of *Viva Maria!*'s interest for West Germans. Finally, this chapter considers the film's significance for 1960s engagement with violence elsewhere. In sum, Malle's film, like its West German reception and *Die Toten auf Ihre Plätze!*, proves complex and ambiguous to the core, like the textual politics of antiauthoritarianism itself.

Viva Maria!

Viva Maria! was released in the FRG in 1966. It features a pastel palette, performance and cabaret sequences, elaborate costumes, visual jokes, nonrealist effects, sublime painterly landscapes, and exaggerated,

---

11 Clare Bielby, "Bewaffnete Terroristinnen: Linksterrorismus, Gender und die Waffe in der Bundesrepublik Deutschland von den 1970er Jahren bis heute," *WerkstattGeschichte* 64 (2014): 77–101, here 88–89.

12 Gregor von Rezzori, *Die Toten auf Ihre Plätze! Ein Filmtagebuch* (1966) (Munich: Goldmann, 1990). Further page references follow in the text.

supposed local color. It evokes genres and styles from musicals to period melodrama, romantic comedy, surrealism, slapstick, Westerns, and action movies. The plot develops chronologically, beginning with the childhood of Bardot's French-Irish character, Maria Fitzgerald O'Malley, or Maria II, from 1891.[13] She grows up taking violent action around the world with her Irish revolutionary father. As they target British interests in Central America in 1907, Maria II's father is captured and orders her to detonate an explosion, knowing it will kill him. She reluctantly complies and escapes to San Miguel, a country in thrall to a corrupt Catholic Church, a dictator, and despotic landowners.

Maria II stows away in a caravan belonging to Moreau's Maria I, a Parisian singer whose stage partner, Janine, has just committed heartbroken suicide. Maria I is a member of a traveling music-hall troupe, alongside conjurors M. and Mme Diogène (the former played by von Rezzori) and their son; marksman The Great Rodolfo; male acrobats Los Turcos; and strongman Werther. The Marias form the cabaret act "Maria y Maria," singing about the beauties of Paris. One night onstage, part of Maria II's costume accidentally comes loose; but because the show must go on, both singers improvise by continuing to pull bits off their outfits and so unintentionally invent the striptease, which they perform at subsequent shows. They become celebrities; Maria II joyfully discovers transient sex, while Maria I dreams of true love. On the road at the height of this success, the horrified troupe sees a village being brutalized by the henchmen of evil landowner Rodriguez, and, instinctively, Maria II shoots one of them.

Captured and held in Rodriguez's compound, the troupe meets a local man, Flores, who has been tortured after leading an uprising. While Maria II is attracted to Flores, he and Maria I fall in love at first sight. Rodriguez brings the two Marias into his grand salon in order to abuse and kill them. But instead, the women gain the upper hand, take control of the machine gun he keeps there, and use it to pulverize the room and its contents, a collection of classic nineteenth-century artworks and antiques. Meanwhile, their fellow artistes use circus skills to escape from their prison alongside Flores and his men. Flores is mortally injured, and Maria I promises to complete his revolution, persuading his compatriots to support her. The initially disapproving Maria II realizes that Maria I, a gifted orator but novice fighter, needs her expertise in armed revolt and joins the revolution. Large-scale battle scenes with many San Miguelian casualties follow, but in the end the troupe liberates the country shoulder

---

13 Helmut Korte and Stephen Lowry outline the film's sequences in detail in *Brigitte Bardot: Materialien und Analysen* (Braunschweig: IMF, 1997): 97–99. Further page references follow in the text.

to shoulder with its brave people and returns to Paris, where it performs a cabaret about its exploits.

Maria, Maria, and Marx: Antiauthoritarians Watch *Viva Maria!*

In West Germany, *Viva Maria!* was generally well received. Its popularity is reflected, for example, by the fact that von Rezzori's memoir was serialized in the *Süddeutsche Zeitung* (1965) and other newspapers and reviewed by Schlöndorff in *Die Zeit*, a piece that doubled as an essay about the film's production.[14] A novel of the film by Malle's cowriter Jean-Claude Carrière appeared in German translation too.[15]

No contemporary West German reviewers perceived serious political messages in *Viva Maria!* Instead, most emphasized its entertaining qualities.[16] The tabloid *Der Kurier* offered an exception in criticizing its comedic portrayal of violence: "Nur bleibt uns manchmal das Lachen im Halse stecken. . . . darf man denn mit so furchtbaren Dingen ein Spiel treiben? . . . Die Regie bemüht sich, das Grausige zu simplifizieren und damit die Realität abzuschwächen. Ist man humorlos, wenn man trotzdem nicht lachen kann? . . . Hier waltet einfach Stillosigkeit" (But sometimes, the laughter sticks in our throat . . . can one make a game of such terrible matters? . . . The director attempts to simplify the horror and so to weaken its reality. If we still can't laugh, does that mean we don't have a sense of humor? . . . This is simply poor taste).[17] *Der Kurier* appeared in West Berlin, where Cold War tensions were high. This paper's unique sensitivity to the film's violence may therefore respond to the divided city's edgy mood; in context, it may be no coincidence that Malle's film found particular resonance among West Berlin's New Left, including Dutschke and the *Viva Maria!* group.

14 Schlöndorff, "Zauberlehrling in Mexiko."

15 Jean-Claude Carrière, *Viva Maria: Roman nach dem Originaldrehbuch von Louis Malle und Jean-Claude Carrière*, trans. Ruth Groh (Munich: Heyne, 1968). This book was first published in 1966. Carrière's plot, like von Rezzori's account of it, differs in some aspects from the film. This chapter discusses the film's storyline only.

16 Cf A.B., "Revolution im Flitterkleid," *Berliner Morgenpost*, February 3, 1966; wf, "Viva Maria," *Rhein-Neckar-Zeitung*, May 3, 1966; HG, "Revolution im Western-Kostüm: Der neue Louis-Malle-Film," *Wiesbadener Kurier*, May 6, 1966; Klaus Hellwig, "Zweimal Zazie in Mexiko: Zu Louis Malles ironischer Filmballade 'Viva Maria,'" *Frankfurter Rundschau*, February 11, 1966. On contemporary German reviews, see also Korte and Lowry, *Brigitte Bardot*, 99–100.

17 Fl.K., "Viva Maria," *Der Kurier*, February 1, 1966.

A key piece of evidence about that antiauthoritarian reception is an essay in *Der Spiegel* (1968) by Dutschke's close SDS associate Rabehl.[18] Titled "Karl Marx und der SDS" (Karl Marx and the SDS), it states that "Die revolutionäre Leidenschaft Brigitte Bardots und Jeanne Moreaus wurde für die radikalen Studenten des SDS im Jahre 1966 zum politischen Vorbild" (The revolutionary passion of Brigitte Bardot and Jeanne Moreau became a political model for radical SDS students in 1966). Rabehl elaborates, "In dieser Film-Fabel hatten zwei Traditionen des revolutionären Kampfes der vergangenen hundert Jahre sich zusammengefunden. Die Anarchistin Bardot drängt mit ihrer antiautoritären Haltung zur Rebellion, während die Marxistin Moreau den richtigen Zeitpunkt des Aufstandes abwägt, den ungestümen Anarchismus mit den wirklichen Verhältnissen konfrontiert" (In this filmic fable, two revolutionary traditions of the past hundred years came together. The anarchist Bardot with her antiauthoritarian attitude presses for rebellion, while Marxist Moreau weighs up the right moment for an uprising, confronts unruly anarchism with the real conditions). Rabehl concludes, "Maria und Maria haben zusammengefunden. Viva Maria" (Maria and Maria have found one another. Viva Maria). This idealized image of the Marias' revolutionary alliance echoes antiauthoritarians' own belief that as they themselves synthesized orthodox Marxist and anarchist traditions, they stood at a historical turning point of their own making.

Rabehl praises "die revolutionären Ereignisse in anderen geographischen Gebieten, der Volkskrieg gegen den amerikanischen Imperialismus in Vietnam und die Kulturrevolution in China" (revolutionary events in other parts of the world, the people's war against American imperialism in Vietnam, and the Cultural Revolution in China). Brown shows that these real-world conflicts were of central interest for West German antiauthoritarians, who valorized revolutionary Ernesto "Che" Guevara's idea, demonstrated in Cuba, that "a small, determined group could make a revolution" (77).[19] In *Viva Maria!* too, the revolution is led by a tiny guerrilla vanguard, the cabaret troupe.[20] Brown observes, in addition, "The most important idea crystallized by [*Viva Maria!*] was the necessity not just of supporting the struggles of the Third World, or of using its theory, but of bringing those struggles home to the First World"

---

18 Bernd Rabehl, "Karl Marx und der SDS," *Der Spiegel* 18 (April 29, 1968): 86.

19 On the significance of that context for Germans, see Jennifer Ruth Hosek's important study *Sun, Sex and Socialism: Cuba in the German Imaginary* (Toronto: University of Toronto Press, 2012).

20 It is telling in context that *Viva Maria!* also evokes Ireland, a country often romanticized in Germany.

(77). The return of Malle's artistes to Paris could be read as bringing the Central American struggle to Europe.

Furthermore, as a French film with an international cast, some of whom play characters of nationalities different from their own, the conspicuously multilingual *Viva Maria!* offered a model for a transnational collective of the kind idealized by Rabehl, Dutschke, and others. The Great Rodolfo's name unites Italian and English, and he has an English accent. Los Turcos ("the Turks" in Spanish) are German. The troupe speaks many languages simultaneously, crosses national borders easily, and manifests seamless solidarity with San Miguelians. In San Miguel, the troupe performs Europeanness, but in Paris, it puts on San Miguelian looks and costumes. In this narrative, national identity is mutable, even a matter of performance bolstered by stage names and costumes. So while in reality, issues of national identity and identification were fraught and complex for West German protesters, the fantasies of *Viva Maria!* map with certain antiauthoritarian, postnational ideals.

Rabehl's essay on *Viva Maria!* draws attention to further ideals of the FRG's New Left too, like the establishment of a "weitgehend herrschaftslose Gesellschaft selbstbewußter Individuen" (society of self-confident individuals which is largely free of authority). Brown argues that activists saw in the film "a revolution of lifestyle that would destroy bourgeois rule at its source, in the relationships and conditions of everyday life" (79). The cabaret troupe is a communal enterprise with no owner or manager, its members sharing goals and solidarity under pressure. Indeed, the very name of the Diogène family evokes classical philosopher Diogenes, who rejected all social norms and citizenship and refused to live in a house or do profitable work. Moreover, the characters' life on the road resonates with antiauthoritarian interest in itinerant lifestyles, and the Marias' caravan is decorated with mermaids, traditionally imagined as living free from domesticity and (masculine) control.

These travels reflect subjective journeys. The New Left considered a rolling-back of sexual inhibitions to be politically emancipatory, and so Rabehl's essay endorses overthrowing "Normen, sogennante Kulturwerte und Sexualtabus" (norms, so-called cultural values, and sexual taboos). Central to antiauthoritarian readings of *Viva Maria!* as endorsement of revolutionary subjectivity was likely its striptease theme, which dovetailed with antiauthoritarian discourse in which cultural forms featuring (images of) naked women were considered both subjectively and politically liberating.[21]

---

21 See, e.g., Bazon Brock, *Ästhetik als Vermittlung: Arbeitsbiographie eines Generalisten*, ed. Karla Fohrbeck (Cologne: DuMont, 1977), 866–67; Bernd Dolle-Weinkauff, "Pop, Protest und Politik: Die Comics der 68er," *Forschung Frankfurt* 2 (2008): 38–45. Cf. also the "Busenattenat" (breast attack) on

As secular, political, sexual, and nonmaternal figures, the Marias undermine a particular tradition of chaste feminine imagery: that of their namesake, the Virgin Mary. While the troupe fords a river, one of the Marias' stage props accidentally floats away. This object is a model of Paris's cathedral of Notre Dame, or "Our Lady," a visual pun suggesting that Marian imagery is finished. This challenge is expressed more explicitly by shrines and votive art (re)dedicated to "Maria y Maria," which start to appear all over San Miguel. The troupe's rejection of "sexual taboos," as Rabehl puts it, is symbolized too by its life in caravans, which can be moved at will and accommodate changing relationships. After Janine's suicide, which leaves Maria I living alone in the wagon they had shared, Rodolfo politely offers to cohabit with her, and she equally politely declines. One morning soon after, Rodolfo emerges from his own caravan alongside an acrobat, hinting that the two men are now together. The collective's defiance of conventional gender roles is also represented by Werther's and the acrobats' flamboyantly floral costumes, which they wear off- as well as onstage.

While M. and Mme Diogène are an established couple, Mme Diogène is also openly involved with Werther. Mme Diogène and Werther dance romantically and publicly, and for some German viewers, their waltz, along with Werther's name, would have resonated with Johann Wolfgang von Goethe's famous novel *Die Leiden des jungen Werther* (The Sorrows of Young Werther, 1774). Its eponymous protagonist is a frustrated artist who suffers owing to an oppressive class society and a distant, authoritarian father in the mold of contemporary Sturm and Drang (Storm and Stress) literature, which thematized violent, destructive father-son conflicts. At a ball, Goethe's Werther dances with an engaged woman and falls in love with her. This love triangle cannot be resolved with bourgeois decorum, and Werther, unable to draw, work, or move on, takes his own life. The contrasts with Malle's comedic, creative, polyamorous circus family are ironic, yet utopian.[22] For instance, the relationship between Mme Diogène and Werther implies that her son's paternity may be unclear, yet this circumstance does not seem to generate conflict on the theme of disturbed filial and paternal relationships. Unlike Goethe's

---

Theodor W. Adorno (1969), in which three women performed a partial striptease at his lectern, breaking off the last lecture he ever gave; there are noticeable echoes of *Viva María!* here, although the effect was shot through with aggression. See, e.g., Wolfgang Kraushaar, *Frankfurter Schule und Studentenbewegung: Von der Flaschenpost zum Molotowcocktail 1946 bis 1995*, 3 vols. (Frankfurt am Main: Rogner bei Zweitausendeins, 1998), 1:418.

22 Werther's story features more tragically in *Der subjektive Faktor*. See Mererid Puw Davies, "Textual/Sexual Politics in Helke Sander's *The Subjective Factor*," in *Gender, Emancipation and Political Violence: Rethinking the Legacy of 1968*, ed. Sarah Colvin and Katharina Karcher (London: Routledge, 2018), 76–94.

self-absorbed, passive Werther, his *Viva Maria!* namesake is a successful artist and able to put sensitivity, empathy, and politics into practice. When the troupe is imprisoned by Rodriguez, he bends open the bars of Flores's cell to allow Maria I in, then bends them back to give the couple privacy, before all join the revolution.

Maria II, too, models a new kind of subject. All her ancestors died in conflict with the British, so she remarks fatalistically of her domineering father's death, "Il a fallu finir comme ça" (it was bound to end that way). That is, he is tied into a toxic legacy that tallies with antiauthoritarian critiques of the bourgeois patriarchal family. But by killing her father, albeit unwillingly, and having otherwise grown up outside repressive familial and social norms, Maria II can be symbolically reborn. On the run in the jungle, she recoils from a snake, recalling Eve in the Garden of Eden. But if Eve falls prey to a serpent and so brings original sin into the world—that is, instigates the transmission of suffering through generations ("Il a fallu finir comme ça")—Maria II avoids the snake, evades Eve's fate, and reverses the traditional demonization of sexuality and the female body in Eve's story.

Maria II's father prohibited her from meeting men, halting her sexual maturity, and so before joining the cabaret she appears either as a little girl or, later, disguised as a teenage boy. By contrast, life with the troupe allows her to become and appear as a fully adult woman. Maria II remains in a state of happy innocence as she discovers her sexuality, and simultaneously becomes a more committed revolutionary. Likewise, for Maria I, emotional, sexual, and political potential are tightly linked, for she is politicized by falling in love with Flores. The cabaret troupe thus provides a nonauthoritarian family driven by the Marias' feminine partnership, which is powerful enough to negate the patrilinear family curse and offer more productive revolutionary politics. Thus, all these characters' rejection of patriarchal authority on a personal level prefigures its political overthrow too.

Rabehl's essay describes "zwei revolutionäre Marias ... die gemeinsam den kulturellen Plunder ... der bürgerlichen Gesellschaft—zusammenschossen und einen Volkskrieg gegen ein Marionetten-Regime eröffneten" (two revolutionary Marias ... who shot to pieces all the rubbish ... of bourgeois society and started a people's war against a puppet regime). Rabehl's observation hints at the importance antiauthoritarianism placed on culture as a battleground. This emphasis derived in part from strands in avant-garde thought that assert that aesthetic revolt may be a precondition for political revolution and that, therefore, classical art must be destroyed. Such impulses fed into 1960s protest through the influence of subversive groupings like the Situationist International (SI). For antiauthoritarians in that tradition, elitist high art was fatally compromised by capitalism and sublimated vital drives in harmful, perverse ways. Instead, they were interested in cultural forms that appear to erase divisions between art and life and between theory and practice, as the avant-garde demanded. Consequently, some antiauthoritarians sought to bring art into the streets and other public spaces; for example, when they staged Situationist-inspired protests.[23] For similar reasons, they valued pop culture for its supposed demotic, desublimating political potential, as exemplified by their admiration of *Viva Maria!*

Rodriguez considers his electrically-lit art collection to underwrite his moral worth. When he has the Marias brought to his salon, he plays an opera, François-Adrien Boieldieu's and Eugène Scribe's *La Dame blanche* (The White Lady, 1825), on his gramophone to showcase his appreciation of culture. Yet he has men whipped as they work his generator and intends to abuse and murder the women to the strains of the classical music. Thus, *Viva Maria!*, in keeping with the Critical Theory that influenced antiauthoritarians, interprets the nineteenth-century art that Rodriguez collects, as well as the religious art associated with the backward Church and its torture chambers, as evidence of barbarism. That is, Rodriguez's fetishization of art and electricity, as well as his alliance with organized religion, stand, in Rabehl's words, for "all the rubbish ... of bourgeois society." Simultaneously in this sequence, with its emphasis on Rodriguez's collection of flashy visual artworks, *Viva Maria!* aligns with Situationist critiques of society in its entirety as a spectacle to be challenged.

In context, then, the heroines' destruction of Rodriguez's artworks, which triggers San Miguel's uprising, evokes avant-garde tradition. Here, the Marias literalize the notion of iconoclasm, in keeping with a hallmark of antiauthoritarian textuality—namely, a disturbing oscillation between literal and figurative meanings.[24] And as the balance of power shifts from Rodriguez to the Marias, the diegetic sound of opera is replaced by an extradiegetic reprise of a number the Marias perform earlier in the film, "Les p'tites Femmes de Paris" (The Little Parisiennes). The women take action to the soundtrack of one of their own cabaret numbers and so dramatize a programmatic leap from high to popular art. Not coincidentally, "Les p'tites Femmes de Paris" later becomes the bugle call of revolution. And by using cabaret skills to start the revolution, the artistes embody the demand to unite art and life.

Comedy is a key tool in this project. In 1966, West Berlin antiauthoritarian Ulrich Enzensberger remarked, "Seit VIVA MARIA [weiß]

---

23 Cf. Mererid Puw Davies, *Writing and the West German Protest Movements: The Textual Revolution* (London: imlr books, 2016).

24 Davies, *Writing*; Mererid Puw Davies, "'Burn, Baby! Burn!': Paris, Watts, Brussels, Berlin and Vietnam in the Work of Kommune I, 1967," *Forum for Modern Language Studies* 54, no. 2 (2018): 136–56.

man, daß Revolution Spaß macht" (Since VIVA MARIA we've known that revolution is fun).[25] That is, he recognized the liberating potential of play and clowning. In stylistic terms, *Viva Maria!* alludes to surrealism, a precursor to the SI that is linked to ideas about revolt and revolution in politics, and visual and cognitive dissonance in art, often centered on irony and humor. Another distinctive form of comedy in *Viva Maria!* is its parody of films set during the Mexican Revolution (1910–20).[26] For Marxists like Dutschke and Rabehl, it may have brought to mind Marx's comment that historical phenomena occur twice, "the first time as tragedy, the second time as farce."[27] So, while film scholars Helmut Korte and Stephen Lowry (95–96) note that *Viva Maria!*'s parodic character makes it impossible to read clear messages off it, that very epistemic uncertainty aligns with antiauthoritarian interest in ambiguity in relation to politics, violence, and representation.

Watching Differently

Equally striking in Rabehl's essay on *Viva Maria!*, however, are its misrepresentations, for on closer examination its description of the two Marias does not match the film at all. Rabehl argues that Maria I stands for a rational, Marxist approach to revolution, while Maria II represents unruly anarchism. But in fact, it is Maria I who fits Rabehl's characterization of an anarchist pushing for quick action. While Maria II does grow up with unorthodox political violence, she dislikes and discontinues it after losing her father. Her precise, long-range shooting of Rodriguez's man draws on her technical training but is motivated by emotion, not politics. She says simply, "C'était plus fort que moi" (I couldn't help it) and subsequently maintains her apolitical stance. Indeed, Maria II counsels Maria I against revolution, albeit in part because of personal rivalry over Flores. And when Maria II does step into the political action, she does so to save her friend, not the uprising. Neither woman therefore matches Rabehl's notion of a patient, calculating approach to revolution.

Rabehl's essay may show that he and his comrades did not engage with *Viva Maria!* as fully as he claims. Possibly then, the film was less central to the movement than posterity has it. Or more likely, as Brown

25 Quoted in "aus der SDS-Korrespondenz Nr. 2, Juni 1966," Kommune I, *Quellen zur Kommuneforschung* ([Berlin: Kommune I], 1968), n.p.
26 Cf. Hellwig, "Zweimal Zazie in Mexiko"; Korte and Lowry, *Brigitte Bardot*; von Rezzori, *Die Toten auf ihre Plätze*; Schele, "Cowboy and Alien"; Southern, *The Films of Louis Malle*.
27 Karl Marx, "The Eighteenth Brumaire of Louis Bonaparte" (1852), accessed April 29, 2022, https://www.marxists.org/archive/marx/works/1852/18th-brumaire/ch01.htm.

writes, antiauthoritarians "saw in the movie what they wanted to see" (78). Rabehl's essay suggests that what they wanted to see was a revolution painlessly and entertainingly achieved in almost no time at all, in ways that gratified libidinal and symbolic as well as political needs. This conclusion underscores the film's fantasy potential for activists; simultaneously, it indicates the need for more critical scrutiny of Rabehl's interpretation.

Rabehl suggests that *Viva Maria!*'s representation of revolution affirmed antiauthoritarian admiration for Third World revolutionaries.[28] Earlier in the film, however, representation of Central Americans is almost unequivocally negative. According to film scholar Nathan C. Southern, they initially appear "lecherous, filthy, stupid, drunken."[29] He goes on to argue that when the Marias' troupe witnesses Rodriguez's men attacking the village, viewers are confronted critically with their previous enjoyment of the film's stereotypes as they realize that San Miguelians have been formed by their terrible treatment. Subsequently, Southern argues, the film jettisons its negative clichés when the heroic Flores and his brave associates are introduced. Their sacrifice is embodied by Flores, who is explicitly, if parodically, portrayed as Christlike, for in prison his arms are bound to a wooden beam like a cross.

Flores, however, played by an actor from the US, George Hamilton, stands out from his compatriots. For instance, he dresses in European or North American style, while other San Miguelians tend to wear traditional-looking costumes. In addition, the film's second half continues to portray San Miguelians like Rodriguez negatively, and the people's revolution is only saved by the Marias and their troupe. The suggestion could be that the San Miguelians have to suffer passively before rescue by white Europeans, a tiny number of whom are more effective in action than are large crowds of local people. Apart from Flores's dramatic end, bloodshed is downplayed. There are hundreds of casualties in the film's action sequences, but the countless San Miguelian dead are mainly silent, nameless extras. Finally, the closing Parisian cabaret glosses over these losses and sufferings.

The film reinforces stereotypes in other ways too. When the troupe, harboring fugitive Maria II, crosses the border into San Miguel, Black British military personnel in exquisite uniforms sit at a tea table with spotless linen and complain in cut-glass tones about the inferior quality of the tea. At first sight, this scene amusingly complicates binary notions about colonialism, nationality, and ethnicity. But as these men perform their border control, they peer into the caravan where Maria II is asleep.

---

28   Here, the now dated, limited terms Third and First World reflect the usage of the time.
29   Southern and Weissberger, *The Films of Louis Malle*, 96.

Not realizing that she is a wanted terrorist, they decline to wake her, and they let the wagon pass. On the one hand, the men respond humanely by not disturbing Maria II. But on the other, there is a focus on their stares, accentuated visually by being framed in a doorway. So at a deeper level, as Black men gaze at a sleeping blonde woman and forget their duty, images of supposedly primitive, mindless sexuality provoked by defenseless white beauty are evoked.

On a different level, beyond the film's diegesis, von Rezzori suggests that *Viva Maria!* was implicated in exploitative practices. He describes the accidental death of a twenty-one-year-old Mexican extra, Pio Olmos Rodriguez, sole breadwinner for his three young brothers, during the chaotic filming of a battle. Von Rezzori remarks of the funeral, onto which ongoing noisy filming intrudes, "Ich sehe keinen Kranz, den die Produktion gestiftet hätte. Man wird es mit ein wenig Geld geregelt haben" (188; I can't see a wreath from the filmmakers. They'll have fixed things with a bit of money). He reports hearing also that ten men were killed during the recent making of a US film in Mexico (187), implying that foreign productions were routinely dangerously careless on location.

West German antiauthoritarians were capable of reading popular cinema critically, as shown by their reception of a controversial, supposedly documentary film, *Africa Addio* (*Africa: Blood and Guts*, 1966), directed by Gualtiero Jacopetti and Franco Prosperi. West Berlin demonstrators challenged its racist images of African people, highlighting allegations that its makers had even arranged real killings to film.[30] For all the differences between *Viva Maria!* and *Africa Addio*, the former could in principle be open to comparable critical readings. Thus, antiauthoritarians' enthusiastic reception of *Viva Maria!* points up the inconsistency, and complexity, of their engagements with the Third World.

Also ambiguous is *Viva Maria!*'s representation of women, as Sander's later allusion in *Der subjektive Faktor* shows. Bardot's and Moreau's characters lead a successful revolution in the manner of French artist Eugène Delacroix's celebrated painting *La Liberté guidant le peuple* (Liberty Guiding the People, 1830). Here, Liberty is a woman, naked from the waist up, bearing a revolutionary tricolore flag and a gun and leading fighters; perhaps not coincidentally, the Notre Dame cathedral is seen in the background. This ostentatiously nonrealist image, along with

---

30 See, e.g., Ulrich Enzensberger, *Die Jahre der Kommune I: Berlin 1967–1969* (Cologne: Kiepenheuer & Witsch, 2004), 71–74; Siegward Lönnendonker, Bernd Rabehl, and Jochen Staadt, *Die antiautoritäre Revolte: Der Sozialistische Deutsche Studentenbund nach der Trennung von der SPD; Band 1: 1960–1967* (Opladen: Westdeutscher Verlag, 2002), 296; Slobodian, *Foreign Front*: 137–46. For an analysis of the film itself, see Peter Pleyer, "Neger und Weiße in dem Film Africa Addio," *Rundfunk und Fernsehen* 15, no. 3 (1967): 271–89.

the painting's title, indicates that Liberty is an allegorical figure in classical tradition. As striptease performers, the Marias too can be understood as parodic personifications of Delacroix's lightly-clad Liberty. That tradition of allegorizing women's bodies is in turn perpetuated by Rabehl's casting of them as embodiments of political beliefs. So, even as the film celebrates the Marias' destruction of Rodriguez's Bluebeard-like collection of nineteenth-century artworks that, like Delacroix's, ostentatiously display (partially) nude female figures, it playfully restores such imagery. This reading tallies with Sander's suggestion in *Der subjektive Faktor* that for women activists, such contradictory imagery was, at best, difficult to navigate.

Indeed, to the extent that *Viva Maria!* has feminist potential, it may lie in aspects uncommented on by Rabehl. Most notably, the film is led by two women stars at the height of their fame. As Southern notes, it blends genres that normally center men as protagonists; namely, action, buddy, and road movies and Westerns.[31] The film also upends tropes of melodrama. The Marias' partnership is not sentimentalized, since they disagree over love and politics. They are briefly rivals for Flores, and in melodrama, such love triangles are often highly emotional and disastrous for women. By contrast, Maria II quickly, discreetly, and pragmatically decides to support Maria I's choices, asserting the value of women's friendship, solidarity, and shared political action. And if German literary tradition makes death a common consequence of women's sexuality and agency, in ways that resonate perhaps with Janine's lovesick suicide, the Marias evade this trend too.

The striptease theme in *Viva Maria!* might seem at first sight to impede a feminist interpretation of the film, relying as it seems to do on highly conventional sexualization and commodification of women's bodies. Yet at a more implicit level, and read against the grain, *Viva Maria!* paradoxically challenges the operations of conventional striptease. The Marias wear so many layers onstage that at the end of their routines, while they have removed their outer clothing, their elaborate undergarments still cover their bodies extensively. This approach no doubt allowed the film to avoid controversy in its day. But read more subversively, it challenges the very notion of striptease. Not long before, Roland Barthes in *Mythologies* (1957) analyzed this form and its accessories: "Feathers, furs and gloves go on pervading the woman . . . even once removed . . . the

---

31 Southern considers *Viva Maria!* the first mainstream women's buddy movie; *The Films of Louis Malle*, 94. It contrasts with other genres that interested antiauthoritarians; e.g., James Bond films. Cf. Martin Buchholz, "James Bond, oder Schule für Sadisten," *konkret* (January 1966): 10–12. In male-centered Bond films women are serial love interests, propel the plot, and soon vanish, often through violence. In *Viva Maria!*, Flores and Maria I's male lovers take that role.

nakedness which follows remains itself unreal, smooth and enclosed."[32] For Barthes, striptease is a highly ritualized performance of nudity, rather than real exposure of the body. *Viva Maria!* goes further still, in being not striptease itself but a highly ritualized performance of some of its conventions, and refuses to present nudity altogether. As such, it foils expectations doubly.

The double figure of "Maria y Maria" counterpoints the status of the Virgin Mary "alone of all her sex,"[33] and this dual figure is disruptive throughout *Viva Maria!* For example, key to the Marias' triumph in Rodriguez's salon is their exploitation of the many large mirrors that hang there. The women move so that their multiplying images seem endlessly to whirl around him, and he becomes transfixed, hypnotized, and helpless. The mesmerizing power of the double Marian figure is amplified by its proliferation, and the soundtrack underlines this theme too. In *La Dame blanche*, a villain's attempt to usurp an estate from a passive, forgetful hero is foiled by a clever, active heroine. There are parallels with Flores's initial failure to seize Rodriguez's compound, rectified by the Marias, who restore it to its rightful owners, the people. Crucially, the opera's plot turns on its heroine's disguise, or self-doubling, as a ghostly white lady. This idea is accentuated further when the opera music gives way to the extradiegetic reprise of "Les p'tites Femmes de Paris." This song's lyrics praise Parisiennes who dazzle their suitors when more than one of them appears at once, just as Rodriguez loses his mind when he sees the Marias endlessly doubled in his mirrors. Viewers are thus reminded of the remarkable sequence in which the Marias had previously performed this number, in which complex, nonrealist visuals moved outside the diegesis to play kaleidoscopically on the women's doubled images.

These sequences highlight the destabilizing potential of the double female figure. Classically, doubling effects in art are often linked to the destructive Uncanny as described by Sigmund Freud in his essay "Das Unheimliche" (The Uncanny, 1919). That effect has at its heart a debilitating, traumatic fear of paternal aggression. By contrast, *Viva Maria!* emphasizes a ludic doubling that upsets order in a more pleasurable, less frightening way, for Rodriguez is not killed or injured physically by the two Marias, only confused. The film thus hints that a subversive, feminine Uncanny could work differently from Freud's canonical masculine version, moving away from wellsprings in patriarchal violence.

---

32 Roland Barthes, *Mythologies*, trans. Annette Lavers (London: Vintage, 1993), 85.
33 Marina Warner, *Alone of All Her Sex: The Myth and Cult of the Virgin Mary* (London: Weidenfeld & Nicolson, 1976).

Hauntings

Von Rezzori's *Die Toten auf ihre Plätze!* documents the making of *Viva Maria!* in Mexico. It contains details of the film's development and script omitted from the final cut, anecdotes, and essayistic passages, some of which echo the film's themes. For example, it emphasizes the surrealist character of both the film and the shoot itself, albeit no doubt with an element of retrospective self-stylization.[34] Likewise, mirroring the dynamic of Malle's cabaret troupe, von Rezzori stresses the cosmopolitan character of cast and crew. He ascribes to it a composite, multilingual European identity; for example, when he describes *Viva Maria!* as a raid on the US territory of the Western: "Nicht allein Frankreich, ganz Europa zieht damit gegen Amerika in die Schranken. Die Trikolore flattert stolz voraus" (32; Not just France, all of Europe is entering the lists against America. The tricolore flutters proudly before us). Von Rezzori was well known in 1960s West German letters but was at that time a stateless Parisian. He was born in 1914 in Czernowitz (present-day Chernivtsi, Ukraine) when it belonged to Austria-Hungary. After the end of the Habsburg Empire, when Czernowitz, as Cernăuți, became part of Romania, von Rezzori gained Romanian citizenship, but he lost it in the turbulent Second World War years. In *Die Toten auf ihre Plätze!*, he emphasizes this statelessness, which seems compatible with Malle's images of mutable linguistic and cultural identity.

The memoir's very title suggests the Uncanny, for it refers to the making of battle scenes involving many extras playing casualties and corpses, who would be directed to resume their places at the start of each take. Therefore, in this title the dead rise repeatedly, in classically uncanny ways. The text itself is permeated with such imagery too. In Mexico, von Rezzori feels "als hätte ich wie Peter Schlemihl meinen Schatten hingegeben" (26; as though I had given away my shadow like Peter Schlemihl). This allusion is to Adalbert von Chamisso's Romantic tale "Peter Schlemihls wundersame Geschichte" (The Wondrous Story of Peter Schlemihl, 1814), in which the eponymous hero sells his shadow to the devil with terrible consequences. Von Rezzori comments of a costume fitting: "Ich ... versuche mich in dem unheimlich bekannten fremden Menschen, der mir aus dem Spiegel entgegenschaut, mich selbst wiederzuerkennen" (45; I ... attempt to recognize myself in the uncannily familiar stranger who is looking out at me from the mirror). Thus, the memoir references the strange yet disturbingly familiar double that has deep roots in Romantic texts like von Chamisso's.

More ominous, uncanny play between fictional representation and reality is present in von Rezzori's account of Pio Olmos Rodriguez's

---

34 See e.g. von Rezzori, *Die Toten auf ihre Plätze!*, 78.

violent death during filming. In this man's passing, a death imagined by the script became real. Yet von Rezzori writes that in reality, the corpse looked unreal, like a mannequin—thus invoking another great motif of the Uncanny, the inability to distinguish between a doll and a human. This description implicitly acknowledges the potential of the young man's demise to haunt *Viva Maria!* Indeed, it intimates uncanny qualities in film itself, a spectral double of life that has become independent of its original, like Schlemihl's shadow.

Even von Rezzori's Mexican landscape seems to be doubled, or haunted. He writes, "*Czernowitz holt mich immer ein.... Der erste Blick auf Mexico, die Stadt, war ein Wiederfinden ... von der bedrängten unwirklichen Wirklichkeit eines Traumgesichts.... Finde ich hier in Mexico City ein Echo meines verlorenen Czernowitz—oder war vielleicht jenes für mich unwirklich gewordene Czernowitz ein in die Zeit zurück- (oder voraus-?) geworfenes Echo von Mexico City?*" (16–17, italics in original; Czernowitz always catches up with me.... My first sight of Mexico, the city, was a reunion ... characterized by the distressingly unreal reality of a vision from a dream.... Am I finding an echo of my lost Czernowitz here in Mexico City—or was that Czernowitz, which had become unreal to me, an echo cast backward (or forward) in time by Mexico City?). Lost Czernowitz is evocative for literary-minded readers, because it produced a flowering of multilingual culture before the Second World War. Later, von Rezzori reflects, "Ich bin heimgesucht von Erinnerungen an Rumänien. Ich bin heimgesucht von Mexiko" (56; I am haunted by memories of Romania. I am haunted by Mexico). In other words, von Rezzori's Mexico is shadowed by a lost European past that comes back to him in uncanny form; even in the here and now of modern European filmmaking, the relationship of past and present is complex.

Just as for Freud, the Uncanny is a marker of past repressed violence, reminders of European history break at times into von Rezzori's Mexican adventure. He mentions, for instance, that his French costar Paulette Dubost (Mme Diogène) "speiste mit Hitler" (12; had dinner with Hitler), and Poldi Bendandi (Werther) had been an Italian prisoner of war in the Second World War. The location for Rodriguez's compound is an estate belonging to "ein Deutscher, 1946 nach Mexiko gekommen ... ein stämmiger Herr in fortgeschrittenen Jahren, Bayer, mit ... straffer militärischer Haltung.... Bewegt er sich über das Gelände, so pfeift er gelegentlich schrill nach seinem Hunde" (104; a German, who had come to Mexico in 1946 ... a stocky man in his later years, a Bavarian, with ... rigid military bearing.... When he walks over the site, he occasionally whistles shrilly for his dog).

This man makes an appearance with his family when part of his property is set on fire for filming purposes: "Heute großes Jubelfest: die Hacienda wird angezündet. Der deutsche Besitzer ... kommt ... um mir zu sagen, daß seine Frau mich kenne . . . als Leserin des 'Spiegel.' Er selbst . . . habe früher auch den 'Spiegel' gelesen, . . . aber . . . wie alles neuerdings wiederum in Deutschland, stehe auch der 'Spiegel' zu sehr unter dem Einfluß der Juden. Er pfeift schrill nach seinem Hund und geht zu seinen Damen zurück" (121; Great festivities today: the hacienda is set on fire. The German owner comes . . . to tell me that his wife knows me . . . from reading *Der Spiegel*. He used to read it himself . . . but . . . just like everything else in Germany recently, *Der Spiegel* is too much under Jewish influence. He whistles shrilly for his dog and returns to his ladies). While von Rezzori makes no explicit comment, the information provided about the German hints strongly that he could be an unreformed Nazi exile, possibly a fugitive from justice. Elsewhere in the memoir, the narrator recalls reporting on the Nuremberg trials, so the significance of the details he gives about this German is unlikely to be lost on him, or his readers.

Furthermore, readers may have recognized resonances between these passages and the widely known poem "Todesfuge" (Deathsfugue, 1948) by Jewish Holocaust survivor Paul Celan, another German-speaking native of prewar Czernowitz and émigré Parisian in the 1960s. Celan's poem features a murderous camp in which a German "master" is associated with burning and ashes, writes to a lady in Germany, and whistles for his dogs. All these images resonate with von Rezzori's descriptions, so that in them, the filming seems eerily to conjure Nazi crimes. Thus, von Rezzori's Mexico is powerfully haunted by the recent European past, and the memoir juxtaposes a far darker version of the Uncanny with the Marias' liberating doublings.

Die Toten auf ihre Plätze! points also to the difficult status of Mexico itself in these fantasies. The German's estate is in a place called Cuautla, which, as von Rezzori notes, was burned down by revolutionary leader Emiliano Zapata Salazar and his forces during the Mexican Revolution. So the 1965 fire, set by filmmakers to tell an imaginary story, not only evokes violent European history for von Rezzori and his readers. At the same time, it covers over Mexican history, only to be partially uncovered again, in a distanciated, parodic form, by *Die Toten auf ihre Plätze!* In other words, in Malle's and von Rezzori's Eurocentric gaze, layers of history from different times and places simultaneously displace, occlude, and reveal one another in palimpsestic ways.

Uncanny Projections: Some Conclusions

This chapter's interpretations of *Viva Maria!* highlight its appeal to the West German New Left as expressed by Rabehl in 1968. In his account, the film is a symbolic dramatization of orthodox Marxist and anarchist theoretical positions, sexual and subjective liberation, and aesthetic revolt, all of which were vital for antiauthoritarians. Importantly too in the context of this volume, his reception of *Viva Maria!* illuminates West German activists' developing thinking about violence in distant locations, for in 1966, interest in postcolonial conflicts was growing, and activists started to see them as revolutionary models.

For Rabehl, therefore, Malle's story of violence elsewhere is an instructive allegory for domestic politics. It seems that here, the transposition of key antiauthoritarian themes to a distant time and imaginary place helps to crystallize, clarify, and idealize them. This effect is amplified by the fact that the tale is projected, too, onto the fictional universe of the action and Western genres and inflected by a comedic surrealism. Thus, reflection on violence elsewhere in *Viva Maria!* and its appeal to protesters can expand into thinking about narrative modes or genres as artistic elsewheres too, which may bring audacious ideas into focus especially vividly for viewers like Rabehl.

Yet in 1966, many activists were still influenced by pacifism and humanism, and significant political violence was not on the agenda in the FRG. Moreover, memory of war only twenty years before, and the threat of the Cold War, especially in recently divided Berlin, were vivid, as *Der Kurier*'s film review hints. Therefore, while the idea of revolutionary liberation was compelling in principle, the prospect of civil war at home in practice was not. By contrast, *Viva Maria!*'s cartoonish violence in a patently unreal elsewhere allowed viewers the gratification of identifying with a successful revolution at little human or political cost and enormous gain. The era's intellectually sophisticated cinemagoers would have noted the film's parodies, which perhaps would have allowed them to enjoy its violent spectacles without necessarily taking them entirely seriously. Thus, there is likely a knowing, ludic self-stylization at work in antiauthoritarian praise, like Rabehl's, of *Viva Maria!* It may be in part for this reason too that antiauthoritarian viewers were able to overlook the negative stereotypes of Central Americans and others in *Viva Maria!*, which work against ideals of transnational solidarity; the contemporary and more controversial *Africa Addio*, widely criticized for racism, seemed to lack such self-conscious ironies.

Malle's film is similarly contradictory in its gender politics. It purports to tell a story about liberated women. Yet it does so by means of clichéd, conventionally sexualized images. In a sexist culture of protest, these images may make the notion of women's (symbolically or physically violent) political agency more palatable, because it is less palpable, less realistic, and hence arguably less challenging to a conventional, masculine gaze. Yet this chapter has argued too that at a less evident level, the film suggests striking gendered innovations in cultural tradition, for the Marias' victory in Rodriguez's salon both evokes Freudian ideas about the Uncanny and reverses them by means of a virtuoso performance of feminine doubling. In this scene, fantasies of elsewhere set the stage for a more unorthodox Uncanny, which is not driven by terror of masculine authority and aggression but is instead joyful and feminine. The sequence ends not in wounding but in confusion and laughter: the distant location of the Marias' salon revolution may help to make such novel ideas thinkable. In sum, all these very different aspects of the film's gender politics hold one another in tension.

Hence, *Viva Maria!*'s uses of violence elsewhere are complex and ambiguous. In these respects, analysis of the film and its reception draws attention to some of the limitations of antiauthoritarian thinking. It suggests that for parts of the 1960s New Left, fantasies about violence elsewhere as depicted by Bardot, Malle, Moreau, and their colleagues served not only to spell out some revolutionary ideals in exhilarating ways. Simultaneously, they simplified and distanced acute challenges close to home, with regard, for instance, to Third World politics, the prospect of domestic direct action, and the nascent women's movement.

In addition, *Viva Maria!* and the wider complex of texts around it draw attention to further orders of violence elsewhere. Von Rezzori's memoir draws attention to the film's uncanny dimensions, which imply that beneath the glossy surface of Malle's pan-European production, and its enthusiastic West German reception, there are substrates of unarticulated, violent history. It unexpectedly links the sunny world of *Viva Maria!* to the violent German and European past, half a world away, and this dimension too may help account for activists' emphatic response to Malle's film. For the 1960s generation that had grown up in the shadow of Nazism and German history, a fantasy of old-time San Miguel no doubt appealed by bracketing out the difficult German past and present. In this fiction, British imperialism, Church corruption, and grotesque San Miguelian villains draw viewers' gaze away from Nazi territorial expansion and crimes, German colonial projects, and the actions of their own parents or elders. At the same time, the film makes national identity into an inconsequential, even evanescent matter. In all these ways, *Viva Maria!* may have attracted young West Germans precisely because it allowed them to rewrite the past in compensatory ways, "imagining themselves" into a heroic narrative.

Finally, and importantly, *Die Toten auf ihre Plätze!* points to aspects of violence elsewhere that are excluded from Malle's finished film. This book shows that the film covers over the real history of the Mexican Revolution, represented by the site at Cuautla, with a playful fantasy about an imaginary one. It also reveals that the film itself brought about the death of a Mexican man, Pio Olmos Rodriguez, in the present, in the pursuit of entertainment for first-world audiences, although it never articulates that loss. Thus, cinemagoers in West Germany who did not read *Die Toten auf ihre Plätze!* may not have known of Pio Olmos Rodriguez.

In these respects, *Viva Maria!* seems to obscure both historical and contemporary violence in distant Mexico, making it all the more appealing a screen onto which West Germans could project their own story. But, in part as a result of their viewing habits in an era of accelerating global media coverage, they would simultaneously have been becoming increasingly aware, at least in general terms, of past and present violence in the Global South and the problems posed by a Eurocentric gaze. In some sense, therefore, viewers might have sensed that screenings of *Viva Maria!* in West Berlin were haunted by obscure knowledge of violent deaths elsewhere. That elusive awareness of seemingly forgotten, simultaneously distant and proximate violence forms part of the ambiguity of both *Viva Maria!* and its West German reception.

3: Images as Weapons: DEFA, Studio H&S, and the Global Cold War

Seán Allan[1]

DURING THE FORTY YEARS of the existence of the German Democratic Republic (GDR; East Germany), images of violence elsewhere were deployed by the East German government to boost its credentials as a progressive state standing on the right side of history. In the 1950s and 1960s, images of the Spanish Civil War—and in particular the contrasting roles of the fascist Condor Legion and the leftist Thälmann Brigade— were reproduced in a range of media in order to highlight the allegedly "fascist" roots of the neighboring Federal Republic of Germany (FRG), while at the same time justifying the establishment of the Nationale Volksarmee (National People's Army [NVA]) in the GDR. East German opposition to the Vietnam War meanwhile provided GDR politicians with the opportunity to reach out to the decolonizing states in Asia, while at the same time enhancing the country's reputation as forward-looking in the eyes of disaffected youth in Western Europe.

Studio H&S, the only significant independent documentary studio in the GDR, was a key player in the production and dissemination of such images, and its cycle of Vietnam films, produced between 1966 and 1984, left little to the imagination.[2] For the production of perhaps the most infamous film of this cycle—*Piloten im Pyjama* (Pilots in Pajamas, 1967)[3]—filmmakers Walter Heynowski (1927–) and Gerhard

---

1   I would like to acknowledge the support of the Undergraduate Research Scheme at the University of St Andrews and, in particular, the contribution of Gwendoline Choi to the research for this article.
2   On the work of studio H&S, see also Martin Brady's chapter in this volume.
3   The standard English translation of the film's title is slightly misleading. "Pajamas" refers to the prisoners' striped clothing. Although the term "pajama" has now become synonymous with nightwear, at the time of the film's production it was commonly used to refer to the loose clothing worn during the day by ordinary Vietnamese men and women. All translations are the author's own unless otherwise stated.

Scheumann (1930–98) were invited by the North Vietnamese to Hanoi, the capital of the Communist Democratic Republic of Vietnam (DRV), where they conducted a series of interviews with eight American pilots who had been shot down in combat and juxtaposed the pilots' commentaries with images of Vietnamese suffering. None of the pilots had been accorded POW (prisoner of war) status, and this issue, together with the fact that some were visibly injured or suffering, goes some way to explaining why, for many years, critics were reluctant to engage with the film or dismissed it as a crude work of propaganda. More recently, however, scholars such as Nora Alter, Sarah Blaylock, Lauren Cuthbert, and Patricia Simpson have argued that these Vietnam films are, aesthetically speaking, considerably more complex than scholars have been willing to acknowledge.[4] As I shall argue, at one level the violence with which we are confronted in films like *Piloten im Pyjama* and the much later documentary *Amok* (1984) reflects the alienation and instrumentalization of human beings under capitalism. At another, the images of violence in Vietnam and the USA (in the case of *Amok*)—images of violence elsewhere—can be read as a warning and reminder of the threat posed by US imperialist ambitions to peace in Europe and to the very existence of the GDR.

Although displays of sexuality and eroticism were broadly accepted in East German cinema and television, the same cannot be said of depictions of violence and brutality. For instance, one of the distinctive characteristics of the well-known *Märchenfilme* (fairy-tale films) that the DEFA (Deutsche Film-Aktiengesellschaft) studio, the GDR's state-owned film-production company, produced for children is the replacement of the often violent dénouements of the literary texts with more humane resolutions that accorded better with a socialist model of education grounded in humanist ethics.[5] It was not just in children's cinema, however, that scenes of violence were avoided; productions targeted at adults such as the popular TV crime series *Polizeiruf 110* usually avoided acts of brutality such as murder and rape and focused instead on nonviolent crimes

---

4   See Nora M. Alter, *Projecting History: German Nonfiction Cinema, 1967–2000* (Ann Arbor: University of Michigan Press, 2002), 13–42; Sarah Blaylock, "Bringing the War Home to the United States and East Germany: *In the Year of the Pig* and *Pilots in Pajamas*," *Cinema Journal* 56, no. 4 (2017): 26–50; Lauren Cuthbert, "'Ich hatte Befehle': Multidirectional Memory and the Vietnam War in Heynowski and Scheumann's *Piloten im Pyjama* (1968)," *German Life and Letters* 75, no. 4 (2022): 521–39; Patricia A. Simpson, "Allegories of Resistance: The Legacy of 1968 in GDR Visual Cultures," in *Celluloid Revolt: German Screen Cultures and the Long 1968*, ed. Christina Gerhardt and Marco Abel (Rochester, NY: Camden House, 2019), 201–18.

5   See for instance, Qinna Shen, *The Politics of Magic: DEFA Fairy-Tale Films* (Detroit, MI: Wayne State University Press, 2015).

such as blackmail, burglary, and juvenile delinquency, which were usually attributed to alcoholism, the corrupting influence of Western capitalism, or a combination of both. Although the notion that DEFA and genre cinema might somehow be incompatible has been discredited,[6] horror remains a genre conspicuous for its absence; and gratuitous on-screen violence as a form of sensationalized entertainment had no place within East German film production. In addition, as Rosemary Stott notes in her study of East German policy on the importation of films from the USA and Western Europe during the 1970s and 1980s, feature films that, as director and actor Lothar Bellag put it, "schamlos Krieg und Gewalt verherrlichen" (shamelessly glorify war and violence), were automatically excluded from selection.[7]

As a result, most East Germans—especially those with restricted access to West German television—had only limited exposure to the kind of sensationalized on-screen brutality served up by Hollywood action films and so were perhaps not as desensitized to the phenomenon of gratuitous violence as their Western counterparts. Although on-screen violence as a form of entertainment was effectively taboo in the GDR, the screening of violent resistance and military conflict appeared fairly regularly on East German television and in cinemas. For the most part, such violence was confined to historical dramas set during World War II and documentaries focusing on either German fascism or the anticolonialist struggle during the postwar period. And it is striking that the politicized violence depicted in both these genres is almost always situated elsewhere; that is to say, in locations that, either temporally or geographically, were far removed from the contemporary GDR. A great many of the antifascist films produced by DEFA depicted acts of extreme violence committed in the name of German fascism during the 1930s and World War II. Alternatively, they drew upon Georgi Dimitroff's 1935 definition of fascism in terms of economics ("the open, terrorist dictatorship of the most reactionary, the most chauvinistic and most imperialist elements of finance capital")[8] to portray the USA, Great Britain, and, of course, the neighboring Federal Republic as essentially "fascist" states whose support

---

6 See the section "Genre and Popular Cinema" in Seán Allan and Sebastian Heiduschke, eds., *Re-Imagining DEFA: East German Cinema in Its National and Transnational Contexts* (New York: Berghahn, 2016), 191–270.

7 Lothar Bellag, "Opening Address: Kongress des Verbandes der Film- und Fernsehschaffenden der DDR vom 15–17 September 1982 in Berlin" [= BArch DY 30/vorl. SED 32750]. See also Rosemary Stott, *Crossing the Wall: The Western Feature Film Import in East Germany* (Oxford: Lang, 2012), 24.

8 Georgi Dimitroff, "The Fascist Offensive and the Tasks of the Communist International in the Struggle of the Working Class against Fascism: Main Report Delivered at the Seventh World Congress of the Communist International, August 2, 1935," in *The Communist International 1919–1943: Documents*, ed.

for military intervention in the Global South during the Cold War could be conceptualized as a form of (postwar) imperialist expansionism fueled by the legacy of (prewar) colonialist aspirations.

With the founding of East Germany in October 1949, DEFA's efforts were increasingly directed toward the creation of a socialist imaginary in which the fledgling GDR was portrayed as a progressive state. The roots of this state, it was argued, could be traced back to left-wing opposition to German nationalist tendencies from 1870 onward and, in particular, to the rise of fascism following the collapse of the Weimar Republic. One key source of inspiration for the construction of a founding myth was the (alleged) self-liberation of Communist prisoners from the Buchenwald concentration camp; but another, equally important, component of this socialist imaginary was bound up with the involvement of German Communists in the Thälmann Brigade fighting on the side of the Republicans in the Spanish Civil War.

This envisioning of violence elsewhere as a means of alluding to the postwar division of Germany is evident in films such as Karl Paryla's *Mich dürstet* (I'm Thirsty), which was released in 1956 to mark the twentieth anniversary of the Spanish Civil War. Set in Spain in 1936, Paryla's film shows how the arrival of Republican soldiers from Madrid helps a young peasant, Pablo, transform his village into an effective antifascist force. When Pablo's lover, Magdalena, is killed by a German bomb during an air-raid attack on his village he is filled with a hatred of everything German. His subsequent involvement with the International Brigades, however, teaches him that not all Germans are fascists, that the antifascist struggle transcends national boundaries, and that a progressive political regime is something that requires active military intervention. While the didactic thrust of Paryla's rather wooden production is hardly subtle, it did nonetheless reflect the rapidly evolving landscape of German-German politics during the Cold War and, above all, the issue of postwar rearmament. East German cinema- viewers could hardly have failed to map the contrasting representations of German military action in the film onto the political developments of 1955 and, in particular, the recent integration of the Federal Republic into the NATO alliance.

Seen from the perspective of the Cold War in the mid-1950s, *Mich dürstet* explicitly invites the viewer to posit a line of continuity between Nazi Germany's support for Spanish fascism in the 1930s and the willingness of the "fascist" Federal Republic to put troops at the disposal of NATO in the 1950s. At the same, the film paved the way for an acceptance of the establishment in 1956 of the NVA in the GDR as the heir apparent to the Thälmann Brigade. As Stefan Soldovieri has argued,

---

Jane Degras, 3 vols. (Oxford: Oxford University Press, 1965), vol. 3 (1929–43): 355–70, here 359.

however, such mythologizations of German involvement in the Spanish Civil War were by no means confined to DEFA or to the GDR.[9] The release in the West of Harald Reinl's unambiguously anti-Communist film inspired by the climate of McCarthyism, *Solange du lebst* (As Long as You Live, 1955), in which a young (fascist) German pilot, Michael— shot down in combat and nursed back to health by the (anti-Republican) Spaniard Theresa—helps "liberate" her Spanish village from the supposedly oppressive rule of the Republican forces, clearly addressed the need to provide West German citizens with similarly positive images of German suffering and sacrifice in military combat during the run-up to rearmament in the Federal Republic.

Released four years after *Mich dürstet*, Frank Beyer's *Fünf Patronenhülsen* (Five Cartridges, 1960) reflects the extent to which the Spanish Civil War had undergone a significant revision in the East German historical imagination following Nikita Khrushchev's denunciation of Joseph Stalin, and a greater openness in the Soviet Union regarding its involvement in the conflict.[10] Up until that point GDR historians—taking their cue from Soviet historians—had denied any knowledge of Soviet involvement in Spain, and, tellingly, there are no references to the Soviet Union in *Mich dürstet*. In Beyer's *Fünf Patronenhülsen*, by contrast, the participation of Soviet officers is foregrounded in the person of the communications officer, Wasja, who dies the death of a heroic martyr. Even more important for an understanding of the film's presentation of violent conflict, however, were recent developments in the East German Ministry for National Defense and, in particular, the creation of the NVA in 1956. Although the NVA remained a professional army until 1962, compulsory military service had already been introduced in the neighboring Federal Republic in 1956. Fearful that rumors of compulsory military service in the GDR would swell the ranks of those already emigrating to the West, the ruling Sozialistische Einheitspartei Deutschlands (Socialist Unity Party of Germany, SED) also drew on the Spanish Civil War as a source of inspiring images of military action. Untainted by any association with Adolf Hitler and World War II, these images could be mobilized to bolster feelings of solidarity in its own population for the ongoing struggle against fascism in the global Cold War.

---

9   Stefan Soldovieri, "Germans Suffering in Spain: Cold War Visions of the Spanish Civil War," *Cinémas* 18, no. 1 (2007): 53–69.

10 As Josie McLellan notes, "Until Stalin's death, the USSR denied any military involvement in Spain . . . preferring instead to portray itself as a genuine adherent to the Non-Intervention Pact." Josie McLellan, *Antifascism and Memory in East Germany: Remembering the International Brigades, 1945–1989* (New York: Oxford University Press, 2004), esp. 178–80.

DEFA's remit was not confined to the production of feature films but also included the production of *Der Augenzeuge* (The Eyewitness), the first newsreel series to be produced in postwar Germany.[11] Although the production of newsreels, documentaries, and feature films was handled centrally during the founding years of the GDR, by 1952 a dedicated unit, the DEFA-Studio für Wochenschau und Dokumentarfilme (DEFA Studio for Newsreels and Documentary Films) had been established in order to expand the production of political documentaries in particular. The highly favorable conditions for documentary film production in the GDR can be explained, at least in part, by the crucial role such films played in the East German government's attempts to secure recognition as a sovereign state during the 1950s and 1960s. The major obstacle for the GDR was the so-called Hallstein Doctrine that formed a key plank in the foreign policy of the neighboring Federal Republic from 1955 to 1969, whereby the latter threatened to break off diplomatic relations with any state that recognized the sovereignty of the GDR. Lacking any formal diplomatic presence beyond the member states of the Warsaw Pact and desperate for international recognition, the GDR became heavily reliant on the exercise of soft power via the screening of political documentaries and newsreels—notably the *DDR Magazin* (GDR Magazine)—in the cultural missions it had established in a number of capital cities.

Given the extent to which productions such as the *DDR Magazin* were designed to promote the GDR as a sovereign state in its own right, it is hardly surprising that international relations feature prominently in almost every episode. From the GDR's perspective, Cuba, the developing nations in postcolonial Africa, and the emerging Arab states in the Middle East represented the most promising avenues for fruitful cooperation. There was, however, also a huge investment in the state's coverage of the conflict in Indochina and Vietnam in particular. Like the Soviet Union and other Warsaw Pact states, the GDR openly supported the North Vietnamese in their struggle against the USA. Indeed, the Vietnam conflict was particularly propitious for the East German government because it constituted a rare example of an area in which public opinion in the GDR and official SED policy seemed to be in almost complete alignment. As was noted in a United States Information Survey of 1966, "While East Germans are constitutionally skeptical of regime propaganda on all issues, the official line may have more credibility on V[iet]N[am] than all other issues. One of the main counteracting sources of information for East Germans, Western TV, has not been

---

11   The first episode was screened on February 19, 1946, and the last on December 19, 1980.

notably effective in presenting the US case."[12] The war itself provided an opportunity not only to portray the USA as an imperialist aggressor bent on a war of destruction but also—and perhaps more importantly from the SED's point of view—to condemn the West German government for its support of the US-led coalition. Throughout 1965 and 1966, Chancellor Ludwig Erhard in the Federal Republic found himself under constant pressure from President Lyndon B. Johnson to back the US war effort by committing not only West German money but also troops to the conflict in Vietnam.[13] Since involvement of the Bundeswehr was politically untenable (and would have been in clear breach of the constitution), Erhard had little choice but to pay the "offsets" demanded by the US administration as compensation for maintaining the kind of American military presence in Western Europe that was seen as essential to ensure the security and viability of West Berlin.

At the same time, as Peter Busch has noted, there was a concerted media campaign in the GDR to exploit these diplomatic tensions with a view to discrediting the standing of the Federal Republic.[14] In what was clearly intended as an allusion to the intervention of the Condor Legion in support of the fascist regime during the Spanish Civil War, an article published in the East German daily, *Neues Deutschland* (New Germany), in the autumn of 1965 claimed (erroneously) that 120 members of the West German air force were involved in a bombing raid in Vietnam alongside American forces.[15] In the course of this media campaign there was constant speculation not only about West German involvement in the manufacture of chemical weapons in South Vietnam[16] but also about

12 "Vietnam and World Opinion: Analysis and Recommendations," August 1966, National Archives RG 306, USIA, Office of Research, folder "Special Reports, 1964–1982."

13 See Eugenie M. Blang, "A Reappraisal of Germany's Vietnam Policy, 1963–1966: Ludwig Erhard's Response to America's War in Vietnam," *German Studies Review* 27, no. 2 (2004): 341–60.

14 Peter Busch, "'The Vietnam Legion': West German Psychological Warfare against East German Propaganda in the 1960s," *Journal of Cold War Studies* 16, no. 3 (2014): 164–89.

15 See "Bundeswehr ist an Aggression in Vietnam beteiligt," *Neues Deutschland* (September 4, 1965): 1.

16 See "'Entblätterung' sagen die USA," *Neues Deutschland* (March 11, 1966): 1, which also reported that a production plant for poison gas in South Vietnam was the largest project being financially supported by the Bonn government. See also "Bonner Meinungsterror in Westberlin," *Neues Deutschland* (February 8, 1966): 6, where the Bonn government's determination to clamp down on antiwar protests in West Berlin is reported together with a photograph of a demonstrator carrying a placard with the words "Kein GAS auch in Vietnam" (No Gas in Vietnam Either).

the Bonn government's alleged attempt to exploit the situation in order to acquire nuclear weapons.[17] Last but not least, Marxist analyses of the relationship between capitalism and war seemed to be borne out by the way in which the Federal Republic appeared to contribute to and support the US war effort through the purchase of large reserves of American currency, thereby stabilizing the dollar.[18]

Atrocities committed by US soldiers during the Vietnam campaign featured regularly in *Der Augenzeuge* and were recycled in the *DDR Magazin* information films targeted at foreign audiences. Released on December 5, 1969, *Der Augenzeuge* No. 50 pulled no punches in condemning the infamous My Lai massacre and juxtaposed a selection of the images of violence circulating worldwide following the revelations of November 13, 1969, with footage of the massive demonstration against the Vietnam War held on November 27 in East Berlin.[19] Traumatic images of the war were also reproduced in a range of other media—including illustrated volumes of antiwar poetry such as Volker Braun's *KriegsErklärung* (1967)[20]—and fueled the kind of solidarity campaigns organized under the auspices of the Vietnam Committee of the Friedensrat der DDR (GDR Peace Council) that peaked in the early 1970s.[21] Finally, East German opposition to the war also provided an opportunity for the GDR to promote itself as a forward-looking state in the eyes of antiwar campaigners in the West; and as the single-themed *DDR Magazin* no. 4 (1971), entitled "Solidarität mit Vietnam" (Solidarity with Vietnam), suggested, in supporting the North Vietnamese, the GDR and its Eastern bloc allies would be aligning themselves with the eventual victors in the conflict.

Perhaps the most widely viewed films in the East German media reporting on the war in Vietnam were those produced by Heynowski and Scheumann from the late 1960s onward. Their *Piloten im Pyjama* was just one of a range of documentary works to emerge from Studio

---

17 "Beteiligung Bonns und Aggression soll Atompläne in Europa sichern," *Neues Deutschland* (January 20, 1966): 7.

18 See Gerd Horten, "Sailing in the Shadow of the Vietnam War: The GDR Government and the 'Vietnam Bonus' of the Early 1970s," *German Studies Review* 36, no. 3 (2013): 557–78, esp. 563–64.

19 The report of this edition of *Der Augenzeuge* is reproduced (with an English voice-over) on *DDR Magazin* No. 26 (1969).

20 Volker Braun, *KriegsErklärung* (Halle an der Saale: Mitteldeutscher Verlag, 1967). On Braun's book, see J. J. Long's chapter in this volume.

21 On the activities of the Friedensrat, see Günter Wernicke, "The World Peace Council and the Antiwar Movement in East Germany," in *America, the Vietnam War, and the World: Comparative and International Perspectives*, ed. Andreas Daum, Lloyd Gardner, and Wilfried Mausbach (Cambridge: Cambridge University Press, 2003), 299–320, esp. 308–18.

H&S that sought to expose the ideological underpinnings of American (and West German) "imperialism." Heynowski and Scheumann had both grown up during the era of German fascism and had established themselves after the war as journalists in the Soviet zone of occupation.[22] Both had considerable experience of working for GDR television in the early 1960s and were among the first to recognize the medium's potential as a means of reaching a wider public. Neither, however, allowed himself to be constrained by the small-screen format, and the radical character of their televisual work reflects a willingness to engage with visual and acoustic techniques more commonly associated with art house cinema.

This stylistic approach is already evident in Studio H&S's 1966 film *400 cm³*, a five-minute short that was screened in East German cinemas before being broadcast on GDR television for the first time in March 1967 and that featured a modernist soundtrack by the avant-garde composer Paul Dessau.[23] Designed to encourage East Germans to donate blood in support of Vietnamese casualties, the sophisticated editing and camerawork show the faces of the East German blood donors and overlays these with images of Vietnamese suffering.[24] In the course of this brief film, the relaxing and clenching of the donors' fists gradually ceases to be part of a medical procedure and is transformed instead into a gesture of political defiance that is intensified by the citation of Friedrich Hölderlin's poem of 1800, "Der Tod für das Vaterland" (Death for the Fatherland). Even in the mid-1960s, the relevance of Hölderlin's patriotic (anti-Napoleonic) ode—a work that calls for a war of liberation against a better equipped, but less motivated, invader—was an unambiguous call to arms

---

22 For a concise overview of the collaboration of the two filmmakers, see Rüdiger Steinmetz, "Heynowski & Scheumann: The GDR's Leading Documentary Film Team," *Historical Journal of Film, Radio and Television* 24, no. 3 (2004): 365–79.

23 For Dessau the commission represented an ideal opportunity for ideological rehabilitation as his advocacy of modernist (dodecaphonic) modes of composition had brought him into conflict with established positions in East German musicology in the early 1960s. See Walter Heynowski, "Walter Heynowski: Einen Film macht man 1:1," in *Das Prinzip Neugier: DEFA-Dokumentarfilme erzählen*, ed. Ingrid Poss, Christiane Mückenberger, and Anne Richter (Berlin: Neues Leben, 2012), 59–97, here 81. For an extended discussion of Dessau's composition, see Martin Brady and Carola Nielinger-Vakil, "'Altes wird aufgerollt': Paul Dessau's Posthumous Collaborations with Brecht," *Brecht Yearbook* 42 (2018): 85–101. On *400 cm³*, see also Martin Brady's chapter in this volume.

24 Horten cites a Stasi report from Leipzig dated August 29, 1966, that suggests an initial reluctance on the part of GDR citizens to respond to the East German government's appeal for solidarity with the Vietnamese cause during the years 1964–66. See Horten, "Sailing in the Shadow of the Vietnam War," 577n36.

that resonated with East German citizens. While at one level the propaganda value of *400 cm³* is obvious, the film's complex aesthetic structure together with its distinctive use of the wide-screen format "Totalvision" offers a foretaste of the way in which Heynowski and Scheumann's documentaries would explore—and redefine—the potential of television as a critical medium in the GDR.

By the time *400 cm³* was first transmitted, Heynowski and Scheumann were firmly established in the East German media landscape following the success of *Der lachende Mann* (The Laughing Man, 1966), a documentary about the West German mercenary and former Wehrmacht soldier Friedrich Müller fighting in the Congo against the leftist supporters of the former president Patrice Lumumba, who had been murdered in 1961. Now enjoying the backing of the rising political star Erich Honecker, the DEFA-Gruppe Heynowski und Scheumann (DEFA-Group Heynowski and Scheumann) was established on February 28, 1967. Although the group still operated officially under the auspices of DEFA, it had its own budget (including access to some 300,000 Deutschmarks), had permission to recruit the West German cameraman Peter Hellmich, and was exempted from the usual requirement to have its films formally signed off by the DEFA studio management. Following the success of the group's next project, *Piloten im Pyjama,* it was allowed, quite exceptionally in the GDR, to operate as a completely autonomous production unit under the name Studio H&S from 1969 to 1982. Not only could most of the team travel freely outside of the GDR, but they were also allowed to retain the foreign currency generated by sales to capitalist countries and, as a result, could purchase sophisticated editing equipment from the USA and Western Europe with which they could generate further income.[25]

First screened on April 17, 1967, on prime-time GDR television, Heynowski and Scheumann's monumental documentary *Piloten im Pyjama* was, in part, a response to the USA's "Operation Rolling Thunder." The protracted bombing campaign, which was designed to destroy the infrastructure of North Vietnam and cut support for the leftist National Liberation Front guerrilla activity in Saigon and the south, lasted from March 2, 1965, to November 2, 1968. Shot in a prison near Hanoi, *Piloten im Pyjama* is divided into four parts of between sixty-five and ninety minutes—"Yes Sir," "Hilton Hanoi," "Der Job" (The Job), and "Die Donnergötter" (The Thunderchiefs)—and each part features a series of extended individual interviews with the eight pilots captured by the North Vietnamese after ejecting from their planes. Interviewed

---

25 A more detailed account of the founding and economic basis of the studio is presented in Rüdiger Steinmetz and Tilo Prase, *Dokumentarfilm zwischen Beweis und Pamphlet: Heynowski & Scheumann und Gruppe Katins* (Leipzig: Leipziger Universitätsverlag, 2002), esp. 45–67.

by Scheumann, each pilot is asked essentially the same questions, their responses are dubbed into German, and the interviews are interspersed with sections of newsreel footage depicting the effects of violent military action that expose the self-contradictory character of the pilots' responses.[26] The film suggests that each of the pilots was interviewed voluntarily, something that would appear to be confirmed, albeit within the artificially constructed world of the documentary, by the foregrounding of the refusal of two pilots to take part or even face the camera. One of the pilots interviewed, Robinson Risner, later claimed in his memoirs, however, that the answers he delivered to camera were scripted by his captors and that he cooperated under duress.[27]

Inevitably, much critical attention has been focused on the treatment of the POWs under the Geneva Convention and the ethics of involving the pilots in the film.[28] The matter is further complicated by the fact that at the time the film was shot, the downed pilots—tellingly always referred to as "Luftpiraten" (air pirates) in the film—were regarded by the North Vietnamese as war criminals who could not be accorded the status of POWs because the USA had not officially declared war. Not surprisingly, the film provoked strong reactions across both Eastern and Western Europe when it was released;[29] and although the American broadcaster NBC had acquired the rights to the series in 1968 and showed individual stills from the film in its evening news bulletins, it never actually screened the series in its entirety.

The fact that Heynowski and Scheumann were quite happy to let viewers arrive at their own conclusions as to whether the pilots had been

26   An (English) transcript of the film script is available on the US Prisoner of War network, accessed March 31, 2021, https://www.pownetwork.org/nvp/pilots_in_pajamas.pdf. Unless otherwise stated, all English translations are taken from this transcript.

27   Robinson Risner, *The Passing of the Night: My Seven Years as a Prisoner of the North Vietnamese* (New York: Random House, 1973), 161–75. For a similar set of allegations, see John G. Hubbell, *P.O.W.: A Definitive History of the American Prisoner-of-War Experience in Vietnam, 1964–1973* (New York: Reader's Digest, 1976), esp. 136–37 and 224–25.

28   These questions were debated in the West German news magazine *Stern* (Heft 43, 1967) in an interview with the filmmakers. The interview is reproduced in the volume released to accompany the film: Walter Heynowski and Gerhard Scheumann, *Piloten im Pyjama* (Berlin: Verlag der Nation, 1967), 408–15, esp. 413–14. See also Amos Vogel, *Film as a Subversive Art* (London: Weidenfeld & Nicolson, 1974), 171, and Heynowski's rebuttal, in Poss, Mückenberger, and Richter, *Das Prinzip Neugier*, 80.

29   For a selection, see "Aus dem internationalen Wirkungsraum," in *Dokument und Kunst: Eine Werkstatt—Ein Thema—Elf Jahre—Dreizehn Filme; Vietnam bei H&S* [= Arbeitshefte No. 27], ed. Robert Michel (Berlin: Akademie der Künste der Deutschen Demokratischen Republik, 1977), 172–80.

compelled to take part suggests that to argue about such questions is to miss the point of what their film is actually about.

Clearly, *Piloten im Pyjama* is a highly partisan undertaking; but it is anything but a conventional work of propaganda. Indeed, I would go further and argue that it is not really a documentary in any conventional sense of the term but an aesthetic construct that is better described in Brechtian terms as a cinematic "Lehrstück" (learning play). The Vietnam War was often referenced, in the words of the *New Yorker* magazine's Michael J. Arlen, as "the living-room war" on account of the extensive television coverage it received, the bulk of which was provided by embedded camera crews belonging to American broadcasters.[30] As Heynowski was at pains to point out, however, "Obwohl man so viel über Vietnam gesehen hat, hat man meiner Meinung nach zu wenig gesehen" (Although we have seen so much about Vietnam, in my view we've seen too little).[31] It is in this sense that we should understand Scheumann's programmatic statement: "Der Dokumentarfilm, wenn er schon mit einem Anspruch auftritt, soll ja mehr als nur berichten" (If it is to be of value, documentary cinema must do more than just report).[32] What is required, the filmmakers suggest, is a process of educating the viewer to embrace a critical mode of seeing: "Dazu kann ich nur sagen, daß es natürlich auch für den Dokumentarfilm so etwas wie die Entwicklung einer Zuschaukunst geben muß, eine Forderung, die Brecht im Hinblick auf das Theaterpublikum gestellt hat. Wir leben doch in einer Welt der Bilder. Es gibt doch so etwas wie eine Inflation von Bildmaterial, das jeden Tag über Fernsehsysteme usw. angeboten wird" (All I can say to that is that what is needed for documentary cinema of course is a development in the art of seeing, a need that Brecht addressed in the case of theatergoing audiences. We are living in a world of images. There is such a thing as an excessive escalation of images that are offered daily on television).[33] Viewed in this context, *Piloten im Pyjama* can be seen as an attempt to disrupt conventional modes of viewing and to encourage the viewer to adopt a critical attitude toward the images on display and thereby to develop a more nuanced understanding of the motivation of the participants and their lack of moral agency.

Nonetheless, it is important not to overlook what remains concealed beneath the surface of this modernist montage. While the viewer is invited to consider the contradiction between the images of destruction and the pilots' rationalization of their actions, the role of the interviewers, translators, editors, and other intermediaries, by contrast, is consistently

---

30   Michael J. Arlen, "Watching Vietnam on TV," *New Yorker*, May 27, 1967.
31   Michel, *Dokument und Kunst*, 98.
32   Michel, *Dokument und Kunst*, 101.
33   Michel, *Dokument und Kunst*, 101.

presented as something to be taken simply on trust and is never foregrounded for critical scrutiny. Accordingly, the style of the film might be seen as an example of what Martin Brady and Carola Nielinger-Vakil have termed "modernist blatancy"—whereby acoustic and visual dissonance is deployed in the service of a partisan standpoint—with all the contradictions that this entails.[34] Nonetheless, however contradictory such an approach may be, its target —as in almost all of Heynowski and Scheumann's work—is the alienation of all human beings under capitalism. Accordingly, while the filmmakers' depiction of violence elsewhere is ostensibly a report "about" the conflict in North and South Vietnam, it also embraces much wider issues including the legacy of fascism in the contemporary era, the right of socialist states to self-determination, the geopolitical divisions of the Cold War generally, and the division of Germany in particular.

In the first part of the documentary, "Yes Sir," the film announces its own programmatic agenda: "Vietnam. Wir haben die Angriffe gesehen—und ihre Ziele—Wir haben am Himmel die Mörder gesehen—und auf der Erde ihre Opfer. Was geht vor in diesen amerikanischen Bombenwerfern? Wie sieht es in ihren Köpfen aus?" (Vietnam. We have seen the air strikes—and their targets—We have seen the murderers in the sky— and their victims on the ground. What's going on in these American bombers? What's going through their minds?). In his quest for an answer, Scheumann puts the same questions to each pilot, asking for his name, rank, serial number, and education before moving on to probe him about his educational background and religious convictions (almost all self-identify as Protestant or Roman Catholic). Right from the outset, there is something deeply disconcerting about the juxtaposition of extreme close-ups of the pilots' sweating bodies (Fig. 3.1) and the laconic manner of Scheumann's interrogation, which is, by turns, both deadpan and patronizing. Yet despite the pseudo-objectivity of this "fact-finding" mission, the performative aspect of Scheumann's repeated patterns of questioning suggests that what we are watching is not some work of cinema verité but rather a deliberately and meticulously engineered aesthetic construct that both foregrounds and conceals its own construction.

Just as the visual dimension of *Piloten im Pyjama* can be seen as a stark corrective to the superfluity of images of Vietnam to which contemporary viewers had been exposed, so too is the language deployed in the film stripped of hyperbole and reduced to a sober functionality that is designed to position the viewer as an objective judge of the evidence, regardless of how obvious the conclusions to be drawn may seem. The constant repetition of essentially the same formulaic questions—and the

---

34 Brady and Nielinger-Vakil, "Altes wird aufgerollt," 91. See also Brady's chapter in this volume.

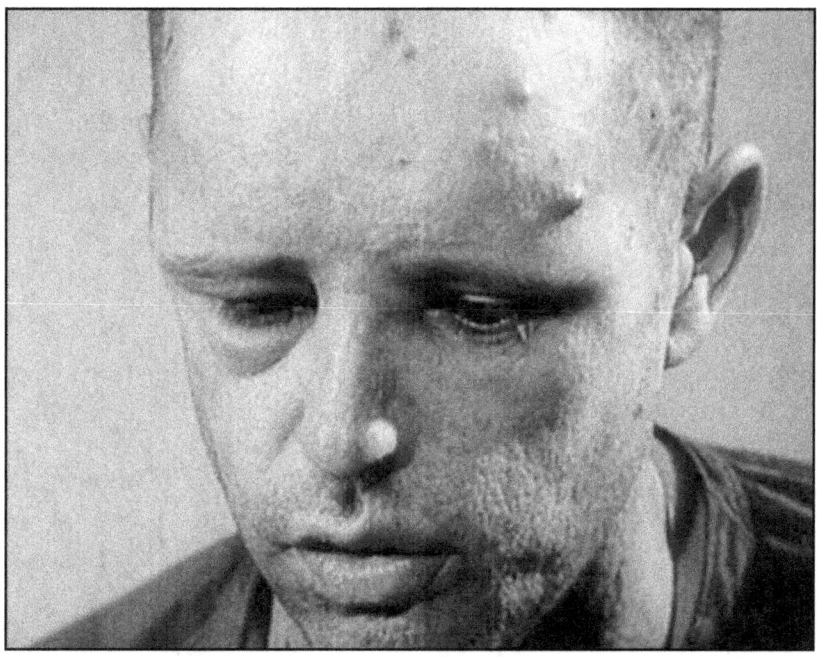

Figure 3.1. *Piloten im Pyjama* (Pilots in Pajamas, Studio H&S, 1967). ©DRA/StudioH&S.

pilots' equally formulaic answers—makes for a script that is, for the most part, predictable and lacking in suspense. This dislocation of image and affect is further amplified by means of a discordant soundtrack by the avant-garde composer Reiner Bredemeyer (1929–95). By the same token, the nonnaturalistic camerawork of Hans Leupold, Gerhard Münch, and Peter Hellmich draws on expressionistic effects—sometimes uncannily reminiscent of the close-up cinematography of the body in *Fünf Patronenhülsen* (Figs. 3.2 and 3.3)—with an intensity that serves to reemphasize the disjuncture between the distorted representations of the pilots and the interviewer's purported attempt to compile a dossier of facts that would somehow offer an objective explanation of "what is going through their minds."

This process of repetition is a crucial component in the film's underlying (modernist) aesthetic strategy and is just one of a number of cinematic devices that distinguish this and other Studio H&S productions from more conventional anti-American propaganda circulated by the SED. This strategy relies not on the mobilization of affect through the repetition of images of violence and intolerable suffering (although there are plenty of examples of that) but rather on the exposition of a chillingly rationalistic analysis of the dehumanization of an individual human being

Figure 3.2. *Piloten im Pyjama* (Studio H&S, 1968). ©DRA/StudioH&S.

and his reassembly as a pilot and extension of the mechanical weaponry he ostensibly "controls." Or to cite the prologue of Bertolt Brecht's 1926 drama, *Mann ist Mann* (Man Equals Man), "Hier wird heute Abend ein Mensch wie ein Auto ummontiert / Ohne daß er irgend etwas dabei verliert" (Tonight you are going to see a man reassembled like a car / Leaving all his component parts as they are).[35] In Heynowski and Scheumann's stylized "interviews" the pilots' responses assume a deadbeat character that is, by turns, naive, lacking in self-reflection, and even provocative. Yet their answers, so the film suggests, merely reflect the extent to which their personalities—if indeed that is the right term—are an effect of the capitalist system in which they have been brought up.

The Brechtian aesthetic underpinning *Piloten im Pyjama* is also evident in the repeated use of props that assume a symbolic function in the documentary's visual economy. Nothing is quite what it seems: the flip-flops the pilots wear—so we are told—have been fabricated from the tires

---

35 Bertolt Brecht, *Mann ist Mann*, "Zwischenspruch," in *Werke: Große kommentierte Berliner und Frankfurter Ausgabe*, ed. Werner Hecht, Jan Knopf, Werner Mittenzwei, and Klaus-Detlef Müller, 30 vols. (Frankfurt am Main and Berlin: Suhrkamp and Aufbau, 1988), 2: 123.

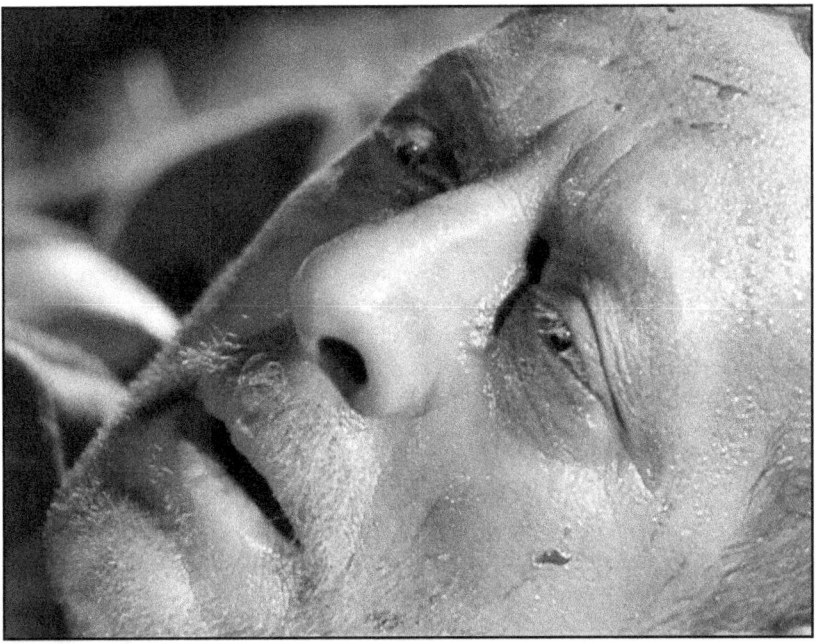

Figure 3.3 *Fünf Patronenhülsen* (Five Cartridges, Frank Beyer, 1960). ©DEFA-Stiftung/Günter Marczinkowsky, Karl Drömmer.

of American planes shot down by the North Vietnamese air defenses; and a piece of charred material handled by one of them turns out to be a clump of rice that has been incinerated following a US bombing raid. When the pilot Ringsdorf has his pistol returned to him, his reaction— "Nein, ich habe keinen Wunsch, einen Revolver zu handhaben" (I have no desire to handle a pistol)—transforms the resulting frame into a gestic tableau that exposes the blatant contradiction between the social, political, and military codes to which he ostensibly subscribes and his basic desire to survive at any cost. For as he explains, "Damals, damals waren meine Gedanken, ist meine Chance zu leben oder zu sterben, also wählte ich natürlich die Chance zu leben" (At the time my thoughts were, have I got a chance to live or to die, so naturally I selected the chance to live). Indeed, in the insistence with which it teases out contradiction, *Piloten im Pyjama* offers its own deconstructive analysis of the workings of propaganda: as the prisoners comment on the respect shown to them by their captors and on the medical treatment they have received, they, like the viewer, are forced to reflect on the way in which each culture seeks to define itself by means of a demonized construct of a hostile Other. In promoting such an argument, however, Heynowski and Scheumann's film also (perhaps unwittingly) critiques a similar tendency in the GDR to demonize the US military and does so at a moment in history in which the increasingly loud voices of antiwar protesters in the USA such as Jane Fonda could be seen as evidence of the existence of a better, more progressive America.

Unsurprisingly, the revelation that the American pilots regard themselves as obedient military personnel who, in their words, are "just obeying orders," is exploited to establish a parallel between prewar German fascism and its apparent enduring legacy in the global Cold War: "Auch die Piloten der Legion Condor seiner Zeit in Spanien haben nichts anders getan als 'etwas zu bombardieren'" (In their day the pilots of the Condor Legion also did nothing in Spain except "bomb something").[36] Moreover, as Scheumann comments during the interview with Ringsdorf, the obvious *mauvaise foi* of such a stance is evident not only in its striking similarity to the defense mounted during the Nuremberg trials but also in the slogans of the antiwar protesters in the USA whose placards and badges posit a similarity between the US military policy in Vietnam and Adolf Eichmann's implementation of the final solution in Nazi Germany. But for the East German audiences watching *Piloten im Pyjama*, perhaps the most telling revelation is the fact that prior to their deployment in Vietnam, all the pilots interviewed had served in the Federal Republic and all profess a willingness to deploy nuclear weapons if ordered to do so. In this way, *Piloten im Pyjama* serves as a reminder that the conflict in Vietnam is essentially a proxy war—violence elsewhere—that is intimately bound up with geopolitical concerns much closer to home. As might be expected, politicians of the Christian Democratic Union and Christian Social Union such as Kurt-Georg Kiesinger and Franz-Joseph Strauß are singled out for criticism in *Piloten im Pyjama* because of their uncritical support for US intervention in Indochina; but so too is the man the SED constantly sought to undermine publicly on account of the potential appeal of his more liberal concept of socialism; namely, the politician and—at that time—foreign minister in the Grand Coalition, Willy Brandt of the Sozialdemokratische Partei Deutschlands (Social Democratic Party of Germany).

Piloten im Pyjama is a hard-hitting film that not only underlines the continuities between prewar fascism and the global Cold War but

---

36 In her highly illuminating reading of the film, Cuthbert invokes Michael Rothberg's theory of "multidirectional memory" and argues that "the connections forged in *Piloten im Pyjama* are a form of multi-directional memory-making; Heynowski and Scheumann draw a red thread between East Germany and North Vietnamese identities in the name of socialist solidarity, but filtering these North Vietnamese stories through their German experience they are also able to begin to re/interpret the recent Nazi past through connections drawn between Germans and American pilots at the centre of the documentary." Cuthbert, "'Ich hatte Befehle,'" 525.

also, via its analysis of the conflict in Vietnam, argues for the right of self-determination free from external interference in other socialist states like the GDR. It is important to remember that it was not until September 4, 1974, that the USA established full diplomatic relations with the GDR following the admission of the Federal Republic and the GDR as members of the United Nations on September 18, 1973. At the time of the film's release in 1967, memories of the Berlin crisis of 1961 were extremely fresh in popular memory, and the viewer is constantly invited to draw links between divided Berlin and the political conflict in Vietnam. Accordingly, the film shows West Berliners in front of the Schöneberg city hall demanding the bombing of North Vietnam and also shows a series of prominent West German politicians (including Kurt Georg Kiesinger, Franz Josef Strauß, and Brandt) pledging their support for the American cause. When Major Thorsness confirms that his plane is capable of carrying nuclear weapons, the ensuing images of US military personnel visiting the attractions of East Berlin assume a sinister significance and are framed as an act of military reconnaissance rather than a tourist outing. In all these ways, the film presents the violence "elsewhere in Vietnam" as a foretaste of what could happen if the "antifascist protection wall" (as the Berlin Wall was termed in the East German political lexicon) should be threatened.

Yet what makes this film so much more than a one-dimensional work of propaganda and explains its enduring fascination is its deconstruction of the American pilots' mindset. Almost all of them have families and children of their own, and most claim to be religious, but all of the pilots seem almost pathologically unaware of the contradictions between their private and public existences. When Ringsdorf is asked, "Sind sie eigentlich nur ein Teil Ihrer Maschine oder ein Mensch mit Verantwortung?" (Are you simply an extension of your plane or are you actually a responsible human?), it is hard to avoid the conclusion that we are watching an individual who has been robbed of his moral agency. In this respect the lingering close-ups of the abject body—almost the inverse of the heroic masculine body foregrounded in Frank Beyer's *Fünf Patronenhülsen*—underline the multiple processes of disempowerment to which they have been subjected, first as dehumanized agents of the US military, and now as enemy POWs in flip-flops and "pajamas."

In this context it is helpful to invoke Charlotte Klonk's theorization of what she terms the "Nicht Porträt" (the "Un-Portrait").[37] Klonk uses the concept of the "Nicht Porträt" to capture the type of image circulated in the context of the RAF hostage-taking in the Federal Republic during the late 1970s and exemplified by the video images of Hanns Martin

---

37 Charlotte Klonk, *Terror: Wenn Bilder zu Waffen werden* (Frankfurt am Main: Fischer, 2017), 120.

Schleyer released on October 13, 1977, "bei dem man sich zwar dem Aufgenommenen ganz nah fühlt, dessen Gesicht aber zugleich merkwürdig fremd, fern und unzugänglich bleibt" (where one may feel quite close to the photographed subject, but whose face at the same time seems strangely alien, distant, and out of reach).[38] Moreover, as Klonk notes, to a large extent this aesthetic effect is itself created by the repetition of similar images. Although deployed in an altogether different context, Klonk's concept of the "Nicht Porträt" seems to capture Heynowski and Scheumann's presentation of the pilots as abject figures and invites us to see the "air pirates" not simply as perpetrators but also as victims of a system of capitalism that is itself the cause of their alienated consciousness.

When viewed in this context, Heynowski and Scheumann's film also hints at a shift of attitudes in the pilots. Toward the end of the final part, one of the airmen, Abbott, declares, "Ich wünsche, dass dieser Konflikt, die Bombenangriffe aufhören, und dass Friedensverhandlungen, diesen, wie Sie ihn nennen, schmutzigen Krieg beenden" (Yes, I'd like to see an end of the conflict, of bombing and peace negotiations to stop this, say, as you call it, the dirty war). In this way, *Piloten im Pyjama* gestures toward a more progressive "other America" that, in the eyes of the SED, came to be embodied in figures such as Paul Robeson and Angela Davis; an America that in the film itself is referenced via the likes of Dale Noyd, who refuses to train pilots to fight in Vietnam, and the conscientious objectors David Summers, Michael Johnson, and Dennis Mora, who were sent to prison.

Although Studio H&S produced another memorable cycle of films in the mid-1970s focusing on Chile and the US-backed coup against Salvador Allende, it never lost sight of the conflict in Vietnam, and Heynowski and Scheumann returned there on several occasions. In some of their films, notably *Remington Cal 12* (1972), a short documentary highlighting the devastating violence inflicted by modified shotgun cartridges that, although outlawed in the USA for use on animals, were being tested in Vietnam, we are returned to the tenor of *Piloten im Pyjama* and the sober analysis of the link between violence and capitalism. Increasingly, however, Studio H&S films of the mid-to-late 1970s adopted a historical perspective looking back at the early days of the conflict and the struggle of the indigenous population to rebuild their lives in its aftermath. In *Die Teufelsinsel* (Devil's Island) of 1976, for instance, we are reminded of the roots of the conflict in Vietnam and the links between colonialism and capitalism as the former prisoner Le Quang Ving takes the filmmakers on a tour of the inhuman conditions under which he was held prisoner in the early 1960s by the South Vietnamese and the French. By the late 1970s, however, it was becoming clear that the human cost

38 Klonk, *Terror*, 120.

of the Vietnam War was not simply confined to Vietnam itself but—as films like Michael Cimino's *The Deer Hunter* (1978) and Francis Ford Coppola's *Apocalypse Now* (1979) underlined—was manifesting itself in contemporary society in the USA. In this context it is striking that the violence elsewhere depicted in Studio H&S's film of 1984, *Amok*, is not Vietnam but 1980s California.

The subject of *Amok* is the so-called McDonald's Massacre in San Ysidro of July 18, 1984, in which the forty-one-year-old gunman, James Huberty, shot and killed twenty-one bystanders and injured a further nineteen. Once again, Heynowski and Scheumann's short film functions as a critical metadocumentary that juxtaposes CBS's sensationalist news coverage with a series of banal commercial breaks in order to posit a connection between contemporary capitalism, the rhetoric of commercial TV, and the presentation of violence in the mainstream US media. As the film unfolds, it becomes increasingly clear what drew Studio H&S to this particular incident; namely, the gunman's (widely reported) claim that he was a Vietnam veteran.[39] Repeatedly the camera zooms in on the headline "Augenzeuge: Es war wie in Vietnam" (Witness: It was just like in Vietnam). The stark contrast, however, between, on the one hand, footage of ambulance crews urgently attending to injured Californians and, on the other, images of isolated abandoned Vietnamese corpses reminds the viewer that even in death, not all are equal, and that violence is a quite different phenomenon when it occurs closer to home rather than elsewhere.

Throughout its existence, Studio H&S produced some of the most uncompromisingly analytical investigations of violence to be shown on East German television. To dismiss their films on the grounds that they are crudely propagandistic is, however, to downplay both their aesthetic complexity and the way in which their deployment of a series of modernist devices—discordant music, unconventional cinematography, and repetition—turns these films into self-reflexive metadocumentaries that reveal the limitations of conventional media reporting in capitalist countries and highlight the need for viewers to be educated in the art of seeing. Nonetheless, like DEFA's feature films from the 1950s about the Spanish Civil War, the films of Studio H&S do not amount to a critique of violence per se; on the contrary, they seek to emphasize the importance of violent resistance in the ongoing struggle against fascism during the Cold War. In focusing on violence elsewhere and in Vietnam in particular, Heynowski and Scheumann remind the viewer that—like capitalism—the

---

39 The Pentagon publicly denied that Huberty had served in Vietnam. See the article in the *New York Times* of July 20, 1984, https://www.nytimes.com/1984/07/20/us/neighbors-term-mass-slayer-a-quiet-but-hotheaded-loner.html.

Cold War is essentially a global phenomenon with proxy wars fought out all over the world. At the same time, the fact that the pilots in *Piloten im Pyjama* have all been stationed in the Federal Republic, flying planes capable of deploying nuclear weapons, serves as a warning that the next phase of this violence might take place not elsewhere, but on the home soil of a divided Germany.

4: *KriegsErklärung* (Declaration of War): Volker Braun's Cold War Camera

J. J. Long[1]

FROM THE PERSPECTIVE OF Western Europe, North America, and much of the Eastern bloc, the Cold War might have seemed an era of peace and stability, albeit fragile. In fact, as historian Paul Chamberlain has argued, it was an era of colossal and deadly violence across much of the Global South and the world, where proxy wars were fought with military and financial backing from the US and USSR as part of the superpowers' struggle for global hegemony.[2]

Of these proxy wars, the involvement of the United States in Vietnam's civil war had the most profound impact on Germany. The Federal Republic of Germany (FRG; West Germany) supported its US ally and indirectly funded the war through the purchase of US currency reserves in order to stabilize the dollar.[3] At the same time, the Vietnam War became the major focus of protest movements between 1965 and 1975 and a political and ethical touchstone that shaped an entire generation.[4] The government of the German Democratic Republic (GDR; East Germany) was opposed to the Vietnam War, seeing it as an imperialist campaign led by the United States with the aim of preventing the rise of independent socialist countries. It supported North Vietnam politically and economically and in the early 1960s was among the first European states to recognize the rebel South Vietnamese National Liberation Front, supplying it with military aid. At home, the ruling Socialist Unity Party

---

1 This chapter is dedicated to the memory of my late friend and colleague, Andrea Noble. I take my title from the project "Cold War Camera," which she co-led. The publication arising from this project is *Cold War Camera*, ed. Thy Phu, Erina Duganne, and Andrea Noble (Durham, NC: Duke University Press, 2022).

2 See Paul Thomas Chamberlain, *Cold War's Killing Fields: Rethinking the Long Peace* (London: HarperCollins, 2018).

3 Gerd Horten, "Sailing in the Shadow of the Vietnam War: The GDR Government and the 'Vietnam Bonus' of the Early 1970s," *German Studies Review* 36 (2013): 557–78, here 563.

4 Mererid Puw Davies, *Writing and the West German Protest Movements: The Textual Revolution* (London: imlr Books, 2016), 76–77.

(Sozialistische Einheitspartei; SED) sponsored frequent solidarity campaigns and fully exploited the propaganda value of Vietnam, attacking the FRG's support for the US intervention as further evidence of its willing collusion in a neo-imperialist global strategy.[5] During the Cold War, then, violence elsewhere was central to the political culture of both Germanies.

"Elsewhere" is a kind of deictic term, whose meaning is dependent on the context of the utterance: violence elsewhere is violence in times and places that are deemed to be different from the speaker's (or writer's) own. It is violence to which one may have no direct experiential access but that can be known vicariously, through its representations. Consequently, to understand what violence elsewhere can mean, critical analysis of those representations is central. The case of the Vietnam War demonstrates this point vividly: one reason for the continued presence of the Vietnam War in public awareness today is the visual culture to which it gave rise. A small number of Vietnam photographs have attained iconic status: Ron Haeberle's photographs of the My Lai massacre (1968), Nick Ut's *Accidental Napalm Attack* (1972), Eddie Adams's image of the summary execution of an alleged Vietcong by South Vietnamese police chief General Loan (1968), and John Paul Filo's images of the shootings at Kent State University in which the Ohio National Guard fatally opened fire on a student antiwar protest (1970). The dominant approach to these images has been to evaluate their affective power and their political efficacy in the context of US foreign policy and subsequent reckonings with the Vietnam conflict.[6] Scholarly writing on the photography of the Vietnam War circles around this tiny corpus, and the images continue to be reproduced in books about the conflict; in studies of photojournalism, iconicity, historical trauma, and the visual culture of war; and in compilations of "photographic masterpieces." They have also been transformed and remediated in numerous artworks and installations, in films, in magazines, in editorial cartoons, on posters, and on placards.[7]

---

5   Horten, "Sailing in the Shadow," 562; Bernd Schaefer, "Socialist Modernisation in Vietnam: The East German Approach, 1976–89," in *Comrades of Color: East Germany in the Cold War World*, ed. Quinn Slobodian (Oxford: Berghahn, 2015), 95–113.

6   See, for example, Caroline Brothers, *War and Photography: A Cultural History* (London: Routledge, 1997), 202–5; Vicki Goldberg, *The Power of Photography: How Photographs Changed Our Lives* (New York: Abbeville, 1991), 226–45; Barbie Zelizer, *About to Die: How News Images Move the Public* (New York: Oxford University Press, 2010), 218–43.

7   See Wendy Kozol, *Distant Wars Visible: The Ambivalence of Witnessing* (Minneapolis, MN: University of Minnesota Press, 2010), 168–77, and Robert Hariman and John Louis Lucaites, *No Caption Needed: Iconic Photographs, Public Culture and Liberal Democracy* (Chicago, IL: University of Chicago Press, 2007), 137–207.

Among the lesser-known creative engagements with Vietnam War photography is Volker Braun's *KriegsErklärung* (Declaration of War). Born in 1939, Braun was one of the preeminent poets of the German Democratic Republic and was often regarded as the successor to his compatriot Bertolt Brecht. In 1955, Brecht had published his *Kriegsfibel* (War Primer). This work consisted of "photo-epigrams": reproductions of news photographs that Brecht had cut from Allied press sources during his years of exile in Sweden and California, accompanied by four-line poems that commented on the photographs in order to offer an account of the Second World War from a conventional Marxist perspective. Twelve years later, Braun published his *KriegsErklärung*, which likewise combines poetic quatrains with news photographs, this time depicting the conflict in Vietnam.[8] Most critical commentary on Brecht's *Kriegsfibel* reads it as a corrective to a capitalist, Western interpretation of the Second World War,[9] and Braun's *KriegsErklärung* can be seen as an attempt to achieve the same for the Vietnam conflict. Visualizing violence elsewhere becomes a question of interrogating the media's perspective on the war by reframing the visual artifacts that construct that perspective.

Reframing the image is no simple matter, however, for from the very beginnings of its history photography has been inextricably linked to the political economy of capitalism, in terms of commodity exchange and all levels of social regulation. And as recent commentators have shown, photography was soon enlisted in the dual regime of surveillance and spectacle, which in turn constituted a powerful disciplinary apparatus for the production and regulation of social subjects within the expanding capitalist state.[10]

This history accounts for the deep suspicion of the photographic image, especially news photography, that emerges in theoretical approaches to the technical media developed by German Marxist intellectuals in the interwar period. Postwar photography in both East and West built upon the photographic culture of the Weimar Republic.[11] As a

---

8   Bertolt Brecht, *Kriegsfibel* (East Berlin: Eulenspiegel, 1955); Volker Braun, *KriegsErklärung* (Halle an der Saale: Mitteldeutscher Verlag, 1967), reprinted with revisions in Volker Braun, *Texte in zeitlicher Folge*, vol. 2 (Halle an der Saale: Mitteldeutscher Verlag, 1990), 105–57. Translations are by the author unless otherwise indicated.

9   For a discussion of this literature, see my article "Paratextual Profusion: Photography and Text in Brecht's *Kriegsfibel*," *Poetics Today* 29, no. 1 (2008): 197–224.

10   See John Tagg, *The Burden of Representation: Essays on Photographies and Histories* (Basingstoke, Hampshire, UK: Palgrave Macmillan, 1988), and Leo Charney and Vanessa R. Schwartz, eds., *Cinema and the Invention of Modern Life* (Berkeley, CA: University of California Press, 1996).

11   Sarah E. James, *Common Ground: German Photographic Cultures Across the Iron Curtain* (New Haven, CT: Yale University Press, 2013).

first step, therefore, I would like to zoom in on Weimar, and particularly the writings of Brecht and Walter Benjamin, which provide the immediate theoretical context for my reading of *KriegsErklärung*. Braun's work exceeds the terms of Marxist photographic aesthetics, however. In particular, his geopolitical reframing of the image goes hand in hand with a sustained and ambivalent concern with questions of gender. So in the second part of this chapter, I would like to zoom out, bringing additional theoretical considerations into play, and allow the multifaceted nature of *KriegsErklärung* to come more fully into focus in ways that problematize the East-West binary underpinning Braun's anti-US agenda in the representation of violence elsewhere.

Zooming In

In his theoretical treatise "Der Dreigroschenprozess" (The Threepenny Lawsuit, 1931), Brecht argues that reality cannot be reduced to the visible surface of things but rather has to be understood as a set of functional and abstract social relationships that are inseparable from the workings of advanced capitalism. Consequently, a putatively "realistic" aesthetics based on mimetic reproduction, of which the photograph (in Brecht's view) is an incarnation, is no longer adequate to the reality it claims to represent.[12] And yet elsewhere, Brecht shows himself to be alert to the revolutionary potential of the technical media. In a note on the tenth anniversary of the Communist newspaper *Arbeiter Illustrierte Zeitung* (*AIZ*; Workers' Illustrated News), Brecht argues that in the hands of the bourgeoisie, photography has become a weapon against truth, and goes on to praise the *AIZ* for restoring photography's truth-telling potential. In his essay fragment "Über Fotografie" (On Photography, 1928), Brecht suggests that captioning is key to the political mobilization of the individual image, a point amplified by Benjamin in "Der Autor als Produzent" (The Author as Producer, 1934): "Was wir vom Photographen zu verlangen haben, das ist die Fähigkeit, seiner Aufnahme diejenige Beschriftung zu geben, die sie dem modischen Verschleiß entreißt und ihr den revolutionären Gebrauchswert verleiht" (What we must demand from the photographer is the ability to put such a caption beneath the picture as will rescue it from the ravages of modishness and confer upon it a revolutionary use value).[13]

---

12 Bertolt Brecht, "Der Dreigroschenprozess: Ein soziologisches Experiment," in *Große kommentierte Berliner und Frankfurter Ausgabe*, vol. 21, ed. Werner Hecht, Jan Knopf, Werner Mittenzwei, and Klaus-Detlev Müller (Frankfurt am Main: Suhrkamp, 1992), 448–514, here 469.

13 Bertolt Brecht, "Zum zehnjährigen Bestehen der A-I-Z," in *Große kommentierte Berliner und Frankfurter Ausgabe*, vol. 21, ed. Werner Hecht, Jan

This project is the driving impulse behind Volker Braun's *KriegsErklärung*. In normal parlance, a "Kriegserklärung" is a declaration of war, but in this instance it also means an explanation of war. Braun's pun alludes to the conception of photography that emerges in the writings of Brecht and Benjamin: it is a both a demystifying medium that can reveal truths that are generally not visible ("Erklärung" as explanation), and a political weapon ("Erklärung" as a declaration of war on Western propaganda). But it can only fulfill these functions in combination with text.

KriegsErklärung was written in two parts in 1966 and published the following year. The first part was written for a "solidarity matinée" entitled *Der ferne Krieg* (The Distant War) put on by the theater company that Brecht had established, the Berliner Ensemble, to raise funds for the North Vietnamese. It is entitled "Geschäftsbericht" (Company Report) and thematizes the US side of the conflict. The second part, "Bericht vom Volk" (The People's Report), concentrates on the North Vietnamese experience of the war and was commissioned by the GDR Peace Committee. Critics in East and West Germany alike dismissed the work: although well-meaning in its political orientation and moral outrage, it was thought that the fact that Braun writes about countries of which he has no experience renders the work unconvincing.[14] These views, however, ignore the visual dimension entirely. But paying full attention to the photographic representation of violence elsewhere and its combination with text, it becomes possible to offer a far more productive reading of *KriegsErklärung*.

Braun substantially shortened and revised *KriegsErklärung* for reissue in his *Texte*. One obvious difference between the two versions is the layout. In the first edition, the photographs are printed on the verso of each two-page spread and are bled to the edges. The quatrains appear on the recto side, along with additional contextual captions explaining what is shown in the image and often providing dates. In the *Texte*, the images are reduced in size, are not bled to the edges of the page, and the quatrain appears beneath them, with the much-reduced contextualizing captions now occupying the verso of each spread. The visual impact of the

---

Knopf, Werner Mittenzwei, and Klaus-Detlev Müller (Frankfurt am Main: Suhrkamp, 1992), 515. Bertolt Brecht, "Über Fotografie," in *Große kommentierte Berliner und Frankfurter Ausgabe*, vol. 21, 264–65. Walter Benjamin, "Der Autor als Produzent," in *Gesammelte Schriften*, vol. 2, ed. Rolf Tiedemann and Hermann Schweppenhäuser (Frankfurt am Main: Surhrkamp, 1977), 683–701, here 693. This section of the chapter summarizes an argument that I develop at length in "Paratextual Profusion."

14 See Ian Wallace, *Volker Braun: Forschungsbericht* (Amsterdam: Rodopi, 1986), 10, for commentary and further references.

work is thereby diminished, and its import becomes more general and less specific. The analysis that follows is based on the *Texte*, but I make reference to the first publication, where the changes have a substantive effect on the overall interpretation.

At the heart of Braun's project is the juxtaposition of the two photo-epigrams that end the first part and start the second part of *KriegsErklärung*. The photograph is the same in both cases.[15] It shows a woman in the foreground. She is wearing dark clothing with a pale headscarf, and her raised left foot suggests that she is breaking into a run. In her left arm she clutches a baby, its head thrown back and its fists clenched. The woman has grabbed a slightly older child by the arm and appears to be dragging it along. A short distance behind the woman, a uniformed soldier walks toward the camera, a rifle slung over his right shoulder and a bayonet in his right hand. In the background is a wooden frame, which lies at a peculiar angle to the picture plane and which could be a bed or a veranda. There seem to be other wooden constructions to the right of the image, while much of the upper portion of the picture is an indeterminate blur. The captions on the verso side of each two-page spread suggest that this blur is a burning village: the first caption is "Das Feuer" (Fire), the second, "Der Rauch" (Smoke).

The quatrains ascribe two different meanings to the image:

Das sieht die Welt. Sie stellts
  beleidigt fest:
Greuel und Greuel, und der
  Mensch ist roh.
Mehr sieht sie nicht. Das alles
  kam da so
Wie Wind, Sintflut, Waldbrand
  und Pest.

Das ist zu sehn: die Mutter
  hilflos flieht
Mit nackten Wesen, aus dem
  Rauch gefischt.
Nun seht hindurch. Das
  geschieht da nicht
Unänderlich wie der Rauch
  vom Feuer zieht.

[This is what the world sees.
  It registers, offended:
Atrocity upon atrocity, and
  humankind is coarse.
More than this it does not see.
  It all just happened
Like wind, flood, wildfire and
  plague.]

[This can be seen: the mother
  flees, helpless,
With naked creatures fished
  out of the smoke.
But look through this.
  It does not happen
Immutably, like smoke rising
  from a fire.]

---

15 This photograph is Horst Faas's "Vietnam Village Razed" (1963), Fig. 1 in Artemis Zervou, "The Unknown Vietnam Series by the Sculptor Christos Kapralos, 1965–1969," translated from Greek by the author; English text edited by William Summerfield, accessed September 14, 2023. https://www.nationalgallery.gr/en/art-topics/i-agnosti-seira-vietnam-tou-glypti-christou-kapralou-1965-1969/.

These two poems turn on different kinds of seeing. In the first, the act of seeing is the superficial registration, by the consumers of the international press, of atrocity and human coarseness. This superficiality leads to an assumption that such phenomena happen in the same way as natural disasters. The concrete image of a woman and her children in a state of extreme vulnerability becomes universalized as a general message about the human condition and the inevitability of war. The implication is that in the absence of any discernible cause that involves human agency, such a mode of viewing leads to political apathy and an acceptance of armed conflict as part of the natural order. The only outcome of viewing these images is transitory outrage ("beleidigt"): a consequence-free release of affect with no consequences for political action.

The second poem begins with a more explicit act of visual registration: a mother flees helplessly, gathering up naked children from the smoke. There is in fact no visible smoke in the foreground of the picture from which the mother has rescued the children; Braun's caption adds something that is not present in the image to reinforce the rhetorical point that the human agency involved in gathering up a child is not the same as the generation of smoke as a necessary by-product of combustion. Sight is, again, the sense on which this nonsimile depends. In the original version of the second quatrain the third line begins, "Doch sehen wir mehr" (Yet we see more). In the revised version, however, we are urged to "hindurchsehen" (look through)—to look beyond appearances and to understand the causes that lie behind them. Reading the photographs, and interpreting them appropriately, becomes a matter not just of seeing more but of seeing through. The epigram itself offers no explanation for the war. Its purpose at this juncture is to establish a particular protocol of reading that then extends both backward and forward, underpinning Braun's own interpretative practices in some cases but functioning more generally as an injunction to subject photographs to an active form of reading that seeks out the absent causes of the image rather than simply registering its contents.

There is a further complexity here, however, which is that the photograph is almost certainly a composite print in which at least two negatives have been used to produce an image that is photographic but does not depict a scene that actually occurred in its entirety in front of the lens. The background, and in particular the frame-like structure to the left of the image, appear to be discontinuous with the foreground. The frame seems to float in space, is not perspectivally aligned with other elements of the scene, and casts no shadow. Abigail Solomon-Godeau argues that the "reality effect" of photographs is due to a multiplicity of factors: they appear to be self-generated, bearing no signs of their making. Although the precondition of the photograph is (in most cases at least) the presence on the scene of the photographer, the latter is manifestly absent from the image. Unlike an image on canvas or paper, a photograph is fully embedded in its material substrate and cannot be thought of as separate from it, and the structural convergence of the eye of the photographer, the camera's lens, and the eye of the spectator confer on photography the quality of pure presentness.[16] The combination of the optical and chemical aspects of photography gives it a particular accuracy and allows it to be integrated into all sorts of discursive formations as evidence or as a truth-telling medium.[17] One of these formations is the discourse of the press, where photographs generally "show" things that corroborate or form the subject of a written report. Their reality effect underscores the accuracy and factuality of journalistic reporting more generally. And yet Solomon-Godeau's comments alert us to the fact that photographic truth is *constructed* by the photographic apparatus. A montage of this kind makes explicit the moment of construction that is always present in the act of photographing, no matter how much the photograph might masquerade as a natural product.

Once we realize this, it becomes possible to read the second of Braun's poems in quite a different way. The injunction to "hindurchsehen" becomes a matter not only of seeing through the superficialities of the scene in order to understand the causes of violence elsewhere but of seeing through the image to reveal its constructedness. If, in Braun's poem, the second instance of "Das" (This) refers not only to the events depicted but also to the image itself, we are dealing with a commentary on photography that denies its status as an index of the real and opens it up to interrogation and contestation. This in turn links Braun's project back to the writings of Weimar theorists and practitioners. For as in Brecht and Benjamin, the caption becomes the means by which this interrogation of the image takes place.

At the start of *KriegsErklärung* is a set of photo-epigrams that explain the war entirely in terms of capitalist expansion and the profit motive. The first epigram imagines US president Lyndon B. Johnson and vice president Hubert Humphrey justifying the war on the grounds that company balance sheets are in such a good state. Epigram I/4,[18] which consists of a montage depicting the New York Stock Exchange, continues the argument for capitalism as the driving force of the Vietnam War.

---

16 See Abigail Solomon-Godeau, *Photography at the Dock: Essays on Photographic History, Institutions, and Practices* (Minneapolis, MN: University of Minnesota Press, 1991), 180.
17 Tagg, *Burden of Representation*.
18 In the *Texte*, the epigrams are numbered sequentially within each section. I use roman numerals to differentiate between parts one and two, and Arabic numerals to identify the specific epigram.

Figure 4.1. "Die New Yorker Börse" (The New York Stock Exchange).

The image itself, with its discontinuous space and consequent perceptual disjunctions, creates an impression of hectic activity, which is here allied to bureaucratic information management, as shown by the prominent filing cabinets and the numerous pieces of paper that seem to circulate within the image. The quatrain once again contains the injunction to look or to see:

Seht hier die höheren Mächte schweben
Sie tragen euer Urteil unterm Latz
Hier steigt und fällt die Chance zu überleben.
Sehts schaudernd an: das ist ein Kriegsschauplatz.

[Behold the higher powers floating
They bear your fate beneath their bibs
The chance of survival rises and falls here.
Look upon it and shudder: it is a theater of war.]

The addressee of the command to look is unclear: is this poem addressed to the reader at large, in which case capitalism is something that decides the fate of everybody? Or is the addressee specifically the North Vietnamese subject, in which case capitalism is the driving force behind the war and wields power over life and death in a literal sense? This ambiguity carries over into the final line, which equates the stock exchange with a theater of war. The sign "SHELTER" with a right-facing arrow at the very top center of the image seems to literalize the metaphor, as does the command to "look" at the "Kriegsschauplatz" (theater of war), a term that foregrounds assumptions about the visuality of warfare that are so deeply embedded in the language we use to describe it. The metaphor implies, first of all, that the operations of capitalism, as manifested in the stock exchange, rely on a level of competitive masculine aggression that is akin to warfare. But it also suggests that the stock exchange is the place where the war in Vietnam is ultimately waged: decisions taken here determine the conduct and outcomes of violence elsewhere. A fundamental aspect of visualizing violence elsewhere, then, is visualizing violence on the domestic front. In doing this, Braun uses a photomontage that does not so much show violence as perform it: space is fractured and discontinuous, bodies lose their integrity (note, for example, the number of heads whose torsos are invisible), and the eye of the viewer is assaulted by an overwhelming quantity of detail without any compositional ordering.

There is, however, more to this photo-epigram. The image teems with white men in suits and spectacles, talking, reading with pen in hand, or simply gazing ahead while performing an unidentifiable administrative task. Random accoutrements of masculinity hover toward the left-center of the image: a duffel bag, a porkpie hat. And the quatrain tells us that these men carry the fate of people "unterm Latz"—beneath their drop-down button flies (of the kind found on Lederhosen and dungarees). The men are not actually wearing these garments, however, so at one level this is easily dismissed as a piece of crudeness whose motivation is the need to rhyme with "Kriegsschauplatz."[19] And yet the notion of men making decisions on the basis of what they've got in their trousers makes a more serious point about masculinity, which ties in with a thematization of gender that we see throughout the *KriegsErklärung*. I will

---

19 For example, by Stefan Wolle, *Der Traum von der Revolte: Die DDR 1968* (Berlin: Links, 2008), 34.

return to this question later; suffice it to say now that the association of phallic masculinity with aggression and the prosecution of war draws on long-established tropes, with which Braun engages critically elsewhere in *KriegsErklärung*.

In the opening epigrams of *KriegsErklärung*, the visualization of violence elsewhere as a function of the violence inherent in capitalism and the profit motive goes hand in hand with an emphasis on military technology. Epigram I/2 shows the helmet of an infantryman from the rear as he crosses a field of long grass, as four Huey helicopters fly overhead. The soldier in the foreground acts as a kind of Rückenfigur, a figure seen from behind that functions as a surrogate for the viewer within the frame itself and whose perspective the viewer is invited to adopt as his or her own. The viewer is thus recruited as a quasi-participant in the US expeditionary force, characterized by technological efficiency and the command of territory and airspace. The emphasis on the helicopter, which became an emblem of US technological superiority and "clean" warfare, was entirely typical of early-stage photographic and televisual reporting of the Vietnam War in the United States.[20]

Braun continues the emphasis on military technology in the third epigram of the collection, which reproduces an advertisement for the Glenn H. Martin Aerospace Manufacturing Company. The photograph, whose prominent halftone dots show that it has been cut from a newspaper, is an aerial shot of a destroyed bridge. Aircraft were first deployed in war not as weapons of destruction but for reconnaissance purposes, turning the airplane, as Christoph Asendorf puts it, into "eine Maschine zum Sehen; es vereinigt die Fähigkeiten zur Aufnahme, Speicherung und Wiedergabe. Das ausgerüstete Aufklärungsflugzeug zeigt, daß das direkte Sehen immer mehr vermittelten Formen weicht" (a vision machine: it unites the capacity to record, store, and play back. A fully equipped reconnaissance plane shows that direct seeing increasingly gives way to mediated forms).[21] The increasingly mediated nature of vision, and the convergence of optical and military technologies, have been a constant of warfare throughout the intervening century.[22] One consequence of this is that killing increasingly takes place at a distance, and war becomes both visualizable and describable in purely technical and impersonal terms.[23] The original caption attached to the photograph of the destroyed bridge reads, "Creative

---

20 Gerhard Paul, *Bilder des Krieges, Krieg der Bilder: Die Visualisierung des modernen Krieges* (Munich: Schoningk/Fink, 2004), 325.
21 Christoph Asendorf, *Super Constellation: Flugzeug und Raumrevolution* (Vienna: Springer, 1997), 36.
22 This is the thesis polemically advanced by Paul Virilio in *War and Cinema: The Logistics of Perception*, trans. Patrick Camiller (London: Verso, 1989).
23 Zygmunt Bauman terms this the "social production of moral invisibility." See his *Modernity and the Holocaust* (Cambridge: Polity, 1989), 24–27.

Figure 4.2. "Kreativität" (Creativity).

engineering at Martin made it happen . . . *and North Viet Nam has the bridges out to prove it.*" The action here is between US military engineering and North Vietnamese civil engineering, with a complete elision of human agency and human consequences. By aligning the viewer's perspective with the gaze of the aerial military observer, the image invites the reader to see Vietnam once again as a clean war, waged by advanced technological means and involving no identifiable casualties. Furthermore, it domesticates the military gaze by reproducing it in a newspaper to be read in the home over breakfast, and commercializes it in the context of an advertisement.

The caption on the verso page reads, simply, "Kreativität," foregrounding the sheer perversity of the equation "creativity = destruction," while the quatrain draws attention to the military-industrial complex:

Die Flüsse nicht, der Himmel aus den Ufern tritt.
Die großen Brücken gehen schwach in die Knie.
Das Schicksal weissagt ihnen Martin Company.
Vietnam geht hoch und der Profit.

[Not rivers, but the sky bursts its banks
Great bridges collapse weakly at the knee
Their fate is prophesied by Martin Company
Vietnam explodes as profits rise.]

Like the photo-epigram of the woman fleeing her village, this epigram again refuses the equation of war and natural disaster, with the metaphor of the sky "bursting its banks" highlighting how *un*natural it is for bridges to be destroyed from the air. The double meaning of "hochgehen" here—to explode and to increase—links the annihilation of North Vietnamese infrastructure to the profits generated for arms manufacturers by the expenditure of military force, reinforcing the message of the stock exchange epigram. While Braun's rhetoric continues to elide human agency in favor of impersonal forces, he locates the cause of the destruction not in "creative" engineering but in the profit motive. Braun's caption is the verbal adjunct necessary to demystify the photograph, insert it into a different set of causal relationships, and transform the passive consumption of military-industrial propaganda into a critical engagement with how images work and the contexts they privilege and elide. This is the practice of "Hindurchsehen."

Having thus, in the opening epigrams of "Geschäftsbericht," established the link between capitalism and the prosecution of war in Vietnam, Braun offers, in the "Bericht vom Volk," an alternative vision of military and socioeconomic organization. Repeatedly, we are shown images of individuals working on a small scale. In the second epigram of "Bericht vom Volk," we see a blasted landscape in which the trees have been defoliated, with only the trunks now pointing skyward. Smaller stakes have been driven into the ground, and wires strung between the tree trunks to create a helicopter trap. Three small figures can be seen in the middle distance, going about the work of erecting the trap. The quatrain refers back to the Martin Company epigram: "Die Bäume stehn jetzt laublos aus den Wiesen / Wie Speere. Dem Himmel geben Drähte Halt" (The trees now stand leafless in the meadows / Like spears. The sky is kept up by wires). Here, the work of the villagers is pitted against technological destruction visited upon their village from the air, and this topic becomes a recurrent concern of the "Bericht vom Volk."

In epigram II/6, the poet finds his own courage growing at the sight of women sewing in the shadow of a concealed antiaircraft gun that will prevent the US forces, here described as "murderers," from progressing further. The structure of the image, with a large, camouflaged flak installation in the background protecting the peaceful activity of the women in the foreground, emphasizes the necessity and fundamentally defensive nature of the (potential) violence, and thereby justifies it. There appear to be three male soldiers manning [*sic*] the gun emplacement, reinforcing a gendered division of labor: men are the protectors of women in war, and the latter thus take on the role of potential victims rather than being agents in the conflict. The communal nature of the scene, however, once again accentuates the sense of a people working collectively to defeat a

Figure 4.3. "Flakstellung in einem Dorf bei Thai Nguyen" (Flak Installation in a Village near Thai Nguyen).

technologically superior enemy. Nowhere is this more apparent than in the preceding epigram, which shows three men in the act of smelting metal for weapons in a makeshift jungle workshop. Strange spatial relationships and the relative sizes of the two men in the foreground suggest that this is another composite print. The significance of the image lies, however, not in its veracity but in the contrastive relationship to the images of the Huey helicopters and the aerial destruction of the bridge in "Geschäftsbericht": the impersonal forces of US imperialism are being countered by the "Volk," using whatever sparse resources they can muster. The success of this endeavor is claimed in epigram II/10, which shows four men carrying part of the tail fin of an F-105 Thunderchief fighter-bomber. The point, once again, is that for all its technological superiority, the US military endeavor can be undermined by freedom fighters with rudimentary armaments.

In terms of its bipartite structure and much of its rhetoric at the level of word and image, then, *KriegsErklärung* offers a dualistic view of the Vietnam War, in which US military aggression, driven by the profit motive and manifesting itself in faceless technological superiority, is opposed to the communal, preindustrial, "Volk"-based war of defense conducted by the North Vietnamese. In this sense, the work is fully ideologically aligned with the East German state's policy on Vietnam and, indeed, with the anti-Vietnam War discourse prevalent in West Germany at the same time.

Zooming Out

Zooming in on the immediate theoretical and ideological contexts relevant to the reading of *KriegsErklärung* shows that Braun seeks to demystify press images of the Vietnam War in order to put forward an anticapitalist and anti-US narrative that was aligned with GDR orthodoxy. At the same time, the above discussion repeatedly alludes to the question of military masculinity, which emerges as a central concern of the epigrams. Refocusing on gender opens up new perspectives on Braun's account of the Vietnam War. These are, perhaps, surprising. And they have certainly been entirely overlooked by Braun's critics.

Returning to the twin epigram that forms the center of the book, while the approach to photography and to the causes of war works against passive acceptance, the photograph nevertheless conveys an entirely conventional view of victimhood: the male soldier in the background functions as an agent of violence and destruction, while the mother and her children in the foreground are part of what Wendy Kozol terms "the spectacle of transnational motherhood," which depends on "supposedly universal ideals about gender, maternal care, vulnerability, and innocence."[24]

The mother-child dyad emerges early in Braun's text, in epigram I/6. The photograph shows a military chaplain bearing a small statue of the Madonna and child—an image that continues to epitomize maternal care within the (post-)Christian West. The accompanying poem reads,

> Der Mann Gottes mit vorschobenem Kinn
> Fand die Madonna, die nicht vor ihm floh.
> Sie fürchtet nichts. Sie fällt nicht schreiend hin.
> Sie ist aus Holz, das Kindlein ebenso.
>
> [The man of God with jutting chin
> Found the Madonna, who did not take flight
> She fears nothing. She does not fall wailing to the ground.
> She is made of wood, as is the child.]

The implication is that had the mother and child not been wooden effigies, they would have done one of two things: collapsed wailing; or taken flight, as though these reactions exhaust the scope for female agency in wartime. This implication, though, is possible only because the iconography of passive maternal victimhood was and remains firmly established as a visual intertext. Braun recycles tropes of the female victim that have a long history in the photographic representation of war and continue to dominate the Western press today.[25]

---

24 Kozol, *Distant Wars Visible*, 44–45.
25 See, for example, Brothers, *War and Photography*, 143–58.

Braun's injunction to "hindurchsehen," then, is less clear-cut than it might initially seem. The reason for this is that icons of suffering motherhood tend to elide questions of causality, agency, and specificity and articulate an "ideal of universal maternal care."[26] The fact that Braun's pivotal epigrams remain unspecific in terms of identifying the cause of the fire, combined with the iconography of maternal suffering, runs the risk of reinforcing a perspective on war informed by immutable patterns of gendered violence and victimhood.

This is congruent with the highly conventional representations of female agency elsewhere in *KriegsErklärung*. In the epigram that follows the image of women sewing under a male-operated antiaircraft installation, women are seen in the act of donating rice (II/7). The poem exhorts their brothers to take the rice and "everything," as long as they triumph: "Nehmt das hier, oder alles. Aber siegt!" (Take this here, or everything. Just win!). In the final epigram (II/15), a woman is shown giving a wounded combatant something to drink. Women are portrayed as ancillary participants in the conflict, fulfilling nurturing roles in repeated displays of behind-the-lines domesticity. Photographic representations emanating from North Vietnam offered a very different view of Vietnamese women, foregrounding the role of the militiawomen who were actively involved in the armed struggle on the North Vietnamese side.[27] As Mererid Puw Davies has shown, some of these photographs were known in West Germany, circulating, for example, in the left-wing journal *konkret*. They appealed to the West German left as powerful images of the anticapitalist guerrilla fighter, which some felt could be a template for antiauthoritarian resistance in the West.[28] The massive extent of Vietnamese women's political organization and military mobilization is outlined in Arlene Eisen Bergman's remarkable book, *Women of Vietnam*. Throughout, Bergman emphasizes the willingness of women to forsake domestic and family responsibilities for months or even years at a time in order to devote themselves to military struggle.[29] And yet Braun's account of the US involvement in Vietnam reinforces conventional gender norms and conceives of critique very much in terms of geopolitics rather than social relations.

---

26 Kozol, *Distant Wars Visible*, 45.
27 See Paul, *Bilder des Krieges*, 332. Women saw active military service on both sides of the conflict.
28 Davies, *Writing and West German Protest Movements*, 82; 84.
29 Arlene Eisen Bergman, *Women of Vietnam*, 2nd ed. (San Francisco: People's Press, 1975). Bergman gives a clear sense of the scope of women's involvement in agricultural production and organized militias, including their responsibility for antiaircraft defense (see 129, 171).

At the same time, images of masculinity are more nuanced and varied. Normative forms of military masculinity across industrialized cultures tend to emphasize the coherence and invulnerability of the soldierly body, psychological resilience, and the ability to tolerate pain and overcome fear. Indeed, these are the intended outcomes of modern military training.[30] In *KriegsErklärung*, though, military masculinity is subjected to critique through the representation of the damaged body. Epigram 1/9 is captioned "Söldner Farley nach einem Hubschraubereinsatz" (Mercenary Farley after a helicopter mission).[31] "Söldner" was a term applied by the GDR to characterize military personnel in the West (especially West Germany), in contradistinction to the class-conscious socialist soldier of the GDR. Western military personnel were portrayed in the GDR as "footsoldiers of capital," as Tom Smith puts it, acting not in their own class interests but in those of capitalist profiteers.[32] Farley is depicted sitting on a strongbox in his fatigues, his holster and ammunition belt still in place, leaning sideways on his right forearm, which is itself resting on another, larger strongbox. He is covering his face with his left hand, but the deep furrow from nose to mouth, and his partially visible rictus, suggest that he is in anguish. Rather than a vision of the well-armed soldier participating in a technologically precise war, this image shows a moment of individual psychological breakdown. Braun's original and revised versions of the accompanying poem betoken a significant change in his interpretation of the photograph. The original reads:

's ist Feierahmnd. Das Tagwerk ist vollbracht.
Mord im Akkord, ich Rindvieh mach es mit.
Wir gehen langsam drauf bei Tag und Nacht.
Jetzt hab ich Schiß. Bald bin ich wieder fit.

[Time to knock off. Our daily work is accomplished.
Murder at piece rates. I, a dumb ox, go along with it.
We slowly die by night and day.
I'm shitting myself now, but I'll soon be fine again.]

---

30 See the discussion of the "socialist soldier personality" in Tom Smith, *Comrades in Arms: Military Masculinities in East German Culture* (Oxford: Berghahn, 2020), 36–40.

31 The photograph of Farley is taken from a famous report in *Life* magazine by photographer Larry Burrows ("One Ride with Yankee Papa 13," *Life*, April 16, 1965, 24–34D) and appears as Fig. 23 here: https://time.com/3879815/vietnam-photo-essay-larry-burrows-one-ride-with-yankee-papa-13/feed/. From the original article, it is clear that Farley is distraught because of the death of a comrade, not that of Vietnamese civilians. This circumstance demonstrates the power of the caption to guide the reading of the image.

32 Smith, *Comrades in Arms*, 36–37.

Here, the poem is voiced by the soldier, who describes himself as "Rindvieh"—literally "cattle," with connotations of bovine stupidity or idiocy—and his daily work as routine murder perpetrated for payment. Indeed, the notion of piece rates suggests that payment is made on the basis of murders committed: a truly mercenary transaction. The distress visible on Farley's face is interpreted as transitory fear, and, like a good worker under industrial capitalism, he will regain his labor power after a period of rest. In its original incarnation, then, this epigram is aligned with orthodox GDR interpretations of the Western military.

In the *Texte*, however, the poem is quite different. The poetic persona is now ambiguous: it could be either Farley or an anonymous third person. More significantly, the poem shifts the emphasis away from the act of killing to the psychological effects of warfare on the aggressors themselves:

> 's ist Feierahmnd. Das Tagwerk ist vollbracht.
> Nur geht es nicht der Heimat zu.
> Ganz sachte schleicht sich an die Nacht.
> Die liebe Seele hat nicht Ruh.
>
> [Time to knock off. Our daily work is accomplished.
> But it is not time to go home.
> The night steals in softly.
> His/my dear soul knows no rest.]

Much of this stanza quotes a well-known dialect folk song, "Feierohmd" (Time to Knock Off), written in 1903 by Alsatian folk poet Anton Günther, in which evening rest after a hard day's work is a metaphor for a peaceful afterlife.[33] In Braun's version, however, the creeping nightfall is transformed into a subjective condition of alienation and psychological torment that is existential rather than transitory. In the revised version, Farley is no longer a dumb or bestial murderer but is endowed with interiority, which in turn constructs a relationship of sympathy with the ostensible enemy. Braun thereby problematizes the victim-perpetrator dualism and suggests the possibility of class solidarity across the East-West geopolitical divide.

The problematization of military masculinity continues in the next epigram (I/10), which shows US soldiers who have been wounded and

---

[33] Anton Günther, "Feierohmd," accessed April 28, 2022, http://noten.bplaced.net/weltlich/abschied/Gunther_SIsFeieromd.pdf. This is one of the countless versions of this song available on the internet. "Feierohmd" is a dialect spelling of "Feierabend," a colloquial term for the end of the working day, which in my translation of Braun's poem I have rendered as "time to knock off."

blinded as a result of a napalm attack by their own side. The inclusion of bodies that are damaged or that express, through their gestures, a disturbed mind, redistributes victimhood and vulnerability. This has two consequences. The first is that US soldiers become implicitly feminized, linked to female victims of war in the two central epigrams: US military masculinity is undermined, and with it the illusion that Vietnam was a clean war fought by technological means. The second is that Braun's text can be seen to take up a surreptitiously pacifist stance, especially in its revised version, in which sympathy for and solidarity with Farley become possible. *KriegsErklärung* is not in general a pacifist text: a number of epigrams justify, celebrate, and encourage military action in the service of revolution (for example, II/5, II/6, II/7II/9, II/10, II/15). But this is partially relativized by epigrams I/9 and I/10.

KriegsErklärung is unified at a visual level by the recurrence of the Rückenfigur. In the early epigram (1/2), we saw that the critique of military masculinity and the value of valor is located in the poem rather than in the image itself. But what happens when the device of the Rückenfigur itself offers a much less comfortable viewer position? In epigram II/3, he is part of a group of uniformed South Vietnamese soldiers training their weapons on a mass of young Vietnamese, some of them still children and all of them unarmed or, at most, armed with sticks. The viewer's position is aligned with that of a potential perpetrator of violence against largely defenseless civilians. The quatrain, meanwhile, is an address to the soldiers that carries a message of defiance: the only way to pass is to kill those blocking the street. In the revised version, the factual caption becomes much more general. The original reads, "Südvietnamesische Arbeiter setzen sich gegen Saigoner Söldner zur Wehr" (South Vietnamese Workers Stand Up to Saigon Mercenaries), while the revised version states simply, "Die Straße" (The Street). A concrete incident that in part demonstrates the complexity of the Vietnam War transmutes into an emblematic scene of generalized civilian defiance. For the *Texte*, Braun slightly amends the poem to reduce the element of challenge and increase the passive nature of the workers. The original reads,

> Durch uns hindurch gelangt ihr nach Gia Dinh.
> Im Blut nur könnt ihr gehen, oder nicht mehr.
> Auf unseren Gräbern ist ein Weg dahin.
> Ihr müßt nur einen Schritt noch tun. Kommt her.
>
> [You must pass through us to get to Gia Dinh.
> You can walk in blood or not at all.
> The way there lies over our graves.
> You just need to take a step forward. Come on.]

Figure 4.4. "Die Straße" (The Street).

In the revised version, lines two and four are changed:

> Im Blut könnt ihr gehen in euren Schuhen.
> . . .
> Ihr müßt nur einen Schritt noch tun.
>
> [In blood may you go in your shoes.
> . . .
> You just need to take a step forward.]

The overt provocation "Kommt her" (Come on) has gone, the self-sacrificial passivity of the young civilians is enhanced, and the identity of the soldiers as South Vietnamese mercenaries elided. The uniform and weaponry of the soldiers support the assumption that they are from the US, and the image enacts a series of binaries: between the armed and the unarmed, the military and the civilian, the individual paid soldier and the solidarity of the collective. These binaries are underscored by the dissonant relationship between image and text. The photograph aligns the viewer with the perspective of pro-US forces, while in the poem, dissenting Vietnamese voices address the Rückenfigur and his companions, and by implication the reader as well. In so doing, the epigram positions the reader/viewer as a potential killer of defenseless civilians and simultaneously challenges that position, thereby highlighting the human agency involved in killing and countering the notion of Vietnam as a clean war.

This epigram refers back to the beginning of the book, concretizing the kind of "Tapferkeit" (bravery) required to prosecute an allegedly genocidal campaign: it involves the cold-blooded killing of unarmed civilians. This is a profoundly unheroic image of military masculinity, and it finds its expression, too, in the image around which the whole text pivots: the woman and her children taking flight from a soldier and a burning village. By highlighting the power differential conferred by firearms, Braun exposes the military masculinity of US and pro-US forces as a form of cowardice rather than bravery. At the same time, these three epigrams are the only ones in which armed military personnel confront civilians. All the soldiers are South Vietnamese rather than from the US. Braun thus represents face-to-face killing as a purely Asian matter, as though he is unable to break a taboo that forbids the depiction of white Western subjects inflicting violence on nonwhite Asian civilians.[34]

As the introduction to this volume argues, representations of violence elsewhere are simultaneously images of Germany itself. In the context of Braun's *KriegsErklärung*, the contrast between the North Vietnamese and the Americans functions not only as a condemnation of the Vietnam War but also as a proxy for the relationship between the GDR and the capitalist West (especially West Germany). The one image of West Germany underscores this point. A clearly doctored photograph shows an anti-Vietnam protester in Munich being forcibly led away by police. The accompanying poem establishes West Germany as a vassal state (presumably in thrall to the US) and the police as both maggot-like and brutal. The image of an unarmed civilian being apprehended by armed and uniformed policemen (note the prominent and phallic positioning of the holster on the main figure's right thigh) echoes the images of military-civilian contact in Vietnam, highlighting the oppressive and antidemocratic nature of the West German state. The GDR is implicitly valorized, as a state in which opposition to the Vietnam War was not only permitted but was a key element of foreign policy and, indeed, an enabling condition of Braun's text.

It turns out, however, that Braun's text is about Germany in other ways as well. It remains, for example, deeply informed by conservative assumptions about gender that convey highly conventional notions of women's labor and female agency. For all the legal commitment to gender equality in the GDR, the ideological, political, and social structures of the GDR's patriarchal socialism perpetuated deep-rooted inequality.[35]

---

34 This taboo is one reason for the controversies surrounding publication of photographs of the My Lai massacre and of "Accidental Napalm Attack."

35 See Irene Dölling, "Frauen in der ehemaligen DDR," *Women in German Yearbook* 7 (1991): 121–36, on the gender-political implications of GDR socialism and their lived consequences. On the relevant legal framework as a vehicle of

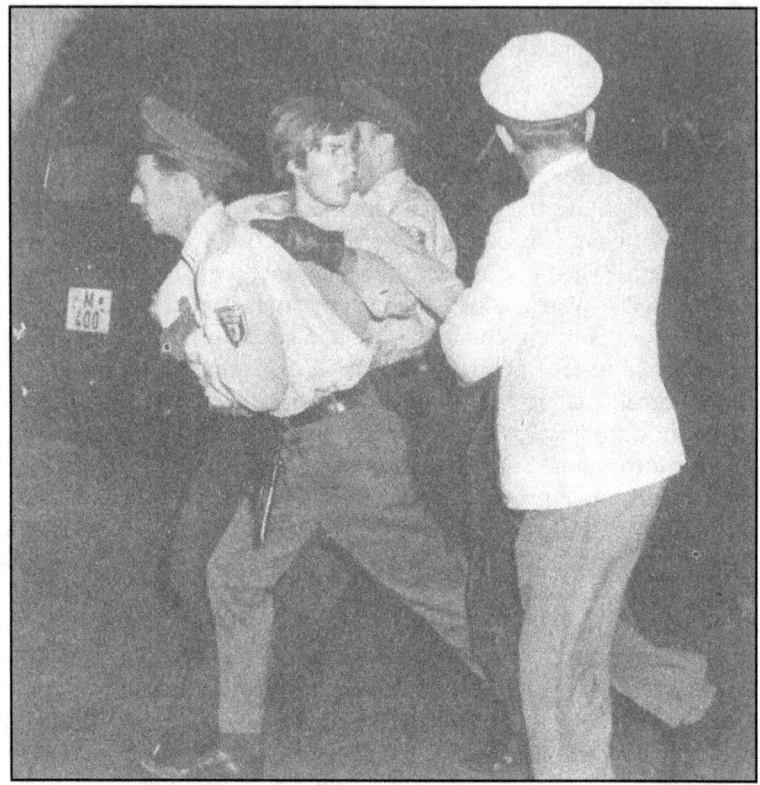

Fig. 4.5: "Im Freistaat Bayern" (In the Free State of Bavaria).

It is well established that women suffered under the dual burden of paid work and childcare/household management. Beyond this, the structure of the labor force was such that women's work was concentrated in a small number of roles in, for example, the service and caring sectors, where they replicated domestic duties in collective social settings. It is perhaps no surprise that Braun reactivates these gender assumptions in his representation of Vietnamese women and portrays war and revolution as fundamentally masculine.

Furthermore, the use of the mother and child as a trope for universal human suffering suggests that Braun cannot fully escape the representational schemata of the global news press when portraying women

---

fundamentally moral values, see Eva Douma, "Die Entwicklung des Familiengesetzbuches der DDR 1945–1966: Frauen und Familienpolitik im Spannungsfeld zwischen theoretischer Grundlage und realexistenter wirtschaftlicher Situation," *Zeitschrift der Savigny-Stiftung für Rechtsgeschichte: Germanistische Abteilung* 111 (1994): 592–620.

in war, despite his intention to "see through" such representations. This goes hand in hand with an orientalist gaze, in which femininity and racial otherness intersect in an image of passive victimhood, and face-to-face killing can only be represented as an "Asiatic" act. The entanglement of race with geopolitics is picked up in the epigram depicting Leipzig students giving blood: humanitarian aid projects such as this enable white Europeans to become the saviors of an Asia in crisis.[36]

The representations of race and gender in *KriegsErklärung* show that for all its criticism of the US, debunking of the global media, and anti-capitalism, Braun's perspective—and by extension the political imaginary of the GDR—remained locked into a set of Eurocentric, orientalist, and patriarchal assumptions. Ultimately, the representation of violence elsewhere in *KriegsErklärung* shows that solidarity with the people of North Vietnam cannot overwrite the ideological congruencies between East Germany and its Western neighbors that persisted through the Cold War.

Concluding Remarks

In sum, Braun's critique of US involvement in Vietnam is developed in two complementary ways. The first is the more obvious of the two: the US is represented in terms of capitalist imperialism, and the war itself in terms of geopolitical maneuvering and economic calculation. The second is less obvious but no less present: a multifaceted critique of a military masculinity. Furthermore, at the heart of *KriegsErklärung* lies a self-reflexive interrogation of the image, using the combination of the verbal and the visual to denaturalize the photograph and subject it to demystifying forms of interpretation. Indeed, the repeated use of the Rückenfigur—itself a self-reflexive device that locates the act of viewing within the image—represents a form of self-reflexivity to the second degree, in the sense that the viewer position implied by the Rückenfigur is repeatedly destabilized by the accompanying poems. *KriegsErklärung* is thus not only a meditation on the gender and geopolitics of the Vietnam War but an interrogation and critique of the very representational forms through which violence elsewhere is mediated to the audience "at home."

---

36 The blood donation campaigns were not trouble-free, however, with some East Germans expressing racist resentment and refusing to provide "white blood" for the "yellow race." See Horten, "Sailing in the Shadow," 569.

5: The Vietnam Veteran in Anna Seghers's *Steinzeit* (Stone Age, 1975)

Ernest Schonfield[1]

THE EAST GERMAN AUTHOR Anna Seghers (1900–1983) "wrote with a deliberately global context in mind."[2] Born Annette Reiling, the daughter of a Jewish art dealer in Mainz, she became a Communist in the 1920s. She went into exile in France (1933–41) and Mexico (1941–47). Her exile informs her work and her commitment to international solidarity.[3] In August 1948 she was a delegate at the Weltkongress der Intellektuellen zur Verteidigung des Friedens (World Congress of Intellectuals in Defense of Peace) in Wrocław, which became the World Peace Council in 1950, where she developed contacts with writers Jorge Amado and Pablo Neruda.[4] Later, Seghers served as president of the East German Writers' Union (1952–78). This chapter will focus on her late novella *Steinzeit* (Stone Age), about a disturbed US Vietnam veteran. *Steinzeit* was first published in the premier literary journal of the German Democratic Republic (GDR; East Germany), *Sinn und Form* (issue 4, 1975), then in book form in 1977 in East Germany and 1978 in West Germany in a twin volume with another of Seghers's novellas, "Wiederbegegnung" (Reencounter).[5] *Steinzeit* is set in Colombia, with flashbacks to the protagonist's time in Vietnam and the USA;

---

1   I would like to thank Douglas Irving for commenting on a previous draft of this essay and for allowing me to quote from his unpublished English translation of *Steinzeit*. Thanks also to Trudy Wallace for giving me books by Anna Seghers that were formerly in the possession of Trudy's late husband, Professor Ian Wallace.

2   Helen Fehervary, *Anna Seghers: The Mythic Dimension* (Ann Arbor: University of Michigan Press, 2001), 1.

3   Marike Janzen, *Writing to Change the World: Anna Seghers, Authorship, and International Solidarity in the Twentieth Century* (Rochester, NY: Camden House, 2018).

4   Christiane Zehl Romero, *Anna Seghers: Eine Biographie 1947–1983* (Berlin: Aufbau, 2003), 59–61.

5   Anna Seghers, *Steinzeit. Wiederbegegnung: Zwei Erzählungen* (Berlin: Aufbau, 1977).

Wiederbegegnung moves between Mexico and Francoist Spain. Both texts reflect the author's understanding of the Cold War as a global conflict.

The US bombing of North Vietnam is the crucial subtext to *Steinzeit*. The title alludes to a statement by General Curtis LeMay (1906–90), which appeared in his 1965 autobiography: "My solution to the problem [of North Vietnam] would be to tell them frankly that they've got to draw in their horns and stop their aggression, or we're going to bomb them back into the Stone Age."[6] LeMay, having directed the bombing of Japan in World War II, was chief of staff of the US Air Force from 1961 to 1965. The US bombing of Vietnam, Laos, and Cambodia has been described by Mark Clodfelter as "the most intense episode of aerial bombing in human history," as the US dropped over seven and a half million tons of explosive ordnance.[7] The Vietnamese government estimates that the death toll was approximately 2 million civilians and 1 million North Vietnamese soldiers; another 3 million people were exposed to health complications owing to the use of herbicides such as Agent Orange, which had previously been used by the British in Malaya in the 1950s.[8] Toward the end of the war, the US bombing campaign "Operation Linebacker II" in December 1972 killed 1,623 people, according to the US estimate.[9] *Steinzeit* references LeMay when one veteran tells another, "Erinnerst du dich an den General, der ganz groß angab, wir würden Vietnam in die Steinzeit zurückbombardieren?" (10; You remember that general who made this big claim that we'd bomb Vietnam back into the Stone Age?). In this way, LeMay's infamous "Stone Age" comment is an essential cue that shapes the reading of *Steinzeit*.

Steinzeit reprises the themes of Seghers's earlier fiction—persecution, flight, and the adventure narrative—into a dense composition of around fifty pages. Its protagonist, Gary, is marked by a history of violence: from childhood beatings by his father to his service in the Vietnam War and his hijacking of a plane. Yet the narrative gives few details of these violent incidents, since it is shaped by Gary's present and his determination to avoid his own past. The text explores various levels of violence, moving among US violence in Vietnam, colonial legacies in Colombia, and violent family structures in the US. On another, latent level, the text rehearses

---

6 General Curtis E. LeMay, with MacKinley Kantor, *Mission with LeMay: My Story* (New York: Doubleday, 1965), 565.

7 Perry Blankson, "Fifty Years Ago: Vietnam's Horror Captured," *Tribune* 15 (2022): 40–43, here 42–43. See also Mark Clodfelter, *The Limits of Air Power: The American Bombing of North Vietnam* (New York: Free Press, 1989).

8 Blankson, "Fifty Years Ago," 41–42.

9 William P. Head, *War from above the Clouds (B-52 Operations during the Second Indochina War and the Effects of the Air War on Theory and Doctrine)*, Fairchild Paper (Montgomery, AL: Air University Press, 2002), 84. Thanks to David McNaught for this reference.

concerns about German history: the protagonist's failure to successfully integrate into civilian life recalls the German *Heimkehrer* (homecoming) texts of the late 1940s, like Wolfgang Borchert's 1947 play *Draußen vor der Tür* (first US production: *Outside the Door*, 1949). The protagonist's animosity toward his father bears comparison to the father-son conflicts of German expressionism and the *Väterliteratur* (father literature) of 1970s West Germany.[10] Halfway through *Steinzeit*, there is even a troubling depiction of a border crossing guarded by armed military police. Therefore, the violence depicted "elsewhere" in *Steinzeit* would have had considerable resonance for readers in both Germanies in the late 1970s.

The present chapter is divided into four sections. First, it considers *Steinzeit*'s narrative technique and content. Second, it focuses on the protagonist, Gary's, disturbed psyche, including his unspoken sense of guilt and the possibility that he is suffering from post-traumatic stress disorder (PTSD). Third, it examines his dysfunctional relationships with other men. The final section will consider the extent to which this apparently "American" story can shed light on our understanding of Seghers herself and her fellow East Germans in the decades after 1945. It will argue that on a deeper, latent level, this story of "violence elsewhere" speaks to the fears and concerns of Seghers and her East German readers.

Steinzeit: Form and Content

It is significant that Seghers focused on the novella form for much of her career, despite the fact that this genre was devalued in East Germany owing to its association with the "irrational" heritage of Romanticism.[11] Yet Seghers had always maintained a distance from Communist orthodoxy by including mythic and "heretical" elements in her work.[12] As Helen Fehervary puts it, Seghers writes "with urgency about a present that is always a *past* present, that is to say, an enchanted present inscribed by topographies inhabited by the dead."[13] Indeed, the densely structured patterning of *Steinzeit* has a certain affinity with Ludwig Tieck's Romantic story *Der blonde Eckbert* (Blond Eckbert, 1797), in which the characters are haunted by their own past crimes as they pass through a magical forest landscape.[14] As early as 1955, Seghers had pushed back against Socialist Realism, arguing that it is essential to depict inner conflict: "was sich im

---

10   Claudia Mauelshagen, *Der Schatten des Vaters: Deutschsprachige Väterliteratur der siebziger und achtziger Jahre* (Bern: Peter Lang, 1995).
11   Janzen, *Writing to Change the World*, 84.
12   Fehervary, *Anna Seghers*, 204.
13   Fehervary, *Anna Seghers*, 2.
14   Thanks to Mererid Puw Davies for sharing this insight.

Inneren der Menschen zuträgt" (what is going on inside people).[15] And in 1975 she observed that a "realist" writer's remit also includes dreams: "Auch Träume, phantastische Gedankenverbindungen, Wünsche usw. gehören zur Wirklichkeit" (Dreams, fantastical thought associations, desires, etc. are also part of reality).[16] Thus, the narrative of *Steinzeit* is not linear but proceeds via a succession of flashbacks and recurring motifs and images. The narrative technique is *erlebte Rede* (free indirect speech)—a form often used by Franz Kafka—which allows the narrative to convey an intimate view of Gary's subjectivity and, at the same time, imply a critical distance from it.

The story begins in medias res: "Die Landung war geglückt" (7; The landing was successful).[17] Fehervary observes that when speaking, Seghers "had the ability to take up her subject matter *in medias res* in a tone and manner of voice that seemed to emanate from the deepest recesses of her psyche."[18] Similarly, in *Steinzeit*, the tone and manner of the narrative are decisive—*how* things happen is just as important as what happens. We hear that Gary has just landed in Colombia, and that he very recently hijacked a plane, but we never hear how and why this happened. Similarly, Gary is a Vietnam veteran who served in the US Air Force (USAF), but we are never told exactly what he did there. Details of his backstory are extremely sparse and scattered—his previous life is largely inaccessible to the reader. In this way, the reader is presented from the outset with the cognitive challenge of reconstructing Gary's backstory from the few details that are scattered through the text.

The plot of *Steinzeit* focuses almost entirely on Gary's time in Colombia as he attempts to disappear. As the story begins, he has just hijacked the plane and threatened to crash it into a nuclear power station. His threat has succeeded, and "[es] war ihm am vereinbarten Ort die Summe ausgehändigt worden" (7; he had been handed a ransom at the arranged location). (The passive construction here conceals more than it reveals.) We read, "Er mußte verschwinden" (7; He had to disappear). Ostensibly this is because of the hijacking, yet it seems that Gary's attempt to "disappear" in Colombia is a response to the horror of the Vietnam War. We only learn a few tantalizing details about Gary's time in Vietnam; for example, when he recalls, "Was alles in Vietnam passiert ist ... die Städte und Brücken, die ich auf ihren Befehl zusammenknallte" (36;

15 Anna Seghers, *Über Kunst und Wirklichkeit*, 4 vols., ed. Sigrid Bock (Berlin: Akademie, 1970–79), 1:240.
16 Anna Seghers, letter to David Scrase, June 10, 1975, in Anna Seghers, *Tage wie Staubsand: Briefe 1953–1983* (Berlin: Aufbau, 2010), 265.
17 Translations of *Steinzeit* into English are by Douglas Irving, from his unpublished English translation (2014; revised, 2022), and used here with his kind permission. Page references to the 1977 German version given in text.
18 Fehervary, *Anna Seghers*, 149.

Everything that happened in Vietnam . . . the cities and the bridges that I blew up at their command). Or when he hears that the Long Biên Bridge in Hanoi is being rebuilt and thinks (this time in an indirect monologue), "Alle seine guten Kriegskameraden hatten also für nichts und wieder nichts ihr Leben aufs Spiel gesetzt" (24; All his good comrades-in-arms had risked their lives for nothing at all). Thus, the Vietnam War is like a framing device. The question here is not *what* Gary did in Vietnam but rather: *why* is he so disturbed? This question is never answered directly—instead, readers have to work it out for themselves. In this way, *Steinzeit* places cognitive gaps at the center of the reading experience. As Jürgen Thomaneck has shown, Seghers uses the technique of omission: what we read is only the tip of the iceberg, and there is always more going on below the surface.[19] This chapter will seek to reconstruct "what is wrong" with Gary by interpreting the hints given in the text.

First, though, it will be useful to outline the salient facts of the narrative. Having landed in Colombia, Gary spends the night at a farm and buys a truck from a farmer. As he drives off, he recalls his friend Henry Maxwell, with whom he spent two years at the USAF flying school in Vietnam. Gary was wounded—we do not learn how. He aggravated his injury artificially in order to be discharged from the Air Force. Upon his discharge, Gary returns to his father's farm, but he cannot stand it. So he goes to a bar, where he finds Maxwell, who suggests that Gary invest his severance pay in a new identity: he knows a hospital porter in Albuquerque who has access to the morgue; he can get a "clean" South American passport for Gary. Metaphorically, it is a chance to wipe the slate clean. Gary asks why he should need a passport; Maxwell gives a laconic response: sooner or later, Gary may need a new identity. Gary takes Maxwell's advice and buys a passport, which happens to be Colombian: his new name is José Hernández. In another flashback, we learn that Gary's mother was Mexican and spoke Spanish with Gary when he was a child; this would enrage his father. His childhood Spanish enables him to adapt quickly to his new identity.

Gary buys a cattle ranch in Colombia and becomes a respected member of the community. He begins a relationship with a woman, Eliza Méndez, but he fears that his past will be discovered. So he heads toward San Sebastián in eastern Colombia and gets a job as overseer on a ranch belonging to a man called González. González has a young son who reminds Gary of his own younger brother. Gary is welcomed by the family, but he does not share their Catholic faith, and he is reluctant when they ask him to attend the confessional. He becomes paranoid and is relieved when he meets Harry Gold, the representative of a

---

19 J. K. A. Thomaneck, "The Iceberg in Anna Seghers's Novel *Überfahrt*," *German Life and Letters* 28, no. 1 (1974): 36–45, here 43.

US company specializing in surveillance equipment. Gary joins Gold's expedition to the Amazon rainforest, bids farewell to the González family, and promises to return within three months—he never does. Gary breaks with Gold when he refuses to give him a share of the profits and heads for the Amazon.

Gary is welcomed by a tribe of indigenous people living on a peninsula in the Amazon. He lives among them, fishing and gathering fruit. It seems as if he has found redemption. Then an anthropologist from the US, Tom Hilsom, arrives; he is studying the indigenous population. Gary is drawn to Hilsom and starts to open up to him. He accidentally lets slip that he was in Vietnam, however, and his paranoia returns. Gary heads off into the jungle again. He joins some woodcutters and makes friends with a young lad, Estébano. The woodcutters give Gary the identity papers of a dead man, Alberto, so he can collect some wages. Another new life beckons. But then the rainy season starts; the woodcutters are picked up by steamship, and Estébano heads home.

Gary has a brief relationship with a woman, Luisa. Then he decides to begin yet another new life as a cattle herder in the Andes Mountains. Two shepherds give him directions to a remote rancho in the mountains owned by a certain Batista Gómez. At the local inn, the innkeeper warns him not to have anything to do with Gómez. Recklessly, Gary presses on, but he gets lost in the mountains. He has a vision of burned faces, followed by the faces of Estébano, young González, and his own younger brother. He crawls through a bush and falls off a cliff. His last thought before he dies is that his parachute will not open. Later, his corpse is discovered by the workers on the Gómez ranch; Gómez pockets the money that was found on the body. Finally, Hilsom deletes the reference to Gary in the fieldwork notebook that he kept. These are the facts of the story. The Vietnam War is not depicted directly in the text but continues to cloud Gary's mind, suggesting that past violence intrudes on the present and shapes it.

Exploring PTSD

Post-traumatic stress disorder is now widely recognized, but this concept only emerged based on studies of Vietnam veterans. It was not until the 1970s that PTSD was formally introduced into the clinical vocabulary, entering the *Diagnostic and Statistical Manual of Mental Disorders*, third edition (DSM-III), of the American Psychiatric Association (APA) in 1980.[20] The APA defines PTSD as "a psychiatric disorder that may

---

20 Julia Huemer et al., "Childhood Trauma," in *Clinical Child Psychiatry*, 3rd ed., ed. William M. Klykylo and Jerald Kay (Chichester, UK: Wiley, 2012), ch. 15, n.p.

occur in people who have experienced or witnessed a traumatic event."[21] Symptoms may include "disturbing thoughts, feelings, or dreams related to the events, mental or physical distress to trauma-related cues, attempts to avoid trauma-related cues, alterations in the way a person thinks and feels, and an increase in the fight-or-flight response."[22] In *Steinzeit*, Gary appears to be suffering from what we now call PTSD, shown by his frequent flight response that drives him into the unknown. Interestingly, historian Dagmar Herzog has shown that the initial definition of PTSD in 1980 included the symptoms of concentration camp survivors in the concept of PTSD, thus helping to bring soldiers' and survivors' traumas into the public consciousness.[23] This finding suggests a certain affinity between Gary's trauma and Seghers's own experience of persecution by the Nazis—although Seghers was a refugee, not a concentration camp survivor (her case is thus related to, yet different from those highlighted by Herzog). As Herzog argues, however, the concept of PTSD "relativizes and blurs the differences between victims and perpetrators," decoupling the trauma from the sociopolitical contexts that caused it.[24] Herzog's point about the "amoralization of trauma"[25] reminds us that although Gary is both a perpetrator and a victim, he cannot be understood in purely psychiatric terms. To understand both guilt and trauma, we have to reconstruct the wider sociopolitical contexts in which they occur.

When Seghers wrote *Steinzeit* in the mid-1970s, the term *PTSD* was only just entering the US clinical vocabulary. It did not feature in the clinical vocabulary of East German psychology, which was dominated by the reflex theory of Ivan Pavlov (1849–1936) and by behavioral therapy.[26] Yet *Steinzeit* resonates with the condition labeled PTSD, for the narrative is structured in terms of a failed quest—the protagonist searches for a refuge, a sanctuary, but this is denied to him. He longs for a quiet life, but the war has left him with a profound disquiet.

Seghers was not the first to depict a Vietnam veteran in this way. Her text draws on *Dschungel und Soldat* (Jungle and Soldier, 1972), a story by

21 American Psychiatric Association, "What Is Posttraumatic Stress Disorder (PTSD)?," accessed October 1, 2022, https://psychiatry.org/patients-families/ptsd/what-is-ptsd.

22 American Psychiatric Association, *Diagnostic and Statistical Manual of Mental Disorders*, 5th ed. (Arlington, VA: American Psychiatric Publishing, 2013), 271–80.

23 Dagmar Herzog, *Cold War Freud: Psychoanalysis in an Age of Catastrophes* (Cambridge: Cambridge University Press, 2017), 112–13.

24 Herzog, *Cold War Freud*, 113, 117.

25 Herzog, *Cold War Freud*, 113.

26 Christine Leuenberger, "Socialist Psychotherapy and Its Dissidents," *Journal of the History of the Behavioral Sciences* 37, no. 3 (2001): 261–73, here 264.

the Norwegian writer Pål Sundvor (1920–92), about a US soldier who participated in the massacre of a Vietnamese village. Before his death, he is tormented by what he has done and buries his rifle.[27] Given that Seghers used Sundvor's text, it seems Gary may well have an unconscious sense of guilt, even though this is never articulated in the narrative. The thought of atoning or apologizing for his wartime actions never occurs to Gary. In this respect, *Steinzeit* also bears comparison with the short story "Das Ende" (The End, 1945), about a Nazi perpetrator called Zillich, who has returned to his Hessian village but is recognized by a former inmate of the concentration camp where he was a guard. He goes on the run and eventually, thinking that he will be exposed, hangs himself.[28] These intertexts suggest that *Steinzeit* is ambivalent about the extent to which Gary is a perpetrator who suffers fear of retribution, or a victim suffering from trauma.

In any case, Gary's participation in the Vietnam War has made him incapable of civilian life. US popular culture of the 1970s abounds in depictions of damaged Vietnam veterans, most notably in the film *Taxi Driver* (1976), directed by Martin Scorsese, where Robert De Niro plays a former US marine who suffers from insomnia and paranoia. In July 1973, the US singer George Clinton and his band Funkadelic released the song "March to the Witch's Castle." The song begins, "February 12, 1973"—this was the date of "Operation Homecoming," the return of 591 American prisoners of war held by North Vietnam following the Paris Peace Accords of January 27, 1973. As the lyrics state: "The war was over, and the first of the prisoners returned . . . / For others, the real nightmare had just begun / The nightmare of readjustment."[29] The song compares this "nightmare of readjustment" to the "March to the Witch's Castle" in the movie *The Wizard of Oz* (1939), featuring a nightmare journey in which Dorothy's companion, the Scarecrow, is torn apart by an army of flying monkeys.

The song's lyrics set up a parallel between Dorothy's quest to return home to Kansas and the troubled veteran's search for a "homecoming." As the song puts it: "Father, we pray that we might understand what has happened to his mind." It is as if the veteran is bewitched, compelled to repeat the nightmarish march through the jungles of Vietnam. Similarly, Seghers sends her protagonist Gary on an uncanny march through the jungles of Colombia and leads him to his doom in the Andes—a natural

---

27 Brandt, "Vorfassungen," 139.
28 See Helen Fehervary, "Anna Seghers's Response to the Holocaust," *American Imago* 74, no. 3 (2017): 383–90, here 388–89.
29 George Clinton/Funkadelic, "March to the Witch's Castle" (1973), accessed August 14, 2022, https://genius.com/Funkadelic-march-to-the-witchs-castle-lyrics.

"witch's castle." Here she reprises a motif from her earlier works, in which characters become entangled and enmeshed with the jungle.[30] The song continues: "Help him understand, that when his loved one remarried / They were truly under the impression that he was dead / And never would return." The same motif is found in *Steinzeit*, when Gary confides to his friend Hilsom that when he returned home from serving "at sea," he found that his fiancée was married to another man (this appears to be a lie). In any case, the lyrics exemplify the figure of the veteran who fails to "come home" and is driven by his demons.

Other disturbed Vietnam veterans include the three ex-soldiers played by Robert De Niro, Christopher Walken, and John Savage in *The Deer Hunter* (1978), directed by Michael Cimino. Depicting them being forced to play Russian roulette by the Vietcong is wildly inaccurate, and yet *The Deer Hunter* delivers a compelling exploration of the self-destructive aspects of what is now called PTSD. This work was soon followed by *Apocalypse Now* (1979), directed by Francis Ford Coppola, which again refunctions the quest genre to explore the horrors of war. It is unlikely that Seghers would have known about these US popular culture responses to Vietnam, yet in *Steinzeit* she could draw on the established Heimkehrer genre of the late 1940s, which has structural similarities to US representations of Vietnam veterans, since both genres referred to lost wars with shameful associations (such as civilian massacres).

Psychiatric studies of former Vietnam pilots indicate psychological problems. In the early 1990s, Dartmouth Medical School conducted one hundred oral histories of Dartmouth College graduates who had experienced combat in Southeast Asia, many of whom were aircraft pilots. Stanley D. Rosenberg regards these narratives as evidence of a specialized subculture or "fraternity" among pilots. He argues that "the men's efforts at narrative self-construction can be seen as attempts to ward off unbearable anxiety."[31] The pilots' narratives emphasized "a shared belief in their special qualities of superiority, intellect, talent, and emotional control that made it possible for them to do extraordinary things."[32] This functional equation of "competence" with "invulnerability" enabled pilots to deal with situations of extreme danger and stress. The danger was real: for example, during Operation Linebacker II in December 1972 alone, fifteen B-52s were shot down, and nine were damaged.[33] Rosenberg observes a connection between these fantasies of immortality, aggression,

---

30 Fehervary, *Anna Seghers*, 144–46.
31 Stanley D. Rosenberg, "The Threshold of Thrill: Life Stories in the Skies over Southeast Asia," in *Gendering War Talk*, ed. Miriam Cooke and Angela Woollacott (Princeton, NJ: Princeton University Press, 1993), 43–66, here 46.
32 Rosenberg, "The Threshold of Thrill," 60.
33 Head, "War from above the Clouds," 84.

depression, and self-destructive risk-taking. He concludes that these veterans may be left with either "the need to continually pursue danger and violence—without which they feel less than alive—or to experience the emergence of a disguised depressive substrate that may be very difficult to tolerate."[34]

The depiction of Gary in *Steinzeit* accords with Rosenberg's findings, which shed light on Gary's compulsive risk-taking. In the opening lines of the story, Gary is convinced of his own superiority: "Das Glück liebt solche Menschen" (7; Fortune smiles on such people). He insists—twice—that he "knows no fear" ("Furcht kannte er nicht"; "Ja, weil ich keine Furcht kenne" (7; He knew no fear; Yeah, because I know no fear). But these are empty assertions. In fact, Gary is afraid that people are on his trail because of the hijacking. He is anxious he will never enjoy life again: "Ihm wurde bang, er könne sich nie seines Lebens freuen, wie er es gewünscht hatte" (12; He grew worried that he could never enjoy life as he had wished). After his attempts at civilian life in Colombia go wrong, Gary heads into the Amazon rainforest. There, his compulsion to keep moving is like an impersonal force that has seized hold of him: "Als ob er sich nicht aus eigener Kraft bewege, sondern durch eine Gewalt, die ihm die Anstrengung abnahm" (26; As though he was being driven not by his own strength but by a force that eased the effort for him). It seems he has internalized the need to take risks and cannot rest in case his past catches up with him. Like German soldiers who justified their actions in wartime by saying that they were following orders or serving their country, Gary has little sense of guilt. In his mind, he is on the run because of money he gained from the plane hijack. He compares his crime with what happened in Vietnam: "Was alles in Vietnam passiert ist, das kam ihnen ehrlich vor" (36; Everything that happened in Vietnam, they thought it honorable). *They* thought it honorable; what *he* thinks is unclear. In his mind, he is on the run for his postwar crimes, and yet Vietnam seems to haunt his every step.

Gary's attitude to Vietnam is highly ambivalent. On the one hand, he heads into the rainforest to escape his past: "Auf jeden Fall würde er dort die Vergangenheit los sein" (24; There, at any rate, he would be free of the past). On the other hand, this journey entails a compulsive reenactment of his experiences in Vietnam: "Oft sah er etwas, was er aus Vietnam kannte, wie es ihm dünkte" (26–27; Often, he saw something he knew from Vietnam, or so it seemed to him). The "etwas" (something) that he recalls from Vietnam remains unspecified—once again, Seghers's technique of omission achieves a haunting effect. Gary is torn between the wish to conceal his time in Vietnam and the longing to reveal his story. Cautiously, he begins to confide in the anthropologist, Hilsom. But

---

34 Rosenberg, "The Threshold of Thrill," 65.

then he lets slip that he served in Vietnam. His cover is blown, and he has to move on again. Hilsom's description of Gary seems to resonate with a diagnosis of PTSD:

> Sicher war Gary verwirrt, ja völlig erschüttert durch seine Erlebnisse in Vietnam, er war herumgezogen, um das Vergangene zu vergessen. . . . Was [er] in Vietnam erlebt hatte, war sicher so tief in ihn eingedrungen, daß er auf die Dauer kein Zusammensein mit anderen Menschen ertrug. (36)

> [His experiences in Vietnam must have left him bewildered, yes, totally shell-shocked. He moved around to forget the past. . . . What [he] experienced in Vietnam must have affected him so deeply that he could no longer bear the company of other human beings for any length of time.]

Douglas Irving's translation of "erschüttert" (shocked) as "shell-shocked" further underlines the connection with PTSD—"shell shock" is the World War I term for what became known in the 1970s as PTSD.

Ironically, Eliza Méndez, Gary's girlfriend for a brief time, also seems to have PTSD due to the fact that her previous lover died suddenly in an airplane crash. Eliza explains to Gary that her bereavement compels her to keep moving around: "Sie gestand ihm, daß sie wie unter einem Zwang herumfuhr, nach dem Tod ihres Freundes" (14; She confessed that she had moved about as if under duress after her boyfriend's death). Eliza's compulsion to keep moving is the image of Gary's condition. After a brief period of stability, Gary's paranoia returns when Eliza invites a stranger to visit them. Gary fears the authorities are on his trail and leaves Eliza without saying goodbye. He cannot recognize his condition, either in her or in himself. It seems Gary's relationships with other men are more significant to him than those with women. It is worth examining these gender relationships in detail because they suggest deep-rooted behavior patterns that go beyond a simple diagnosis of PTSD. As Herzog argues with reference to the work of psychoanalyst and novelist Hans Keilson (1909–2011), PTSD is best understood as a sequential process that includes the prehistory and the aftermath of the traumatic event itself, as well as the "recursive interrelationships" between these.[35] It is therefore appropriate to look more closely into the development of Gary's gender identity.

---

35 Herzog, *Cold War Freud*, 118.

Masculinity and Male Relationships in *Steinzeit*

Gary's militarized masculinity is central here. He is a man with many positive characteristics—he is clever, resourceful, and has linguistic skills. Yet readers can observe that he makes a series of terrible decisions. As Marion Brandt argues, Gary's entire life is "eine Flucht von Anfang an" (a flight from the beginning onward).[36] Gary applies the scorched-earth policy to his own personal life and keeps burning his bridges behind him. His drive to sever attachments recalls James Baldwin's exploration of disturbed masculinity in *Giovanni's Room* (1956). As David, the narrator of *Giovanni's Room*, states, "There is something fantastic in the spectacle I now present to myself of having run so far, so hard, across the ocean even, only to find myself brought up short once more before the bulldog in my own backyard."[37] In both texts, the protagonist has a troubled relationship with an aggressive father that seems to prevent him from forming close attachments. David flees to France; Gary flees his family through military service, which only makes matters worse. In both cases, the past catches up with them. In *Giovanni's Room*, the protagonist's flight seems motivated by the stigma of being queer. In *Steinzeit*, in contrast, Gary never consciously realizes the reasons for his flight; yet his vision of burned faces shortly before his death suggests that he is haunted by the aerial bombardment he carried out. In both cases, relationships with other men seem to promise redemption, but intimacy is blocked, with fatal consequences, as the male characters cannot come to terms with their feelings. In *Steinzeit*, Gary believes that he is in control of his life, but he never stops to reflect on his past experiences, which continue to shape his present. Occasionally the text suggests that Gary urgently needs to face his past, but this need is never fulfilled. He opts for avoidance and displacement, but it seems that some problems cannot be displaced. *Steinzeit* is a story about flight and the inability to take a long hard look at oneself.

Gary's name is significant: it recalls the iconic Hollywood actor Gary Cooper (1901–61). Cooper was known for playing strong, silent types, and was said to represent the image of the ideal American hero, the kind of man Americans aspired to be.[38] Thus he typified a form of hegemonic masculinity, defined by R. W. Connell as "the configuration of gender practice which embodies the currently accepted answer to the problem

---

36 Marion Brandt, "Vorfassungen zu Anna Seghers' Erzählung *Steinzeit*—Beschreibung und Kommentar in bezug auf eine mögliche Interpretation," *Zeitschrift für Germanistik* 2, no. 1 (1992): 138–48, here 145.

37 James Baldwin, *Giovanni's Room* (1956; London: Penguin, 2001), 11.

38 Jeffrey Meyers, *Gary Cooper: American Hero* (New York: William Morrow, 1998), 323–24.

of the legitimacy of patriarchy, which guarantees (or is taken to guarantee) the dominant position of men and the subordination of women."[39] Cooper's understated performances gave him an aura of masculine authority. As a star of the early 1930s, Cooper would have been known to German cinemagoers of Seghers's generation. His roles included Legionnaire Tom Brown in *Morocco* (1930, dir. Josef von Sternberg), and Marshal Will Kane in *High Noon* (1952, dir. Fred Zinnemann). At the end of *Morocco*, Cooper marches off into the Sahara desert, followed by Marlene Dietrich. In Seghers's *Steinzeit*, too, Gary marches off into the wilderness—although unlike with Cooper, there is no one to follow him.

The type of masculinity represented in Cooper's film performances is problematic, however, because of the emotional repression that it requires. This ideal is criticized by Baldwin as follows:

> The American ideal of sexuality appears to be rooted in the American ideal of masculinity. This idea has created cowboys and Indians, good guys and bad guys, punks and studs, tough guys and softies, butch and faggot, black and white. It is an ideal so paralytically infantile that it is virtually forbidden—as an unpatriotic act—that the American boy evolve into the complexity of manhood.[40]

Baldwin wrote this essay in the 1950s, and, of course, gender categories have become less rigid since then. Yet in Seghers's *Steinzeit*, it seems that Gary still aspires to a classic, rugged, cowboy-style masculinity.[41] He gets a job as overseer on the González ranch, working with the vaqueros. The position offers Gary a form of male fraternity that he once experienced in the military. And yet Gary misses the thrill of his time in Vietnam. Like a Wild West pioneer, he heads into the unknown. Gary's cowboy identity alludes to widespread moral concerns about American Wild West films in both Germanies in the 1950s and 1960s.[42] Ironically, the mainstream media in *both* Germanies expressed concerns about the negative effects of cowboy movies and rock and roll music. In East Germany, though, the state took active measures to restrict the spread of

---

39 R. W. Connell, *Masculinities* (1995; New York: Routledge, 2020), 77.

40 James Baldwin, "The Male Prison"; first published under the title "Gide as Husband and Homosexual" in *The New Leader*, December 13, 1954. Reprinted in James Baldwin, *Nobody Knows My Name: More Notes of a Native Son* (New York: Dial, 1961). Quoted in Bill V. Mullen, *James Baldwin: Living in Fire* (London: Pluto Press, 2019), 172.

41 On the myth of the cowboy, see Jacqueline M. Moore, *Cow Boys and Cattle Men: Class and Masculinities on the Texas Frontier, 1865–1900* (New York: New York University Press, 2009).

42 Uta G. Poiger, "A New, 'Western' Hero? Reconstructing German Masculinity in the 1950s," *Signs* 24, no. 1 (1998): 147–62.

American cultural imports and instead promoted a Soviet-style masculinity based on stoic sacrifice.[43]

Gary's masculinity is troubled not only by his wartime experiences but also by an unhappy relationship with his father. In consequence, his relationships with other men seem particularly loaded with anxiety. As a child, Gary was beaten by his father for speaking Spanish, while his older brother would watch and laugh, and his mother would always back them up. Gary was close only to his younger brother, who was only a "Kätzchen" (32; kitten) at the time. Gary discovers that he enjoys speaking Spanish because it is an act of rebellion against his father, "als ob sein Vater darüber dauernd in Wut gerate" (11; as though his father got angry about it every time). Gary is trying to compensate for his childhood beatings and the resulting sense of abandonment: "Er war mutterseelenallein. Er war immer, immer allein gewesen. . . . So ist es am besten. Wer etwas wagt, muß allein sein" (12; He was completely and utterly alone. He had always, always been alone. . . . It's best like that. Whoever takes a risk has to be alone). Thus he rationalizes his loneliness, imagining that emotional attachments could only slow him down. It seems that Gary's masculinity was already in crisis from an early age, and this has been compounded by his wartime experiences. This accords with Susan Jeffords's argument that many cultural representations of the Vietnam War aimed at the recuperation of masculine identity.[44]

Gary is always on his guard with everyone. This is symbolized by the fact that he always keeps the last cigarette in the pack for himself. His friend Henry comments, "Man könnte glauben, die sei dir ganz besonders heilig" (10, Anyone'd think it was sacred to you). Henry is correct: the cigarette symbolizes Gary's reserve, his cult of the self. It is a kind of ritual, revealing the limits that Gary places on his intimacy with other men. This habit relates to a key incident: when Gary was discharged, he wanted to give a packet of cigarettes to his father. On returning home, he discovered that the old man was already dead. Gary smoked all the cigarettes himself; he did not share one with his younger brother, who was hoping to have the last one. Gary now regrets the unshared cigarette, as he admits to Hilsom (33). Thus, while Gary thinks he is better off alone, his need to confide in Hilsom tells a different story. It is Gary's inability to connect that leads to his downfall. He cannot share his experiences with

---

43 See Tom Smith, *Comrades in Arms: Military Masculinities in East German Culture* (New York: Berghahn, 2020).

44 Susan Jeffords, *The Remasculinization of America: Gender and the Vietnam War* (Bloomington: Indiana University Press, 1989). More broadly, one could speculate that the perennial history of male violence around the world suggests that masculinity is often in crisis. Why else would it require such violent displays to maintain itself?

anyone, he cannot even share a cigarette. The cigarette is a metonym—it stands in for his own personal history, which he would like to share but cannot do so for fear of compromising himself. The most eloquent thing about strong, silent Gary is his cigarettes—they reveal the frustration of a man who has never learned how to share.

Without the male fraternity that he experienced in Vietnam, Gary is adrift. Alone in the Amazon rainforest, he begins an imaginary conversation with his absent friend Henry, who "war in seinem Gedächtnis eingenistet" (27; had taken up residence in Gary's head). He compares the Amazon jungle to the jungle they experienced in Vietnam: "Sieh mal, erinnerst du dich, war's so? War's anders?" (27; Take a look, d'you remember, was it like this? Was it different?). He even wonders, "Hat der [Henry] mich deshalb hierhergeschickt?" (27; Has Henry sent me here for this very reason?). Gary starts to doubt his own agency here. Perhaps his friend has "sent" him on a mission? This fantasy underlines the fact that Gary has lost the plot. He is instinctively rehearsing his previous combat experience. On the verge of collapse, he strains upright again, as if he has been commanded to do so: "Er brach oft erschöpft zusammen, er fuhr hoch, wie gehetzt von einem Befehl" (28; Frequently he collapsed in exhaustion and got up again, as if under orders). He has internalized military power structures to such an extent that he continues to discipline himself, almost involuntarily. Strong, silent Gary is driven by forces beyond his control.

When Gary learns that the Vietnam War has ended, the thought flashes through his mind that the war has cost him a great deal:

> Und er dachte: Dafür hat der General befohlen, Vietnam zurückzubomben in die Steinzeit, und unser Fleisch und unsere Knochen hat es gekostet. Mich hat es noch mehr gekostet. . . . Er hätte sich vielleicht gefragt, was es ihn außer Fleisch und Knochen gekostet hätte—denn die Nachricht über den Frieden in Vietnam beunruhigte ihn mehr als die Nachricht von dem angeblich aufgefundenen Luftpiraten—, da setzte sich jemand an seinen Tisch. (20)
>
> [And he thought: this is what the general ordered Vietnam be bombed back into the Stone Age for, and our flesh and our bones were the price. It's cost me more. . . . He might perhaps have asked himself what it had cost him apart from flesh and bone—because news of peace in Vietnam disturbed Gary more than the news of the hijacker who had allegedly been found—when someone sat down at his table.]

The subjunctive verb forms used express the narrator's wish that Gary had continued these reflections. If only he would ask: What did the war cost him? But a good soldier does not ask questions. In any case, the fact that

Gary is more disturbed by peace in Vietnam than by the hijacking investigation shows how much his identity is still invested in the war effort. The US defeat is—for him—a personal injury because it implies that the veterans' sacrifices were in vain. The arrival of the audio equipment salesman Gold is a welcome distraction. He offers Gary a role as a guide on a business trip into the Amazon (thus representing US economic interests in Colombia), and Gary's painful brush with reality is soon forgotten. As in Bertolt Brecht's and Kurt Weill's opera *Aufstieg und Fall der Stadt Mahagonny* (1930; *Rise and Fall of the City of Mahagonny*) about four doomed lumberjacks, male bonding descends quickly like a warm fog, hindering any critical awareness.[45]

What matters most to Gary, it seems, are his failed relationships with other men: his father, his younger brother, Henry Maxwell, Tom Hilsom, and Estébano. Hilsom and Estébano are particularly significant because they hold out the hand of friendship that Gary is unable to accept. Hilsom serves as a foil for Gary because his work involves studying human beings and understanding them.[46] Gary, in contrast, is determined to avoid any understanding of what he has done. As for Estébano, he reminds Gary of his younger brother and of the young son of the ranch owner González. As noted previously, Gary broke his promise to González Junior that he would return. Upon meeting Estébano, Gary imagines that he has the chance to make up for this broken promise: "Fast war es Gary zumute, als halte er doch sein Versprechen und kehre zurück: Worüber hätte sich sonst dieser Junge gefreut, mit seinem fast strahlenden Lächeln?" (38; It almost felt to Gary as if he were keeping his promise after all and returning: why else would this boy Estébano be glad, with his practically radiant smile?). All too soon, Estébano has to return home and bids farewell to Gary. Yet Gary is consoled when the other men tell him they thought that he and Estébano were brothers (40). These young men represent missed opportunities for Gary—relationships that he has systematically avoided.

Gary's final hours are revealing, as images of death and love flash before his eyes. As he climbs into the Andes Mountains, the word "Steinwelt" (stone world) could be an allusion to the title: "Dumpf und grau war die Steinwelt, in die er geraten war" (50; He had stumbled into

---

45 *Steinzeit* touches on some themes that will be familiar to readers of Brecht. Gary's paranoia and his wish to disappear recall Brecht's poem "Verwisch die Spuren" (Cover Your Tracks). Gary's military discipline recall the drama *Mann ist Mann* (*Man Equals Man*) about the conversion of a man into a killing machine. Only one letter separates Gary from Galy Gay, the soldier in *Mann ist Mann*.

46 Katrin Löffler is incorrect when she claims that "Gary bleibt ohne Kontrastfigur" (Gary remains without a foil). Gary's opposite number is Hilsom. Katrin Löffler, "*Steinzeit. Wiederbegegnung.* Zwei Erzählungen (1977)," in *Anna Seghers Handbuch: Leben–Werk–Wirkung*, ed. Carola Hilmes and Ilse Nagelschmidt (Stuttgart: Metzler, 2020), 160–65, here 162.

a dull, gray, stone world). The verb "geraten" (stumble) underlines the involuntary quality of his actions—he is sleepwalking into danger. Yet Gary cannot sleep because he recalls the burned faces of his victims: "Es gab in seiner Erinnerung unzählige zerschundene, versengte Gesichter" (50; In his memory there were innumerable mutilated, scorched faces). Next, Gary sees the people he loves most: Estébano; González Junior; and his own younger brother. Their faces symbolize fraternity and brotherhood. Gary longs to be a good brother; he longs for the radiant smile of Estébano. But it is too late to turn back. He crawls through a bush and falls off a cliff. His last thought: "Der Fallschirm, verdammt, geht nicht auf" (51; The parachute, damn it, won't open). This ending brings the narrative back to its opening sentence, but this time there will be no happy landing for Gary. He remains a Vietnam veteran to the end.

Gary wants to be completely independent—free of all ties. Yet, without any attachments, happiness eludes him. Gary is a man with great potential, but he is fundamentally alienated. His pleasures cannot be enjoyed—every personal attachment becomes a curse to him because it is loaded with risk. He cannot allow himself to get close to another person because of the danger involved. He fears that if someone knew about his past, they could destroy him. He has no self-understanding, but he insists on his own individual sovereignty. It is the sovereignty of an ego that is adrift and driven by forces beyond its comprehension.

Recognizable Parallels for GDR Readers

So far, this chapter has explored *Steinzeit* as a portrait of a Vietnam veteran. It is, however, well known that a portrait often reveals more about the painter than it does about its subject. What does Gary tell us about the situation in East Germany? How does his masculinity compare with the East German military masculinities that Tom Smith has studied?[47] Christiane Zehl Romero argues that it is not enough to read *Steinzeit* in terms of political slogans such as "imperialism" and "capitalism"; "dazu geht sie [die Geschichte] zu nah an die eigene Haut" (the story is too close to the bone for that).[48] Thus it seems advisable to consider the parallels between Gary's experiences and those of Seghers and her readers in the GDR. After all, an entire generation of East German men were veterans of World War II. They too had experienced a military defeat that had to be faced, avoided, or compensated for in some way or other.

On a deeper level, Gary's experiences could relate to those of Seghers herself, or those of her East German readers, or indeed those of any reader. As Romero puts it, "Sinnlosigkeit, Mißtrauen und der einsame

---

47 Smith, *Comrades in Arms*.
48 Romero, *Anna Seghers*, 306.

Tod in einer versteinerten Welt bedrohen alle" (Meaninglessness, mistrust, and a lonely death in a petrified world could potentially threaten us all).⁴⁹ Seghers has invested too much empathy in Gary, too much of her art in him, for readers to shrug him off. Indeed, readers may well find themselves relating to Gary. This concluding section will consider what *Steinzeit* could tell us about East Germany and Seghers herself. Reading between the lines of *Steinzeit*, we can observe a number of parallels with Seghers's own historical context: first, in terms of how (East) Germans reinvented themselves after 1945; second, in terms of the representation of national borders; and third, in terms of everyday experiences of paranoia and mistrust.

Gary's search for a new identity seems to resonate with what happened in Germany after 1945. Not only was Germany transformed into two separate states: many individual Germans, too, had to reshape and reeducate themselves—or rather, they had to appear to do so. There is a stigma attached to defeat in a war, although Germany's defeat also brought welcome opportunities for economic, political, and social reconstruction. Faced with defeat and occupation in 1945, Germans needed to dissociate themselves from what had happened during the "Third Reich." In the mid-1940s, before the division of Germany was formalized in 1949, the narrative soon emerged that the vast majority of ordinary German people were not responsible for wartime atrocities—they had been misled by Adolf Hitler and the Nazi leadership. In addition, the founding myth of the GDR as an antifascist state allowed its citizens to view themselves as blameless. Nevertheless, many individuals had to wrestle with their own biographies and edit them. As Mary Fulbrook puts it, "People going through denazification generally saw the procedures as a hurdle to be jumped.... Biographies were reshaped and facts reinterpreted to fit into whichever framework was most likely to lead to a desired outcome."⁵⁰

Seghers explored this theme in *Der Mann und sein Name* (The Man and His Name, 1952), about a German soldier, Walter Retzlow, who attempts to conceal the fact that he had joined the SS in the last year of the war, taking on the identity of a murdered antifascist resistance fighter. Retzlow gradually learns the error of his ways—he is saved by the love of a good woman and by his commitment to the construction of a new socialist Germany. *Steinzeit* reprises this theme, as Gary reinvents himself with his new passport and his new name. On one level, then, *Steinzeit* is a variation on the *Heimkehrer* (homecoming) fiction genre that Seghers had explored in *Der Mann und sein Name*. But for Gary, homecoming is a failure, and there is no reeducation, no reintegration into society.

---

49 Romero, *Anna Seghers*, 306.
50 Mary Fulbrook, *Reckonings: Legacies of Nazi Persecution and the Quest for Justice* (Oxford: Oxford University Press, 2018), 211–12.

Gary's inability to form new attachments condemns him to keep shifting from one identity to another. This shapeshifting is underlined when he takes on the identity of another dead man, Alberto, and even collects Alberto's wages (41). In order to avoid a reckoning with the past, Gary is propelled from one new identity into another. This strategy would have been recognizable for an older generation of East German readers, for whom their past entanglements with fascism were taboo. On one level, then, *Steinzeit* would have operated as a work of what Michael Rothberg calls "multidirectional memory," inviting audiences to compare different histories of violence.[51] Even though World War II and the Vietnam War are completely different, they are both wars in which civilian massacres took place. Lauren Cuthbert argues that the GDR documentary film on Vietnam, *Piloten im Pyjama* (Pilots in Pajamas, directed by Walter Heynowski and Gerhard Scheumann, 1968), "creates a space in which questions of responsibility, duty, and guilt can be confronted from the standpoint of a perpetrator collective."[52] Much the same could be said of *Steinzeit*. It suggests that Gary is scarred by his criminal actions in the war, and that his failure to engage critically with the past is a route to disaster. East German readers would have recognized that this moral message about "violence elsewhere" could also have applied to themselves.[53]

Steinzeit contains other details that would have been recognizable to East German readers. For example, there is a border scene that seems to allude to the Berlin Wall. When Gary arrives at the Amazon, his relief soon fades when he realizes that the border between Colombia and Brazil is tightly controlled on both sides of the river by military police:

> [Gary] stutzte. Seine Aufmerksamkeit war plötzlich aufs höchste gespannt. An einer Umladestelle . . . gab es mehrere Militärposten. . . . rechts und links des Landungssteges flatterten kolumbianische Fahnen. Dann kam eine Zwischenstrecke, auf der Polizei in raschem Tempo auf und ab ging. Hinter dem Niemandsland war abermals eine starke Reihe Grenzposten erkennbar. Von hier aus erblickte man die Fahnen Brasiliens. (25–26)

---

51 Michael Rothberg, *Multidirectional Memory: Remembering the Holocaust in the Age of Decolonization* (Stanford, CA: Stanford University Press, 2009), 3.

52 Lauren Cuthbert, "'Ich hatte Befehle': Multidirectional Memory and the Vietnam War in Heynowski and Scheumann's *Piloten im Pyjama* (1968)," *German Life and Letters* 75 (2022): 521–39. See also the discussion of *Piloten im Pyjama* by Seán Allan in this volume.

53 The next generation of GDR authors did address the theme of ordinary Germans' complicity with Nazism; for example, Christa Wolf's *Kindheitsmuster* (Berlin: Aufbau, 1976); trans. Ursule Molinaro and Hedwig Rappolt as *Patterns of Childhood* (New York: Farrar, Straus and Giroux, 1984).

[Gary stopped in his tracks. He was on high alert. At a reloading point by the gangway ... there were several military police.... Colombian flags were flapping to the right and left of the jetty. Then came an intermediate strip of ground where police were pacing up and down. Beyond this no man's land, yet another bastion of border guards was discernible. From here the flags of Brazil were visible.]

Gary's unease at the border guards keeping watch on "no man's land" was likely shared by many of the intended readers in the GDR. It is remarkable that Seghers should allude so sharply to the Berlin Wall here, given her public declaration of support for it in 1961 as a defense against "imperialism."[54] Yet there is a certain consistency here: Seghers was a committed internationalist; much of her life's work was devoted to cultural diplomacy between nations. The fluttering flags in the border scene in *Steinzeit* are scary because they suggest the potential for violence: borders are guarded with weapons; they are places where conflict can break out.

This symbolic logic is reinforced when Hilsom observes that allegiance to a national flag can be seen as a form of pagan idolatry: "'Mancher verteidigt das Symbol seines Landes, zum Beispiel das Sternenbanner, bis zum letzten Blutstropfen'" (30; "Some defend their country's icon, for instance the star-spangled banner, to the very last drop of their blood"). Hilsom's point subverts the opposition between civilization and barbarity, suggesting that both are characterized by idolatry. The story continues this subversion of the hierarchy between the "civilized West" and the "Third World" in the depiction of the indigenous people in the Amazon basin. Although their way of life recalls prehistoric hunter-gatherers, Hilsom is amazed at the linguistic diversity of their speech, which indicates a surprisingly advanced level of civilization (30). Yet this cultural diversity was suppressed by *La Conquista*, the Spanish colonization of the Americas: "Die Conquista hat einem ganzen Erdteil ihre Sprache aufgedrängt" (31; The Conquista imposed its language on an entire continent). Ironically, Hilsom seems unaware that he and his compatriot Gold, the audio salesman, are helping to impose US culture and economic interests in the region. Colombia was a key partner of the US, having sent around five thousand troops to serve in the Korean War (1950–53).[55] Seghers is subtly implying the connections between the Spanish Conquista and present-day US economic and military involvement in Colombia. This section of *Steinzeit* would lend itself

---

54 Romero, *Anna Seghers*, 212.
55 Relations between the US and Colombia intensified in the year 2000, when President Bill Clinton launched "Plan Colombia," a huge foreign and military aid program.

to a postcolonial reading, one that could build on the work of Arlene A. Teraoka and Marike Janzen.[56] In any case, the negative depiction of flags and strong borders in *Steinzeit* could perhaps be understood as Seghers wishing to qualify—in an oblique, coded way—her previous support for the Berlin Wall.

On another level, we could also read *Steinzeit* as an exploration of Cold War anxieties experienced by many GDR citizens, including Seghers herself. The keynote of the narrative is paranoia. Gary's fear that the past will catch up with him would have been recognized by many older GDR citizens who were still potentially tainted by their actions during the "Third Reich." Younger GDR citizens, too, knowing that state surveillance was a possibility, would also have been able to relate to Gary's constant mistrust. He fears that the authorities are pursuing him, even though he has no evidence for this fear. It is tempting to read the story's pervasive atmosphere of fear and paranoia as an echo of the Cold War climate in East Germany, perhaps even as evidence of the author's identification with her protagonist. Seghers herself had been a refugee and a victim of war and persecution by the Nazis. She had experienced Stalinist repression, too, which in the early 1950s was often directed against loyal Communists with a Jewish background. During the Rudolph Slánský trial in Czechoslovakia in November 1952, her name had been mentioned, and around the same time the Stasi (East German secret police) began to interrogate her husband, László Radványi, who, the same year, had returned to East Berlin from Mexico.[57]

With reference to Seghers herself, the "Stone Age" of the title seems to recall the term "Ice Age" that Seghers had often used to describe her own situation back in Germany after the war.[58] "Ice Age" refers not only to the Cold War but also to the specific climate of coldness and alienation in Berlin in the late 1940s and early 1950s, when cosmopolitan attempts to promote world peace by Seghers and her internationalist colleagues were thwarted by the remilitarization of the world

---

56 Arlene A. Teraoka argues that Seghers's Caribbean fiction has a "Eurocentric core." Arlene A. Teraoka, *East, West, and Others: The Third World in Postwar German Literature* (Lincoln: University of Nebraska Press, 1996), 26. Teraoka's critique only applies, however, to Seghers's works produced up to 1960; it completely ignores those produced in the last two decades of Seghers's life: for example, *Drei Frauen aus Haiti* (Darmstadt: Luchterhand, 1980); trans. Douglas Irving as *Three Women from Haiti* (New Orleans: Dialogos, 2019). For a more convincing postcolonial reading of Seghers, see Janzen, *Writing to Change the World*, 99–127.

57 The Slánský trial of 1952 was a show trial against fourteen members of the Communist Party of Czechoslovakia. Eleven were sentenced to death, eight of whom were Jews. See Romero, *Anna Seghers*, 135–38.

58 Romero, *Anna Seghers*, 15, 55, 152.

and the remilitarization of both Germanies.[59] In 1948 Seghers wrote to Georg Lukács, "Ich habe das Gefühl, ich bin in die Eiszeit geraten, so kalt kommt mir alles vor" (Everything is so cold here, I feel as if I have stumbled back into the Ice Age).[60] The language here—for example, the verb "geraten" (stumbled)—recalls what happens to Gary in *Steinzeit*: "Dumpf und grau war die Steinwelt, in die er geraten war." Gary's isolation is described using the same lexical field that Seghers had used to describe her own situation in 1948.

Steinzeit can thus be read on a deeper level as a case study in paranoia, which affected both survivors of Nazi persecution *and* former perpetrators themselves, the latter of whom sought to evade responsibility and retribution for previous crimes after 1945. If Gary's desperate avoidance of his past is motivated by paranoia, trauma, and guilt, then it bears comparison to the paranoia, trauma, and guilt of the victims and perpetrators of the Holocaust, who largely remained silent about what had happened. Hilsom almost seems to act as a mouthpiece for the author when he says, "Verfolgung macht immer traurig und isoliert" (30; Persecution always leads to mistrust and isolation). Hilsom's job involves studying human nature. (This aligns him with Seghers—novelists study human beings, too). Silent, macho Gary is shocked to find himself opening up to Hilsom in a way he has never done before. He experiences a feeling of release but is tormented by the idea that Hilsom could betray his confidence. He yearns to trust Hilsom, but: "Dann wieder warnte ihn irgendein Wort, eine Redewendung, seinen Argwohn nie aufzugeben" (30; Then once more some word or other, a turn of phrase, warned him to never drop his guard). In the final sentences of the story, we learn that Gary was wrong to mistrust Hilsom. As Hilsom looks through his journals, he finds the notes that he made about Gary. Suddenly he remembers vividly the time he spent with Gary, even the tone of his voice. Hilsom realizes that Gary wanted to disappear, and he decides to respect Gary's wishes. He carefully deletes every reference to Gary. The story ends, "Als könne jemand in diesem Heft ihn doch noch aufstöbern, löschte er jede Spur für jetzt und immer" (53; In case someone might yet track him down in this notebook, he erased every single trace of him, now and for ever). Hilsom is discreet and honors Gary's wishes—Gary and his life will remain secret forever. This is another example of Seghers's technique of omission. The final deletion of Gary's life by Hilsom challenges readers to find some meaning in the story, even as Gary is consigned to oblivion.

To conclude: *Steinzeit* sheds considerable light on the experience of PTSD and on the aftermath of the Vietnam War. What really makes

---

59 Romero, *Anna Seghers*, 52–53.
60 Anna Seghers, letter to Georg Lukács, June 28, 1948, in Seghers, *Über Kunst und Wirklichkeit*, 4:154. Quoted in Romero, *Anna Seghers*, 15.

Steinzeit such a compelling narrative, though, is the extent to which the author has used her protagonist to explore questions of collective guilt. Gary is both a victim of trauma *and* a perpetrator who shares in the collective guilt of the aerial bombing campaigns. Seghers's omission technique means that she never tackles the question of Gary's wartime guilt directly; instead, she invites her readers to guess at it and to compare Gary's situation with their own. *Steinzeit* challenges its readers to debate different legacies of violence from two very different wars. On one level, Gary's desperate search for a new identity resonates with the GDR's own quest for a new form of humanity, the "Neuer Mensch" (new human) or *Homo Sovieticus*. The narrative intensity suggests that Seghers is using the figure of Gary to explore her own fears and anxieties about unaddressed legacies of violence in Germany. Like the generations of Germans whom Mary Fulbrook examines in *Dissonant Lives* (2011), Gary's life is dissonant, full of unspoken gaps and unacknowledged guilt.[61] He cannot make any sense of his life, and he does not want to. The story gestures toward anxieties that Seghers may have had: anxieties about surveillance and persecution; about the enduring nature of the military mindset; about the idolatry of the nation-state and the fetishism of flags; about unexplored collective guilt; and about the long-lasting effects of trauma. Gary works on many levels, as a former perpetrator who fails to reinvent himself and as a victim who fails to understand his predicament. On another level, he is a kind of everyman figure, and on yet another level, he could be a cipher for Seghers and her readers. As Romero puts it, "Seghers fürchtete nichts so sehr wie die ziellose Vereinzelung" (More than anything, Seghers feared aimless isolation).[62] This is Gary's fate, as he fails to confront his past and flees into aimlessness.[63] Gary's final disappearance serves as a stark reminder to readers that violent legacies must be acknowledged if the demons of the past are to be laid to rest. Finally, readers of *Steinzeit* in the 2020s—another decade of militarization and surveillance—may well observe some parallels with their own lives too. In a context of rival superpowers competing for global influence, "violence elsewhere" is always connected to problems closer to home.

---

61 Mary Fulbrook, *Dissonant Lives: Generations and Violence through the German Dictatorships* (Oxford: Oxford University Press, 2011).

62 Romero, *Anna Seghers*, 52.

63 The crisis of American masculinity caused by the Vietnam War is also explored in Romain Gary's novel *The Ski Bum* (1965) about American dropouts in the Swiss Alps. The French version appeared under the title *Adieu Gary Cooper* (1969). The novel features a character who is crushed by remorse because "he really believed that Gary Cooper was on his way and that the tough, pure and just hero would once again be triumphant. Gary Cooper never came." Romain Gary, cited in David Bellos, *Romain Gary: A Tall Story* (London: Harvill Secker, 2010), 128.

6: "So It Has to Be Said: Hammer and Sickle Here, Hammer and Sickle There": Heynowski-Scheumann's *Die Angkar* (1981) and the Problem of *Khmer Rouge* Violence for the GDR

Martin Brady

Violence

IN JANUARY 1979, the most high-profile and prolific documentary filmmakers in the German Democratic Republic (GDR; East Germany)—Walter Heynowski and Gerhard Scheumann, who together ran their eponymous Studio H&S—were commissioned by the country's ruling party to document the Killing Fields of Cambodia. The resulting trilogy of feature-length documentaries (1980–83) would become a "Solidaritätsgeschenk" (solidarity present) for the victorious Vietnamese, who had defeated the Khmer Rouge of Pol Pot, Ieng Sary, and others on January 7, 1979. In the words of a Politburo protocol of January 23, the filmmakers were not only to demonstrate the brutality of the regime itself but also to expose China's ideological complicity in and military support for Pol Potism, the "hegemonistische Politik der Pekinger Führung" (hegemonic politics of the Peking leadership).[1]

The political program underpinning the resulting trilogy of films on the Khmer Rouge's reign of terror was expounded by the directors themselves in a brief essay published in *Neues Deutschland* (New Germany), the official daily newspaper of the Socialist Unity Party of Germany (SED), in October 1980. It dutifully quotes the terms of their commission almost

---

1   Hannes Riemann, *Eine Herausforderung an jeden Kommunisten: Die Khmer Rouge, der III. Indochinakrieg und Kambodscha im Fokus von Dokumentarfilmen des Dokumentarfilmstudios H&S (1979–1983)*, Schriftenreihe der Thüringisch-Kambodschanischen Gesellschaft, vol. 6 (Erfurt: TKG, 2011), 42. This volume is currently unobtainable, and I am therefore very grateful to Hannes Riemann for providing a copy of his book directly. In what follows, page numbers refer to this version, which differs slightly in pagination from the published book. Translations are by the current author unless noted otherwise.

verbatim and notes, "Der nahezu nahtlose Übergang von Gewaltpolitik des Imperialismus gegen Kampuchea . . . zur Politik des Hegemonismus der Pekinger Führung (die Pol-Pot/Ieng-Sary-Clique ließ nach entsprechender 'Beratung' das Khmer-Volk in der Dimension von Millionen vernichten, um Platz für eine Filiale Pekings in Indochina zu schaffen)" (The almost seamless transition from imperialism's policy of violence against Kampuchea . . . to the Peking leadership's hegemonic policy [the Pol-Pot/Ieng-Sary Clique, after appropriate "consultation," had the Khmer people annihilated in their millions to make room for a branch of Peking in Indochina]).[2]

Heynowski and Scheumann denounce China on no fewer than three occasions in their essay: along with the passage quoted above, we learn about the "von Peking inspirierte[r] Vernichtungsfeldzug" (campaign of destruction inspired by Peking) and that, post-Khmer Rouge, traditional Cambodian dance is alive once again, having survived a "'Kulturrevolution' nach Pekingschem Muster" ("cultural revolution" based on the Peking model).

Following the GDR premiere of Part 1 of the trilogy a month later, an enthusiastic review appears in the same newspaper: it makes no reference to China and its portrayal in the film as jointly responsible for the violence of the Killing Fields.[3] A week later, *Neues Deutschland* reports that the film has premiered in West Berlin as part of the campaign against the 1979 NATO Double-Track Decision, implying that it constitutes a call for peace in the face of an escalating global arms race.[4] A year later, in December 1981, the same paper reviews Part 2 of Heynowski-Scheumann's trilogy—*Die Angkar* (*The Angkar*; literally, "The Organization," 1981), the principal focus of this chapter and even more outspoken in its condemnation of Maoist aggression—and again makes no mention of China.[5] With hindsight these official responses to Heynowski-Scheumann's Cambodia films reveal that a chasm was opening up between their aim of presenting audiences with a damning condemnation of China's involvement in mass violence and the GDR's desire to avert attention from the complicity of a prospective ally.

2   Walter Heynowski and Gerhard Scheumann, "Das Lächeln der Apsara: Impressionen aus Kampuchea," *Neues Deutschland*, October 11–12, 1980, 11.

3   Henryk Goldberg, "Auch aus dem Zorn wächst Kraft für die Zukunft: 'Kampuchea: Sterben und Auferstehen' von H & S" [sic], *Neues Deutschland*, November 13, 1980, 4.

4   "Kampuchea-Film wurde in Westberlin aufgeführt," *Neues Deutschland*, November 18, 1980, 4.

5   Henryk Goldberg, "Ein Film, der anklagt und bohrende Fragen stellt: 'Die Angkar,' eine Arbeit aus dem Studio H & S" [sic], *Neues Deutschland*, December 16, 1981, 4.

As historian Hannes Riemann has convincingly set out, the films coincided with rapid changes in GDR foreign policy in relation to China.[6] The result was that while the first film, titled *Kampuchea: Sterben und Auferstehn* (Cambodia: Death and Resurrection, 1980) was, as we have seen, officially commissioned to uncover the truth about the Khmer Rouge and Chinese complicity in it, the second (*Die Angkar*) was denied a screening on GDR television, and the third, *Der Dschungelkrieg* (The Jungle War, 1983), was censored to expunge all references to Chinese aggression.

In the light of these developments, it is easy to see why the Cambodia trilogy led to a crisis for Studio H&S, resulting in autumn 1982 in its forced closure, the reintegration of the directors into the monopoly state filmmaking company DEFA, and, for Heynowski and Scheumann personally, the loss of sundry privileges and freedoms. This chapter traces the part that the portrayal of violence—Cambodian and Chinese abroad, National Socialist at home—played in this unfolding drama. To understand what Heynowski in 1982 termed the "große Erschütterung und auch Herausforderung" (the great shock and also challenge)[7] of violence in Cambodia—both for the filmmakers and for the GDR—it is first necessary to place the trilogy within the context of Studio H&S's work more broadly.

Truth

Heynowski-Scheumann had a unique status in the GDR. They were the only filmmakers allowed their own studio, at least until 1982, and were free to travel across the globe to capture the most reprehensible manifestations of global imperialism. Their films, around seventy in all, are arguably the most potently propagandist corpus of work the GDR produced. They engage in meticulous detail with atrocities in Vietnam, Cambodia, and Chile, and with the living legacy of the Nazi fascism in West Germany. Initially largely ignored after unification—with the notable exception of an article on the Vietnam corpus by Nora Alter in 1996 and the work of Rüdiger Steinmetz—their films have, in recent years, become better known through retrospectives, one-off screenings, and DVD releases.[8]

---

6   Riemann, *Eine Herausforderung an jeden Kommunisten*.
7   Quoted in Riemann, *Eine Herausforderung an jeden Kommunisten*, 44.
8   See, for example, Nora M. Alter, "Excessive Pre/Requisites: Vietnam through the East German Lens," *Cultural Critique* 35 (Winter 1996-97): 39–79. See also Rüdiger Steinmetz and Tilo Prase, *Dokumentarfilm zwischen Beweis und Pamphlet: Heynowski & Scheumann und Gruppe Katins* (Leipzig: Leipziger Universitätsverlag, 2002).

According to film historian Olaf Möller, quoted on the cover of the five-DVD collection of Studio H&S films released by absolut MEDIEN in 2014, "Die Trennung von Propaganda und Dokument ist Walter Heynowski & Gerhard Scheumann fremd. Eine Wahrheit . . . ist etwas, worum man kämpfen muss, Wahrheit muss man schaffen" (The separation of propaganda and documentation is alien to Walter Heynowski and Gerhard Scheumann. A truth . . . is something one has to fight for; truth has to be created).[9] Shortly before his death in 1998, Scheumann offered a bullish résumé of his and Heynowski's legacy. In his remarks Scheumann concludes that Studio H&S was always at hand when it came to matters of GDR foreign policy: "So bleiben meiner Meinung nach einige Positionen, deren wir uns niemals zu schämen brauchen, sowohl was Chile als auch Vietnam und Kambodscha betrifft. Da hat die DDR im Gegensatz zu dem Staat, der heute der ganze Staat ist, historische Positionen besetzt, und wir können sagen, wir sind mit unseren Filmen dabeigewesen" (There remain, I believe, certain positions in relation to Chile, Vietnam, and Cambodia of which we have no reason whatsoever to feel ashamed. In this context the GDR occupied historically valid positions, unlike the state that now represents all of Germany, and we can say that we were there with our films).[10] Heynowski-Scheumann were certainly able to elevate Marxist-Leninist ideology to the status of truth, as Möller notes. They did so through two related strategies: protracted and meticulous research, on the one hand, and the deployment of a carefully honed corpus of rhetorical visual and linguistic devices, on the other.

Particularly significant in the context of this volume is the fact that no other GDR filmmakers focused as consistently on "violence elsewhere," to the extent that the theme could be deemed the trademark of Studio H&S from the mid-sixties onward. This preoccupation is underscored by the DVD box set: it is divided into five discs, of which three are devoted to series filmed "elsewhere"—Vietnam, Chile, and Cambodia—with only one short film of the twenty-four in the collection, the earliest (*O.K.*, 1965), addressing the GDR directly. Other films focusing on Germany in the discs "Frühe Filme" (Early Films) and "Späte Filme" (Late Films) are only indirectly related to the GDR, focusing on historical and geographical "elsewheres": principally World War II and its legacy in the Federal Republic of Getmany (FRG; West Germany). The latter is a benchmark "elsewhere" from Heynowski's (pre-Studio H&S) attack on West

---

9   *Studio H&S Walter Heynowski und Gerhard Scheumann: Filme 1964–1989*, absolut MEDIEN DVD box set (2014), cover.
10   Quoted in Claudia Böttcher, Julia Kretzschmar, Corinna Schier, eds, *Walter Heynowski und Gerhard Scheumann—Dokumentarfilmer im Klassenkampf: Eine kommentierte Filmographie* (Leipzig: Leipziger Universitätsverlag, 2002), 48.

German policy toward the GDR in *Brüder und Schwestern* (Brothers and Sisters, 1963) through to *Der Mann an der Rampe* (The Man Who Met the Trains, 1989), which identifies the FRG as the home of erstwhile and contemporary Nazism.

In an essay on Cambodia published in the prestigious GDR literary and cultural journal *Sinn und Form* (Sense and Form) in 1982, Heynowski-Scheumann characterize their practice as fundamentally in opposition to journalistic reportage: "Es gibt in unserer Zeit eine Art von Berichterstattung, die an einem fragwürdigen Begriff von Aktualität orientiert ist.... Der Leser, Hörer oder Zuschauer, der von solcher Berichterstattung bedient wird, erfährt immer weniger über immer mehr. Zuletzt weiß er, um es ins Paradoxe zu treiben, nichts über alles" (In our time there is a kind of reporting that is based on a questionable concept of topicality.... The reader, listener, or viewer who is served by such reporting learns less and less about more and more. In the end, to put it in the form of a paradox, he knows nothing about everything).[11] In this essay they defend their extensive use of commentary, now sometimes considered intrusive, arguing that meticulous exegesis is necessary because objects do not always "speak for themselves": "Die stumme Sprache von Gegenständen gibt nicht immer Wahrheit heraus. Wirklichkeit und Wahrheit fallen nur selten sinnfällig zusammen. Es gibt Wesentliches, was von den Erscheinungen nicht ausgedrückt wird, sich oft sogar hinter den Erscheinungen verbirgt" (The silent language of objects does not always reveal truth. Reality and truth rarely coincide in a meaningful way. There are essentials that are not expressed by appearance and that are indeed often hidden behind such appearance).[12] Before turning to the presence of specific objects—hammers and sickles in particular—in *Die Angkar*, it is helpful to identify the source of Heynowski-Scheumann's distinctive rhetorical style in their first series of works addressing "violence elsewhere," the Vietnam films. It was here that the distinctive Studio H&S approach was perfected.

War Primers

The Vietnam corpus, consisting of sixteen films in total, is the most extensive and most discussed body of work from Studio H&S, beginning with the brief blood donation film *400 cm³* in 1966.[13] This diverse but ideologically consistent corpus contains Studio H&S's most

---

11 Walter Heynowski and Gerhard Scheumann, "Die Angkar," *Sinn und Form* 34, no. 5 (September/October 1982): 989–98, here 994.

12 Heynowski and Scheumann, "Die Angkar," 996.

13 See Alter, "Excessive Pre/Requisites"; Steinmetz and Prase, *Dokumentarfilm zwischen Beweis und Pamphlet*.

experimental films, and traces of the techniques developed in them will resurface in *Die Angkar*.

The basic principles of Heynowski-Scheumann's approach are established in *400 cm³*, with its fierce and furious, highly chromatic score for unaccompanied voices by GDR composer and Bertolt Brecht collaborator Paul Dessau.[14] It is also their most daring formal experiment—"vielleicht auch Filmkunst" (perhaps also film art), Heynowski noted in 2003.[15] This film insistently alternates between images of bloodshed and suffering in Vietnam and calm and resolute GDR citizens donating blood for the Vietcong before concluding, in the form of an adapted quotation from Dessau's 1951 setting of Brecht and Pablo Neruda's "Friedenslied" (Peace Song), with a call for peace "den Kindern Vietnams und den Kumpeln von Neisse und Ruhr" (for the children of Vietnam and the workers on the Neisse and Ruhr).[16] Insistent rhythmical alternations and extended passages of repetition are deployed to deconstruct, interrogate, and reassemble the documentary source material (both archive and original) with biting sarcasm and considerable visual and acoustic ferocity. The film is uncompromisingly polemical and unfolds at a rhetorical fever pitch.

Vietnam was the paradigmatic distant war, "far away" according to the French collaborative film *Loin du Vietnam* (Far from Vietnam, 1967),[17] or "Der ferne Krieg" (The Distant War), as GDR poet Volker Braun termed it in the title of a poem.[18] But where the American Weather Underground called on protesters to "Bring the war home," and Che Guevara urged revolutionaries to "Create Two, Three, Many Vietnams," Braun's poem stems from a simple, quasi-documentary observation: he draws attention to the relationship between West Berlin chemical concerns in Wedding and Britz (Neukölln) and the US Department of

---

14   On this film, see also Seán Allan's chapter in this volume.

15   Walter Heynowski interview with Ralf Schenk, in *Das Prinzip Neugier: DEFA-Dokumentarfilmer erzählen*, ed. Ingrid Poss, Christiane Mückenberger, and Anne Richter (Berlin: Verlag Neues Leben, 2012), 81.

16   In 1968, Dessau coedited and contributed to the GDR volume *Vietnam in dieser Stunde* (Vietnam at This Hour), ed. Werner Bräunig et al. (Halle an der Saale: Mitteldeutscher Verlag, 1968), a compendium of texts and images by international artists, writers, and filmmakers denouncing American involvement in Vietnam. Volker Braun contributed three photographs with captions and poems (34–35); the third shows a student at the Karl Marx University, Leipzig, donating blood. On Braun's poems on Vietnam, see J. J. Long's chapter in this book. Heynowski-Scheumann's text, "Hilton Hanoi" (88–92), is one of the longest in *Vietnam in dieser Stunde*.

17   Joris Ivens et al., *Loin du Vietnam* (1967).

18   Volker Braun, "Der ferne Krieg," in *gegen den krieg in vietnam*, ed. Riewert Qu. Tode (Berlin: amBEATion, 1968), 11. Cf. J. J. Long's chapter in this volume.

Defense (here referred to as the *Kriegsministerium* [war ministry]) over the supply of chemical weapons. Braun juxtaposes smoke from the nearby Britz factory, a mere six kilometers from the poet's window, and the distant ("fern") sky over Vietnam out of which chemical defoliant rains; while the factory smoke is "deutlich" (clear), the chemical rain in Asia is "Undeutlich wie ein Gerücht" (Unclear like a rumor). In referring to the barrier between East and West—the "Grenzverhau" (border) separating the poet from the factory in Britz—a parallel is drawn between Germany's fascist past (which led to its subsequent postwar division) and the present threat from West Germany and the US. The binaries of near and far are thus both geographical and historical. Dessau set Braun's poem as one of his *Fünf Melodramen* (Five Melodramas) in 1967, alongside texts by Karl Mickel (the Vietnam poem "Das zerschossene Dorf" [The Village Shot to Pieces]), Ho Chi Minh (the poem "Die rot und goldene Fahne" [The Red and Gold Flag]), and Bertrand Russell.[19]

The dialectics of proximity and distance axiomatic to Braun's "Der ferne Krieg" is the central structuring principle of Heynowski-Scheumann's *400 cm³* and also of Dessau's terse and hard-hitting Vietnam cantata *Geschäftsbericht* (Business Report) of 1966, a setting of five poems from Braun's volume *KriegsErklärung* (Declaration of War)—a reworking and updating of Brecht's 1955 *Kriegsfibel* (War Primer)—which highlight the contrast between human devastation in Vietnam (abroad) and the corresponding economic success in America (at home, at least for the capitalist West): "Vietnam geht hoch, und hoch geht der Profit" (Vietnam goes up in flames, and up go the profits).[20]

For Dessau, Braun, and Heynowski-Scheumann, the new global conflict in Vietnam shamefully resembled the one that had been the subject of Brecht's *Kriegsfibel* a decade earlier. Scheumann noted retrospectively that Vietnam had been an inescapable theme for GDR artists during the mid to late 1960s: "Es gab damals eigentlich kaum einen Dokumentaristen, der an dem Thema Vietnam vorbeigehen konnte" (At the time practically no documentarist could avoid the theme of Vietnam).[21] As an agitational response to the war, *400 cm³* can be labeled experimental propaganda. It incorporates elements of the photo and film essay, found footage, and structural formalism in the service of unequivocal ideological disclosure. It is collaborative and deploys visual, acoustic, and linguistic shock effects.

19 Ho Chi Minh's poem was published in *Neues Deutschland*, May 14, 1960, 7.
20 Volker Braun, *KriegsErklärung* (Halle an der Saale: Mitteldeutscher Verlag, 1967), 11. The year 1966 also saw the premiere of Dessau's substantial cycle of *Kriegsfibel* settings, *Deutsches Miserere*. On *KriegsErklärung*, cf. J. J. Long's chapter in this volume.
21 Gerhard Scheumann in *Arbeitshefte 27: Dokument und Kunst; Vietnam bei H&S*, ed. Robert Michel (Berlin: Akademie der Künste, 1977), 95.

The style is modernist, the message straightforwardly propagandistic—it is, after all, a simple public information film calling on people to donate blood—and the result a kind of blatancy in which ideological conflict is translated into harsh visual and acoustic dissonance. What the imagery of Heynowski-Scheumann and the film's striking music share is not just a febrility of utterance and an amalgamation of simplicity and difficulty—a sense that the viewer should be expected to arrive at an inescapable conclusion by arduous means—but also an enthusiasm for shock-like interruptions of the kind associated with Walter Benjamin's theory of montage.[22] These shock effects also link *400 cm³* to Brecht's *Kriegsfibel*, and a revealing connection to Studio H&S should be noted here in passing: Heynowski was, in 1954, the founder of the Eulenspiegel Verlag, which published the *Kriegsfibel*. I would argue that the key features of the work of Studio H&S—the dialectical interplay of image and text, the fascination with iconography and emblems, the deployment of shocking juxtapositions, the insistent use of critical, satirical, or debunking commentary—have their roots in Brecht's seminal volume.

Brecht's collection of newspaper clippings with accompanying quatrains challenging the ideological assumption of iconic press photographs and their captions is nothing short of an exercise in the deconstruction of propaganda. To take just one example—directly related to the question of "violence elsewhere"—a reproduced photograph of a cigarette-smoking American soldier standing over the corpse of a Japanese fighter, published in *Life* magazine on February 15, 1943, bears the original English-language caption: "An American and the Jap he killed. Pfc Wally Wakeman says: 'I was walking down the trail when I saw two fellows talking. They grinned and I grinned. One pulled a gun. I pulled mine. I killed him. It was just like in the movies.'"[23] Brecht's accompanying poem presents the action, stripped of its historical and geographical specificity, as a sequence of quasi-cinematic "shots" and thereby reveals the absurdity of the situation or, more precisely and more politically, what unites the protagonists (their common fate as victims) rather than what divides them (a war that is not of their own making). Why would three people smile at one another and then shoot? What are the strange circumstances that have led to this seemingly irrational, unmotivated outcome? In his poem on the photo of Wakeman, Brecht implies that the explanation for the tragic outcome has to be sought beyond the encounter depicted,

---

22 See Walter Benjamin's essay "Kunst im Zeitalter seiner technischen Reproduzierbarkeit" (The Work of Art in the Age of Mechanical Reproduction, 1936), February 2005, https://www.marxists.org/reference/subject/philosophy/works/ge/benjamin.htm.

23 Bertolt Brecht, *War Primer*, trans. John Willett (London: Libris, 1998), n.p.

its three protagonists, and the misleading caption. As with Heynowski-Scheumann, the connections must be drawn by the viewer or reader.

Tellingly, in the present context, the *Kriegsfibel* also demonstrates that Brecht was quite willing to construct his arguments theatrically and with recourse to fiction if necessary. One image in the volume, showing four helmets in a puddle, was staged in 1954 using props from the Berliner Ensemble.[24] Similarly constructed tableaux become a hallmark of Heynowski-Scheumann's work: the weaponry or "tote Gegenstände" (dead objects) filmed almost fetishistically in *Remington Cal. 12* (1972) and the striking intertwining of French colonial leg-irons and US handcuffs—a suggestive image of past and present, of colonizer and colonized—in the Vietnam film *Die Teufelsinsel* (Devil's Island, 1976) and the copiously illustrated book that accompanied it.[25] The link between the French leg-irons and US handcuffs is not explicitly stated, although it is difficult to avoid the conclusion that it is, in the terminology of the film's own program, imperialism and (monopoly) capitalism.

Across the Vietnam films and *Die Angkar*, the underlying dialectic is the one pinpointed in the title of Jean-Luc Godard's and Anne-Marie Miéville's 1976 film *Ici et ailleurs* (Here and Elsewhere) in which documentary footage of the Palestinian fedayeen, shot by Godard in 1970 (for a planned pro-Palestinian film, *Jusqu'à la victoire* [Until Victory]), is juxtaposed with staged scenes of a French family watching television at home and critically deconstructed. *Ici et ailleurs* confronts the dilemma of Western European filmmakers appropriating geographically and culturally distant conflicts for local and, Godard-Miéville's film argues, frequently incomparable political struggles. Their self-critical essay on the politics of hereness and thereness repeatedly interrogates the conjunction "and" semiotically and semantically (fig. 6.1), literally (fig. 6.2), and metaphorically. The binary examples of "ici" and "ailleurs" that appear again and again across the film in still photographs, archive film, sound clips, and superimposed text include France and Palestine, Germany and Israel, America and Vietnam. For their part, Heynowski-Scheumann readily acknowledged that their fascination with Vietnam stemmed from the conspicuous similarities between North-South conflict in Vietnam and East-West division at home (for example, in an interview with *Stern* in 1969)[26] and, as we shall see, never hesitated from drawing direct and unapologetically blunt parallels. As Heynowski nicely put it in interview

---

24 Brecht, *War Primer*, iv (notes). The original photograph Brecht had collected was of French helmets.
25 Scheumann, *Arbeitshefte 27*, 133; Walter Heynowski and Gerhard Scheumann, *Die Teufelsinsel* (Berlin: Verlag der Nation, 1977), 134–35.
26 Reproduced in Walter Heynowski and Gerhard Scheumann, *Piloten in Pyjama* (Berlin: Verlag der Nation, 1969), 408–15, here 408.

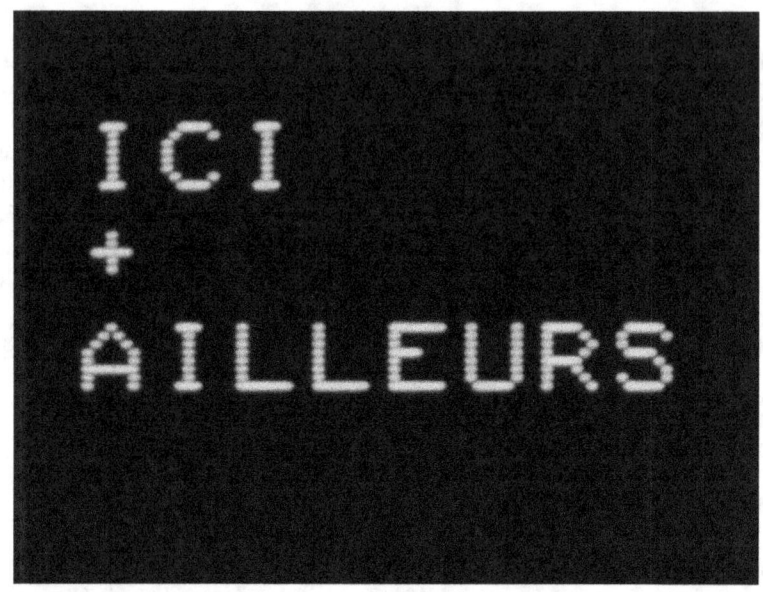

Figures 6.1 and 6.2. Shedding light on "and" (Jean-Luc Godard and Anne-Marie Miéville, *Ici et ailleurs*, 1976; Gaumont Vidéo, 2012).

in 1977, "Ich bin ein Fanatiker der Montage" (I am a montage fanatic).[27] The same, of course, could be said of Godard and Miéville, although the melancholy self-criticism and media critique of *Ici et ailleurs* is very far from the political certainty of Studio H&S.

Cambodia

I have engaged with Heynowski-Scheumann's Vietnam cycle here because it establishes the studio's model for dealing with "violence elsewhere," a model applied consistently in their subsequent work. Following, albeit also overlapping, their Vietnam series, and after nine films on the struggle in Chile, Heynowski-Scheumann turned in 1979, for their third and last major corpus of works on global conflict, to the regime of the Khmer Rouge.

As has been noted already, Heynowski-Scheumann's Vietnam, Chile, and Cambodia films are all directly relevant to the theme of this volume: they deal explicitly and often very graphically with "violence elsewhere." One film, however—one that turned out to be among their most controversial—stands out in the present context for addressing the question explicitly and metatextually: *Die Angkar*. Filming the gruesome aftermath of the Cambodian massacres (1975–79) for the second time, following *Kampuchea: Sterben und Auferstehn* of 1980, the directors confront the paradox that the murderous regime of the Khmer Rouge—which they refer to disparagingly as the Pol-Pot/Ieng-Sary Clique to avoid associating it with legitimate Marxism-Leninism—adopted as its standard a beloved Communist symbol: "hammer and sickle here, hammer and sickle there" (18),[28] as the voice-over reminds us. How can we distinguish, the film asks, between the "so-called communism" of the Khmer Rouge and its ally Mao Zedong and the healthy, progressive Marxism-Leninism of the GDR and Soviet Union? Just five minutes into the film, they pose the question as follows: "Und nun also Hammer und Sichel zusammen mit diesem Pol Pot, dem Schlächter des Volkes von Kampuchea. Eine widerliche Nachbarschaft, die wir hätten übersehen oder gar beseitigen können—wären da nicht jene Ideologen des Imperialismus, die in der Polpoterei eine Variante des Kommunismus erkannt haben wollen. Eine Herausforderung, die wir annehmen mußten" (17; "And now the hammer and sickle together with this Pol Pot, the butcher of the Kampuchean

---

27 Scheumann, *Arbeitshefte 27*, 102.

28 Studio H&S, *Die Angkar* (Berlin: Studio H&S, 1981), 16–17. In what follows, the commentary and English translations are taken from this trilingual (German, English, French) protocol of the film. The book also provides translations of the introductory interview with the directors and a résumé of the film in Khmer, Russian, and Spanish.

people. A revolting juxtaposition, which we would rather have overlooked or even got rid of—if it hadn't been for those ideologues of imperialism who claim to have discovered in Pol-Potism a version of communism. This was a challenge we couldn't ignore," 16). Agonizing with perhaps unexpected candor over this thorny question of who does and does not have the right to adopt the emblems of Marxism-Leninism, *Die Angkar* becomes a self-reflexive effort to extricate the hammer and sickle and the red flag from the hands of the Khmer Rouge, to separate ideological rectitude "here" (in the GDR and Soviet Union) and debasement "there" (in Cambodia and its ally, China). As the directors put it, pointedly adopting the personal pronoun "wir"/"we," in the interview accompanying the published script:

> Denn auch wir waren ja bei der Arbeit auf Tatsachen gestoßen, die uns beunruhigten. Eine solche Tatsache ist die, daß das Massenmorden in Kampuchea unter dem Zeichen von Hammer und Sichel geschehen ist. So etwas kann einen doch nicht gleichgültig lassen, wenn man zu einer Generation gehört, für die die Fahne mit Hammer und Sichel auf dem Berliner Reichstag zu den markanten Einschnitten im Leben gehört. Noch niemals haben wir so deutlich gespürt, daß es bei einer kreativen Hervorbringung immer auch um Selbstverständigung geht. (III)
>
> [We too, in the course of our work, had encountered disquieting facts. One such fact was that the murders in Kampuchea had been carried out under the sign of the hammer and sickle. This cannot be casually passed over by those of our generation, for whom the hammer-and-sickle flag raised over the Reichstag in Berlin in the last days of the war marked a turning-point in life. We had never felt so clearly that creative production is always also a matter of self-clarification.] (XII)

"Self-clarification" here means historical insight into "violence elsewhere" and how it relates to politics at home. As we shall see, split screens in *Die Angkar* go so far as to show violence in (Nazi) Germany and (Communist) Cambodia side by side. Uniquely metatextual within the H&S oeuvre, *Die Angkar* even painstakingly and self-reflexively deconstructs a Chinese-made Cambodian propaganda film. Developing the theme of otherness, geographical and historical, from their earlier Vietnam work discussed above, *Die Angkar* asks questions, at the start of the GDR's final decade, about Communist identity in the face of one of its most violent global manifestations. As Fred Gehler put it in a 1982 review of the film in the GDR journal *Film und Fernsehen* (Film and Television), *Die Angkar* is "eine nachhaltige Lektion über die Austauschbarkeit von Worten, Parolen, Insignien, Emblemen, auch über die Verführbarkeit durch Oberflächen, das Verhältnis von 'einfacher' und 'komplizierter' Wahrheit. Das Finden der Wahrheit ist nicht einfacher geworden—im Gegenteil" (a lasting lesson about the interchangeability of words, slogans, insignia, emblems, also about the seduction of surfaces, the relationship between "simple" and "complicated" truths. Finding the truth has not become easier—on the contrary).[29]

Although the film may not quite amount to evidence for the entry of poststructuralist inquiry into GDR documentary practice, it does certainly raise semiotic questions not found elsewhere in contemporary East German cinema.

Deconstructing Iconography

The first part of the Cambodia trilogy, *Kampuchea: Sterben und Auferstehn*, offers a broader overview of the rise and fall of the Khmer Rouge and was an immediate response to what Heynowski-Scheumann found when they were commissioned by the SED to visit and film post-Khmer Rouge Phnom Penh. The film opens with an iconic image that will frame the first two films: juxtaposed Vietnamese and Cambodian flags following the liberation in 1979. This uplifting image is followed by one of the most striking sequences in the film, a traveling shot through the deserted streets of the capital over dramatically minimal music of composer Reiner Bredemeyer: a simple, haunting descending scale on the piano, accompanied by occasional vocal outbursts resembling screams of horror. In an effective rhetorical twist, this scale will be inverted to a rising one at the end of the film, where the focus is on liberation. In typically experimental fashion, the opening sequence ends with an unexpected freeze-frame as the camera captures the first sign of life spotted by the directors: a pair of pigeons in flight. In what follows, however, the film for the most part uncovers evidence of the Killing Fields, with interviews and documentation relating to victims and perpetrators.

Kampuchea: Sterben und Auferstehn certainly displays the studio's trademark polemical juxtapositions. Most striking, perhaps, is a provocative tableau that places a portrait of Mao Zedong (representing Chinese imperialism and expansionism) alongside a can of Castrol GTX oil (standing in for the US equivalent), which leaves little to the imagination in framing the link between China and the US. The commentary also acknowledges, however, that the atrocities unearthed are at times "das kaum Begreifbare" (barely imaginable). Tendentiously, a volume

---

29 Fred Gehler, "Die toten Augen von Tuol Sleng," *Film und Fernsehen* 3 (1982): 27. Quoted in Ralf Schenk, "Kunst und Klassenkampf: Unvollständige Notizen zu Heynowski & Scheumann," DVD booklet to *Studio H&S: Walter Heynowski und Gerhard Scheumann: Filme 1964–1989.*

of the thoughts of Pol Pot is presented not only in Chinese translation but with Chinese characters superimposed in white over the image, again underscoring the fatal contiguity of Khmer Rouge ideology and the "pseudorevolutionäre Lehre" (pseudorevolutionary teachings) of Mao's "sogenannte Kulturrevolution" (so-called Cultural Revolution). But elsewhere the film acknowledges the need for careful thought: the commentator notes early in the film, "Wir müssen über einige bisher unerhörte Begriffe nachdenken" (We must think carefully about concepts entirely new to us), before acknowledging toward the end that the images of victims and perpetrators do not, of themselves, provide ready insights. "Wir müssen weiterfragen" (We must continue to ask questions), the directors conclude.

Unlike its sequel, to which this essay now turns, the first part of the Cambodia trilogy is relatively circumspect with its historical analogies beyond the inevitable references to "koloniale Ausplünderung" (colonial exploitation), although the secret police headquarters in Phnom Penh is dubbed the "Gestapohauptquartier" (Gestapo headquarters) and an aside toward the end of the film notes that "Blut und Boden, das ging da wieder einmal zusammen" (Blood and Soil were united here once again). Analogies of this kind were also present in the Vietnam films: for example, when H. B. Ringsdorf, one of the downed pilots interrogated in *Piloten in Pyjama* (Pilots in Pajamas, 1967), protests that he was only following orders, he is reminded by the interviewer of the Nuremberg Trials, and *Die Teufelsinsel* not only refers to Buchenwald and Bergen-Belsen but also draws a direct comparison between revolutionaries incarcerated in Côn Sơn and Erich Honecker's imprisonment by the Gestapo.

As an exercise in further, detailed interrogation of the Khmer Rouge, *Die Angkar* investigates the operation of the Tuol Sleng headquarters of the secret police, the aforementioned "Gestapo headquarters" known as "Security Office 21" (S-21). After a contextual introduction, including a definition of the term "Angkar" with recourse to a Khmer-English dictionary, Heynowski-Scheumann turn to the main body of documents that the film, in what amounts to a self-reflexive gesture, will address: photographs. In the abandoned rooms of Tuol Sleng (a former school and now a "genocide museum")[30] the directors found thousands of passport-size identity photos of victims and perpetrators along with piles of forms, reports, registers, and lists. These form the main body of documents interrogated by the film, along with paintings, drawings, and effigies of Pol Pot discovered in the artists' studio attached to S-21.

The filmmakers use the technical devices available to them in the GDR—having taken crucial documents back home—to frame, highlight,

---

30 Official website: Tuol Sleng Genocide Museum, accessed August 21, 2021, https://tuolsleng.gov.kh/.

and challenge the material they find. Strips of bright light (in red and green) highlight relevant details in handwritten and printed texts, words are frequently superimposed onto photographs, and the rostrum camerawork is extremely varied and sophisticated in reproducing the identity photographs. Individual photos are zoomed in and out, multiple images are captured with smooth tracking shots, relevant details are highlighted by selective focus, and images are juxtaposed using split-screen and superimposition.

Six minutes into the film there is a striking and polemical use of animation and color-choreography as it grapples with the multiple uses and abuses of the hammer and sickle. The commentator explains, "Hammer und Sichel—und Pol Pot. Man nehme einen von Pol Pot hinterlassenen Schädelberg und nehme das von Pol Pot benutzte Zeichen von Hammer und Sichel, man gebe beides zusammen und nenne es 'Kommunismus': So entwaffnend einfach ist das Rezept aus der Küche des Kalten Krieges" (19; "Hammer and sickle—and Pol Pot. Take one of Pol Pot's legacies, a heap of skulls, and take the hammer and sickle used by Pol Pot, put them together and call it communism, and you have a disarmingly simple recipe from the cuisine of the cold war," 18). The film does precisely what is described: in a single, complex shot (shot 53) the directors take a still image of a portrait of Pol Pot found in Tuol Sleng below a hammer-and-sickle emblem, superimpose a pile of skulls onto the bottom right-hand corner of this image, and then, in a brief animation, extract the hammer and sickle from the red flag (top left) and transport it diagonally across the image onto the skulls (bottom right). As the emblem is lifted from the red flag, it turns black, suggesting, presumably, that it has been drained of the genuine lifeblood of Marxism-Leninism. The shot then ends—accompanying the phrase "a disarmingly simple recipe"—with a zoom in on the lower right corner of the tableau so that the black-and-white image of the hammer and sickle on the skulls entirely fills the screen, without Pol Pot. This is then followed (in shots 54–57) by alternating positive (Lenin, Vietnam) and negative (Mao Zedong, Pol Pot) historical deployment of the hammer-and-sickle emblem. As a bridge to the ensuing outline of the history of Marxist-Leninist struggle in Southeast Asia, the directors summarize their conclusion from this primer in the use and abuse of emblem as follows: "Hammer und Sichel können, so kompliziert stellt sich die Gegenwart dar, in durchaus unterschiedlicher Ansicht vorgezeigt werden" (21; "the hammer and sickle can in this complicated world of today be displayed with quite different intentions," 20).

This insight is accompanied by a fictional insert—Scheumann in interview rather nicely terms such moments "Organisierung für die Zwecke der Kamera" (organization for photographic purposes)[31]—lasting a mere seven seconds (shot 58, figure 6.3). Hands enter the frame from left and right to place a real sickle and a real hammer on top of one another on a bright red background. This literal-yet-iconic juxtaposition of a hammer and a sickle is strikingly similar to the tableau of helmets constructed in 1954 for Brecht's *Kriegsfibel* from props at the Berliner Ensemble. The only difference (aside from the use of color and moving-image photography) is that Heynowski-Scheumann openly acknowledge the constructedness of their image as the hands are seen carefully placing the tools on top of one another on the red background. Signs, shot 58 implies, are not only constructions but can also be deconstructed.

Deconstructing Propaganda Filmmaking

The most striking case of iconographic or ideological deconstruction in *Die Angkar* is the film's engagement with the Chinese-produced propaganda film made in 1976 for the Khmer Rouge. In a self-reflexive gesture that is, to my knowledge, unique in the history of GDR documentary, the directors probe and unpack this document. Initially they do so in a series of strikingly materialist gestures: they show not only the American Kodak Eastman Company film cans with Chinese lettering (shot 126, figure 6.4)—neatly connecting two malevolent "elsewheres"—but also the test card images (shot 127) not normally projected to an audience. The clear implication is that the filmmakers are engaging in forensic research, and, in an ironically complimentary aside, they acknowledge the quality of the light and color grading. The commentary here accompanying nine shots of the Chinese film (shots 128–136) is remarkable and merits extensive quotation:

> Was hier verlogen ist, ist das Ganze.
> Als die deutschen Faschisten bereits ihr Programm der "Endlösung der Judenfrage"—also die systematische Ausrottung der Juden—betrieben, drehten faschistische Regisseure und Kameraleute für das Ausland einen Film über das Konzentrationslager Theresienstadt unter dem einladenden Titel "Der Führer schenkt den Juden eine Stadt". Nur mit jenem Unternehmen ist diese chinesische Camouflage der Wirklichkeit der Pol-Pot-Herrschaft über Kampuchea zu vergleichen.
> Vor dem Hintergrund heutiger Erkenntnisse denunzieren sich diese Bilder nämlich selbst. Denn daß das Pol-Pot-Regime ein Mordregime war, wird heute nur noch von verbohrten Maoisten geleugnet—wie auch verbohrte Faschisten heute noch die Wirklichkeit der Gaskammern von Auschwitz leugnen zu können glauben. (37–39)

---

31 Scheumann, *Arbeitshefte 27*, 108.

Figure 6.3. Constructing meaning (Heynowski-Scheumann, *Die Angkar*, 1981, absolut MEDIEN, 2014).

Figure 6.4. Chinese propaganda in American cans (Heynowski-Scheumann, *Die Angkar*, 1981, absolut MEDIEN, 2014).

[What is falsified here is the whole.

When the German fascists were already carrying out their program for the "final solution of the Jewish question"—the extermination of the Jews—fascist directors and cameramen made a film for consumption abroad about the Theresienstadt concentration camp with the rather inviting title "The Führer gives the Jews a town". That particular project is the only thing comparable with this Chinese camouflage of the reality of the Pol Pot rule over Kampuchea.

Against the background of facts available today these scenes are a self-condemnation. The fact that the Pol Pot regime was a regime of murder would today be denied only by obstinate Maoists—just as obstinate fascists to this day think they can deny the reality of the gas chambers of Auschwitz.] (36–38)

At this point the directors intercut a color image of a smashed skull (shots 137, 138) before returning to the Chinese film for a further sequence of four shots of Pol Pot visiting a cotton field (shots 140–43). As the skull is interpolated, the self-reflexive gesture is expanded: "(Shot 137) Dieses Bild stammt nicht aus dem chinesischen Film, sondern aus unserer Kamera. Es waren Rodehacken, (Shot 138) die in die Schädel schlugen. Wer von dieser (Shot 139) Realität weiß, der kann diese Inszenierung nicht ohne Grauen betrachten. Immer noch fanden und finden sich Regisseure, die bereit sind, ihren Brotgebern (Shot 140) durch Fälscherdienste gefällig zu sein" (39–41) ("[Shot 137] This shot doesn't come from the Chinese film, but from our camera. It was farming hoes [Shot 138] that smashed them in. Whoever knows about this [Shot 139] reality, cannot watch this scene without horror. There were and there still are directors who are ready to render their employers their services [Shot 140] as counterfeiters," 38). The inference here is unmistakable: Studio H&S's GDR camera is deployed to uncover (unearth, literally and metaphorically) the truth; the Chinese-Cambodian propaganda film's camera is an apparatus that stages untruth (an "Inszenierung").

Parallels are drawn repeatedly in *Die Angkar* to Nazi Germany, to violence that is historically elsewhere but geographically closer to home for the directors: the aforementioned flag hoisted on the Reichstag by the Red Army in 1945 (shots 42–44); barbed wire and the motto "Arbeit macht frei" (Work sets you free) over the gate to Auschwitz (shots 176–77); medical experiments in concentration camps (shot 231) followed by a striking sequence of six shots (shots 232–37) panning out from a full-screen image of victims of Nazi concentration camps on the left to a split-screen with victims of the Angkar on the right, the first (shot 232) with the superimposed text "Nazi-KZ" (Nazi concentration camp) on the left and "Angkar-KZ" (Angkar concentration camp) on the right. Later in the film a comparison is drawn between the barbarity of Pol Pot's guards and the SS-Einsatzkommandos (shot 485), and toward the end a sarcastic rhetorical question is asked, in the context of a discussion of Pol Pot's "anti-communism," as to whether Hitler was "etwa ein Sozialist, nur weil er seine politische Doktrin Nationalsozialismus nannte?" ("perhaps a socialist just because he called his political doctrine National Socialism?" shot 653). The final example cited here leads directly into a further "violence elsewhere" connection, as Pol Pot's and Hitler's misuse of the term "socialism" is compared with that of the Italian Red Brigade "Terroristen" (terrorists, shot 654), who, it is alleged, have nothing whatsoever to do with the workers' movement proper.

It has to be noted that despite the meticulous research undertaken for the film, these comparisons are not always free of oversimplification: in the case of the Theresienstadt (Terezín) film (the official title of which is *Theresienstadt: Ein Dokumentarfilm aus dem jüdischen Siedlungsgebiet* [Theresienstadt: A Documentary Film from the Jewish Settlement Area]) it is not actually true that the film was directed and shot exclusively by fascists, although it is, undoubtedly, a fascist film produced by a fascist regime. The Jewish actor and director Kurt Gerron, imprisoned in Theresienstadt and killed in Auschwitz shortly after completion of the film, was forced to direct it under the supervision of Nazi officials and to work alongside the Czech director Karel Pečený. These circumstances do not undermine the validity of the point being made by the juxtaposition, or indeed its rhetorical force, but do demonstrate that sweeping comparisons can obscure historical detail and complexity.

Conclusion: (Media) Politics and Auteurism

Die Angkar is sometimes referenced in histories of GDR film, and indeed in publications on Studio H&S itself, not for its insights into the Khmer Rouge—for which it deserves to be much better known—but because of its controversial reception and for the part it played, albeit indirectly, in the demise of Studio H&S mentioned above. In his notoriously critical paper delivered at the fourth congress of the Verband der Film- und Fernsehschaffenden der DDR (Association of Film and Television Producers of the GDR) in September 1982—a document that swiftly led to punitive sanctions and the loss of independence for the studio—Scheumann, frustrated by the refusal of GDR television to broadcast *Die Angkar*, cited the film as an example of the problems facing GDR media. The fourteenth of fifteen theses in his controversial paper "Dokumentarfilm im Spannungsfeld von Strategie und Taktik (Gedanken zur Selbstverständigung und zur Diskussion" (Documentary Film as a Trade-off between Strategy and Tactics [Thoughts for Self-Clarification and Discussion]) reads, "Die Rezeption des Film 'Die Angkar' hat bewirkt, dass [*sic*] Zuschauer an die Dokumentaristen die Frage stellten, warum unsere Medien sich . . . über Kampuchea ausgeschwiegen haben. Die Frage zielt nicht darauf, welche Rücksichten dies bewirkt haben mögen, sondern welche Vertrauenswürdigkeit unseren Medien zuerkannt werden darf. Der Dokumentarfilm muß in solchen Fällen darauf verweisen, daß diese Frage an die falsche Adresse gerichtet ist" (The reception of the film "Die Angkar" has caused viewers to ask the documentarists why our media . . . kept silent about Cambodia. The question is not what considerations may have brought this about, but about the trustworthiness of our media. In such cases documentary film must point out that this question is being directed to the wrong address).[32]

Earlier in the same document, in the twelfth thesis, Scheumann pointedly notes that documentary film cannot simply bow to "diplomatische oder wirtschaftliche Hintergründe" (diplomatic or economic backgrounds).[33] The thirteenth opens even more provocatively with the assertion "Wenn der Dokumentarfilm nur als Vehikel der täglichen Medienpolitik benutzt werden soll, muß er verkommen" (If documentary film is used merely as a vehicle for everyday media politics, it will degenerate).[34] Put simply, Scheumann's point is that the search for truth in Cambodia cannot be subservient to GDR *Tagespolitik* (current affairs) and, implicitly at least, that Chinese anger at the Cambodian films—which had led to a walkout by their delegation at a film festival in Bilbao[35]—should not be a reason for denying the films airtime on East German television. As Steinmetz has noted, "Die Thematik [fiel] in die Phase einer veränderten Außenpolitik der DDR gegenüber China . . . und [wurde] im Fernsehen als nicht mehr opportun angesehen" (The subject matter fell within a period of changed foreign policy within the GDR toward China . . . and it was viewed as no longer opportune for television).[36]

As proposed above, the films of Studio H&S can be classified as modernist blatancy—for the most part, Heynowski-Scheumann have no truck with ambiguity. As the image of colonial French shackles intertwined with US handcuffs discussed above demonstrates, they were also happy to construct documentary evidence where necessary to translate ideological conflict into visual and acoustic dissonance. *Die Angkar*, however, is in a number of ways exceptional in H&S's vast catalogue. The certainties of Studio H&S confront some uncomfortable facts, above all in the abuse

---

32 Quoted in Steinmetz and Prase, *Dokumentarfilm zwischen Beweis und Pamphlet*, 157. There are clearly errors in the source material or transcription of this text.
33 Steinmetz and Prase, *Dokumentarfilm zwischen Beweis und Pamphlet*, 157.
34 Steinmetz and Prase, *Dokumentarfilm zwischen Beweis und Pamphlet*, 157.
35 Riemann, *Eine Herausforderung an jeden Kommunisten*, 81.
36 Steinmetz and Prase, *Dokumentarfilm zwischen Beweis und Pamphlet*, 50.

of Communist ideology and iconography by the Khmer Rouge in the 1970s. The directors' own description of the film as "so etwas wie eine optimistische Tragödie" (IV; "[a kind of] optimistic tragedy," XII)—optimist insofar as it ends with liberation from Pol Pot's regime, tragic in terms of the death toll and suffering that preceded it—suggests the contradictions it uncovers. As they note in the interview for the screenplay publication: "Es geht also dem Film 'Die Angkar' nicht nur um die Aufarbeitung eines historischen Tatbestandes. Jeder Dokumentarfilm, der sich nicht nur als Bericht versteht, sollte das Exemplarische seines Gegenstandes suchen und zeigen" (IV; "Our film 'The Angkar' is not designed simply as a recording of historical facts. Every documentary film which is not only a straightforward report should seek and display the lessons to be learned from its subject matter," XIII). For "kommunistische Filmemacher" (IV; "Communist film-makers," XIII), the lessons learned here are uncomfortable, and the untypically long stretches of silence in this film—lasting on one occasion almost a full minute—may be read as textual, or rather structural, evidence of this. In an interview with Ralf Schenk in 2003, Heynowski went so far as to admit that Stalinist atrocities and domestic Marxism-Leninism could not be entirely "ausgeklammert" (bracketed out) in the Cambodian cycle.[37] He even surmises that an awareness of the potential implications of the films at home may have contributed to the harsh treatment of the studio in the wake of Scheumann's 1982 speech.[38]

The roll call of twenty-four photographs (shots 333–56) of victims accompanied by the famous funeral march from Frédéric Chopin's *Piano Sonata No. 2*, the only music deployed in the film, is a particularly striking example of "words failing"—"mais on ne peut plus rien dire," as Jean Cayrol famously puts it in his commentary for Alain Resnais's Holocaust documentary *Nuit et brouillard* (Night and Fog, 1955). On a number of occasions in *Die Angkar* the directors are almost (or even actually) lost for words when faced by the horrific cruelty of the Khmer Rouge, and repeatedly, as we have seen, they feel the need to comment self-reflexively on their own practice. This reveals an unexpectedly personal, quasi-auteurist dimension to the work of Studio H&S that has, too often, been overlooked, and one that Scheumann was himself at pains to stress in the controversial paper he delivered at the Verband der Film- und Fernsehschaffenden der DDR in September 1982: "Tatsächlich ist auch der Dokumentarfilm niemals die Wirklichkeit selbst, sondern immer ein subjektives Abbild der objektiven Welt und insoweit den fiktiven Genres der Kunst verwandt. Im Dokumentarfilm ist der Autor ebenso anwesend wie im Spielfilm" (In fact, documentary film is never reality itself,

---

37 Poss et al., *Das Prinzip Neugier*, 88.
38 Poss et al., *Das Prinzip Neugier*, 88.

but always a subjective image of the objective world and to that extent related to the fictional genres of art. The author is just as present in documentary film as in feature films).[39] In assessing the achievement of *Die Angkar*, this remarkable admission should be viewed in conjunction with the heartfelt admiration for Heynowski-Scheumann's Cambodia films expressed in 2005 by Peter Maguire, author of the study of the Khmer Rouge *Facing Death in Cambodia*. Having studied the films and their scripts and interviewed Scheumann in 1997, Maguire concludes,

> Unlike the majority of individuals debating about the Khmer Rouge, Scheumann wore his political ideology on his sleeve, and though it didn't accord with the preferences or opinions of some policy makers and scholars, his analysis of the situation in Cambodia between 1975 and 1979 was correct. . . . The filmmaker had backed his ideological commitment with a kind of empirical inquiry that simply could not be done from a studio office or a university campus.[40]

Despite the revelations about the origins and spread of "violence elsewhere" uncovered by Heynowski-Scheumann, however, the Cambodia trilogy ultimately fell victim to what Riemann simply and succinctly terms a "Wandel der *politischen Bedingungen*" (change in *political conditions*) at home.[41] The uncovering of truths about Khmer Rouge violence and its links to Beijing, called for by the SED in 1979, became a potential obstacle to foreign policy ambitions in less than two years. It is ultimately this pragmatic consideration, rather than the uncomfortable parallels between democratic (GDR/USSR) and despotic (Khmer Rouge/Chinese) Communist iconography identified in *Die Angkar*—even *Neues Deutschland* was willing to commend the directors for their courage in asking "bohrende Fragen" (penetrating questions)[42]—that led not only to the sidelining of the trilogy and its disappearance from GDR television screens but also to the crisis that brought down Studio H&S in 1982. Despite, and indeed also because of, its troubled reception, the trilogy— and *Die Angkar* in particular—remains a revealing document of political oppression both elsewhere and at home.

---

39 Steinmetz and Prase, *Dokumentarfilm zwischen Beweis und Pamphlet*, 156.
40 Peter Maguire, *Facing Death in Cambodia* (New York: Columbia University Press, 2005), 97.
41 Riemann, *Eine Herausforderung an jeden Kommunisten*, 104.
42 See Goldberg, "Ein Film, der anklagt und bohrende Fragen stellt."

7: Narrating Violent Agency Elsewhere in Inge Viett's *Nie war ich furchtloser* (Never Was I More Fearless, 1996)

Clare Bielby[1]

IN THIS CHAPTER, I explore former Bewegung 2. Juni (Movement 2nd June) and briefly Rote Armee Fraktion (Red Army Faction, RAF) member Inge Viett's representation of what I am terming "violent agency elsewhere" in her autobiography, *Nie war ich furchtloser* (Never Was I More Fearless, 1996).[2] My focus is on the different ways in which violent agency elsewhere offers Viett models for her own militant subjectivity,[3] not least as a West German and a woman militant, where "elsewhere" functions both geographically and temporally. As a retrospective narrative reconstruction of her experiences in the stylized form of an autobiography, the text offers no immediate access to Viett's subjectivity, neither in the narrated past nor the narrating present. But it does provide some indication of what violent agency elsewhere meant to her, and what it was able to provide to the West German militant woman more broadly, in a context in which there was little discursive space to imagine women's politically violent agency.[4]

Viett's text has attracted some scholarly interest.[5] Of particular note here is Christina Gerhardt's seven-page discussion of it in the context of

---

1   Thanks to Mererid Puw Davies and Laura Schwartz for valuable feedback on this chapter.
2   Inge Viett, *Nie war ich furchtloser: Autobiographie* (1996; Reinbek bei Hamburg: Rowohlt, 1999). Further page references follow in the text. All translations are the author's own.
3   I therefore do not explore examples of violent agency elsewhere toward which Viett would have felt hostile; for example, the agency of US soldiers in Vietnam.
4   On the lack of discursive space to imagine revolutionary women, see Sarah Colvin, "'Wir Frauen haben kein Vaterland': Ulrike Marie Meinhof, Emily Wilding Davison and the 'Homelessness' of Women Revolutionaries," *German Life and Letters* 64, no. 1 (2011): 108–21.
5   See Katharina Karcher, "'Ich bin parteilich, subjektiv und emotional'— *Eigen-Sinn* and the Narrative (Re)construction of Political Agency in Inge Viett's

a monograph that explores, among other things, "the international context" of leftist terrorism.[6] Gerhardt's focus, however, is on the differences between Viett's text and the narrative of Volker Schlöndorff's film *Die Stille nach dem Schuss* (The Silence after the Shot, 2000; in English as *The Legend of Rita*), which was inspired in part by Viett's life.[7] One of these differences is the significance Viett attributes to "international events" as a way to understand her politicization.[8] From a historiographical perspective, scholarship has explored the West German New Left from a global or transnational angle,[9] with analyses of the significance for leftist terrorists of their relationships with (and affective investment in) Palestinian militants, the Vietcong, and Latin American guerrilla fighters notable examples.[10] This scholarship has tended to ignore gender, however, and

---

Nie war ich furchtloser," in *Experiencing Postwar Germany: Everyday Life and Cultural Practice in East and West, 1960–2000*, ed. Erica Carter et al. (Oxford: Berghahn, 2018), 85–106; Christina Gerhardt, *Screening the Red Army Faction: Historical and Cultural Memory* (New York: Bloomsbury, 2018), 221–27; Patricia Melzer, *Death in the Shape of a Young Girl: Women's Political Violence in the Red Army Faction* (New York: New York University Press, 2015), 198–209; Clare Bielby, "Narrating the Revolutionary Self in German Post-Terrorist Life Writing: Gender, Identity and Historical Agency," *German Life and Letters* 76, no. 2 (2014): 219–41.

6 Gerhardt, *Screening the Red Army Faction*, 2.

7 Screenwriter Wolfgang Kohlhaase conducted regular interviews with Viett and fellow former woman terrorists Susanne Albrecht and Silke Maier-Witt, who had sought asylum in the German Democratic Republic (East Germany) in the early 1990s. See Gerhardt, *Screening the Red Army Faction*, 221.

8 Gerhardt, *Screening the Red Army Faction*, 11.

9 On global/transnational perspectives, see, for example, Timothy Scott Brown, *West Germany and the Global Sixties: The Antiauthoritarian Revolt, 1962–1978* (Cambridge: Cambridge University Press, 2013); Brown, "'1968' East and West: Divided Germany as a Case Study in Transnational History," *American Historical Review* 114, no. 1 (2009): 69–96. On West German/US connections, see, for example, Martin Klimke, *The Other Alliance: Student Protest in West Germany & the United States in the Global Sixties* (Princeton, NJ: Princeton University Press, 2010); Jeremy Varon, *Bringing the War Home: The Weather Underground, the Red Army Faction, and Revolutionary Violence in the Sixties and Seventies* (Berkeley: University of California Press, 2004). On West German/"Third World" connections, see Quinn Slobodian, *Foreign Front: Third World Politics in Sixties West Germany* (Durham, NC: Duke University Press, 2012).

10 On the importance of Palestinian militants for West German terrorism, see Thomas Skelton Robinson, "Im Netz verheddert: Die Beziehungen des bundesdeutschen Linksterrorismus zur *Volksfront für die Befreiung Palästinas* (1969–1980)," in *Die RAF und der linke Terrorismus*, ed. Wolfgang Kraushaar, 2 vols. (Hamburg: Hamburger Edition, 2006), 2:828–904. On the Vietcong, see Wolfgang Kraushaar, "Der *Vietcong* als Mythos des bewaffneten Volksaufstandes," in Kraushaar, *Die RAF und der linke Terrorismus*, 2:751–67. On Latin American

to neglect women's perspectives.[11] In an otherwise insightful article that examines "1968" in East and West Germany from a transnational historical perspective, for example, Timothy Scott Brown draws attention to "the importance of popular culture in the formation of radical political identities in the 1960s" in ways that are not attuned to gender.[12]

This chapter will first make a case for the particular appeal of violent agency elsewhere for the West German New Left before sketching out the gendered discursive context of left-wing militancy in West Germany, paying particular attention to the discursive space available to articulate women's militant subjectivity. The chapter then focuses on Viett's text. I first consider how she narrates herself as part of an "imagined community of global revolt"[13] where, not least in Viett's capacity as a West German woman militant, that "imagined community" has transhistorical, even transhuman dimensions. I then turn to Viett's construction of the violent agency of the Palestinian militant men she encountered in the Middle East, and what happens when "radical orientalist" fantasies come up against reality.[14] Finally, I explore the few examples of *women*'s violent agency elsewhere in the text. While not exhaustive, my approach allows me to reflect on how violent agency elsewhere, in however contradictory a manner, shaped Viett's construction of her own revolutionary subjectivity.

---

militants, see Jamie Trnka, "The West German Red Army Faction and its Appropriation of Latin American Urban Guerilla Struggles," in *Counter-Cultures in Germany and Central Europe: From* Sturm und Drang *to Baader-Meinhof*, ed. Steve Giles and Maike Oergel (Bern: Peter Lang, 2003), 315–32.

11 Notable exceptions here are Quinn Slobodian, "Guerilla Mothers and Distant Doubles: West German Feminists look at China and Vietnam," *Zeithistorische Forschungen* 1 (2015): 39–65; Mererid Puw Davies, "West German Representations of Women and Resistance in Vietnam, 1966–73," in *Women and Death 2: Warlike Women in the German Literary and Cultural Imagination since 1500*, ed. Sarah Colvin and Helen Watanabe-O'Kelly (Rochester, NY: Camden House, 2009), 229–49. See also Sarah Colvin and Katharina Karcher, eds., *Women, Global Protest Movements, and Political Agency: Rethinking the Legacy of 1968* (London: Routledge, 2019).

12 Brown, "'1968' East and West," 78. While Brown's *West Germany and the Global Sixties* includes a chapter, "Sex," that focuses on women's perspectives, the rest of the book does not reflect on gender, taking the male perspective as universal.

13 Simon Prince, "The Global Revolt of 1968 and Northern Ireland," *Historical Journal* 49, no. 3 (2006): 851–75.

14 Judy Tzu-Chun Wu, *Radicals on the Road: Internationalism, Orientalism, and Feminism during the Vietnam Era* (Ithaca, NY: Cornell University Press, 2013).

Born in 1944 as one of seven children of an impoverished single mother, Viett was placed in foster care aged six, subjected to years of emotional and physical abuse, and raped by a local farmer during her adolescent years. After aborted attempts at further education, various lesbian relationships, and living and working in Hamburg and Wiesbaden among other locales, Viett moved to West Berlin's Kreuzberg district in her mid-twenties, where her politics became increasingly radical as she immersed herself in Berlin's leftist militant scene. Viett joined Bewegung 2. Juni in 1972 soon after its formation, functioning as a core member throughout the 1970s and being involved in two abductions, among other violent actions. Arrested in 1972 and 1975, Viett escaped from prison on two occasions. She reluctantly joined the RAF in 1980 when Bewegung 2. Juni disbanded. After shooting and seriously injuring a police officer in Paris in 1981, Viett fled to the GDR (along with several other RAF members) as part of the so-called RAF-Stasi-connection that she had helped establish.[15] There she twice took on a new identity. She was arrested in Magdeburg in 1990, shortly after the fall of the Berlin Wall, was sentenced to thirteen years in prison in 1992, and received an early release in 1997.

First published in 1996, *Nie war ich furchtloser* was written while Viett was in prison. The text covers her childhood and teenage years in postwar West Germany (chapters 1–2), her politicization/radicalization (chapters 3–4), years "underground" through to the agonizing process of deciding to leave armed militancy (chapters 4–14), then to her time spent in the GDR and eventual arrest (chapters 15–16). The prologue and epilogue are written from the perspective of the narrating present, with the prologue creating a keen sense of the existential urgency of prison writing in ways that echo Sigrid Weigel's claim that the objective of the prison writer is "die Bewahrung seiner Identität" (the preservation of their identity).[16] In Viett's case, this preservation of a sense of self is bound up with the writing of her own and her comrades' hi/story (Geschichte), "meine Verteidigung gegen die drohende Selbstauslöschung in den leeren Jahren der Gefangenschaft" (12; my defense against the impending annihilation of self in the empty years of imprisonment). Viett's book is characterized by an assertive authorial voice that is undermined by the sense of searching and contradiction at the heart of the text.

---

15 See Michael Müller and Andreas Kanonenberg, *Die RAF-Stasi-Connection* (Berlin: Rowohlt, 1992).

16 Sigrid Weigel, *"Und selbst im Kerker frei ... !": Schreiben im Gefängnis; Zur Theorie und Gattungsgeschichte der Gefängnisliteratur* (Marburg an der Lahn: Guttandin & Hoppe, 1982), 8.

Setting the Scene

In the late 1980s, former '68er and eventual German foreign minister Joschka Fischer recalled, "Nachdem ich lange Zeit Schläge eingesteckt hatte, habe ich mit einem gewissen Vergnügen zurückgeschlagen, wie man das als Typ halt gemacht hat. Ich habe auf diese Art meine Courage bewiesen, und ich bin bestärkt worden durch Menschen, die ich bewunderte: Che Guevara, die Kämpfer im Vietcong" (After a long period of taking blows, I hit back, as you did as a bloke, with a certain sense of pleasure. In this way I proved my courage, and I was strengthened by those that I admired: Che Guevara, Vietcong fighters).[17] As well as describing the—for him—self-evidently masculine nature of this violent response to state violence, Fischer draws attention to the significance of "Third World" revolutionary agents.[18] According to Stefanie Pilzweger, who cites him, it was through his "Bewunderung der tapferen und unbeugsamen Guerilleros" (admiration for brave and uncompromising guerrilla fighters) that Fischer was able "seine pazifistische Grundhaltung aufzugeben und körperliche Gewalt zum Einsatz zu bringen" (to abandon his pacifist stance and deploy physical violence).[19]

Guerrilla fighters in Vietnam and other Third World countries were of huge significance to New Leftists in diverse trans/national contexts, as a wealth of scholarship has demonstrated. But they arguably held a crucial, particular function in the context of West German militancy. Brown has emphasized the "urgency" of ideas and practices coming from elsewhere for the West German 1968, on account of the National Socialist past and Cold War present: "The 'national deficit' produced by multiple erasures of National Socialism and West Germany's Cold War status made borrowing a necessity, in both political and cultural terms."[20] Former activist Peter Schneider asserted in 1998 that internationalism was attractive to West German activists first and foremost as it offered "a means of escaping from a despicable skin, the skin of being German";[21] an idea supported by Arlene A. Teraoka and Sara Lennox, who argue, as glossed by Quinn Slobodian, that "West German radicals identified with Third World revolutionaries to exonerate themselves as Germans

---

17 Cited in Stefanie Pilzweger, *Männlichkeit zwischen Gefühl und Revolution: Eine Emotionsgeschichte der bundesdeutschen 1968er Bewegung* (Bielefeld: transcript Verlag, 2015), 299.
18 I use the term "Third World" (henceforth without quotations marks) according to usage at the time.
19 Pilzweger, *Männlichkeit zwischen Gefühl und Revolution*, 300.
20 Brown, *West Germany and the Global Sixties*, 366.
21 Cited in Slobodian, *Foreign Front*, 11.

and claim a position that transcended national sins."²² While this perspective can invisibilize the significance of embodied encounters between West German and Third World subjects, as Slobodian has illustrated,²³ it does shed light on the crucial points of identification, far removed from the National Socialist past, that violent agency elsewhere could offer. But the perpetration of violence remained heavily burdened nonetheless, particularly for the male subject, as Pilzweger observes: "Das kriegerische Männlichkeitsideal des todesverachtenden Guerillakämpfers unterschied sich, was die Einstellung zur Anwendung von Gewalt anging, im Grunde nicht von dem soldatisch-militärischen Männerbild der väterlichen Kriegsgeneration, auch wenn die '68er' dieses entschieden ablehnten" (With reference to the use of violence, the warlike masculine ideal of the fearless guerrilla fighter was in essence no different from the soldierly-military model of masculinity of their fathers' war generation, even though "'68ers" emphatically rejected this).²⁴

As gender-sensitive scholarship has demonstrated, though women were highly involved in New Left revolutionary movements in diverse trans/national contexts, those movements were infused with masculinist ideologies, discourses, and practices. Male figures such as Ernesto (Che) Guevara, Ho Chi Minh, and Mao Zedong achieved iconic status, serving as identificatory and affective foci, while texts by the likes of Frantz Fanon and Carlos Marighella provided theoretical underpinnings that were profoundly masculinist. Aribert Reimann has described West Germany's cultural revolution of the 1960s and 1970s as "männlich codiert" (male-coded), pointing to the "allgegenwärtige Dominanz von deutschen und internationalen Vorbildern eines maskulin-revolutionären Typus" (ubiquitous dominance of German and international role models of a masculine-revolutionary type).²⁵ For Pilzweger, meanwhile, the West German '68er movement was "maskulin-geprägt" (masculine-connoted).²⁶

---

22 Slobodian, *Foreign Front*, 11. See Arlene A. Teraoka, *East, West, and Others: The Third World in Postwar German Literature* (Lincoln: University of Nebraska Press, 1996), 165; Sara Lennox, "Enzensberger, *Kursbuch*, and 'Third Worldism': The Sixties' Construction of Latin America," in *"Neue Welt"/"Dritte Welt": Interkulturelle Beziehungen Deutschland zu Lateinamerika und der Karibik*, ed. Sigrid Bauschinger and Susan L. Cocalis (Tübingen: Francke, 1994), 185–200, here 188.

23 Slobodian, *Foreign Front*.

24 Pilzweger, *Männlichkeit zwischen Gefühl und Revolution*, 300.

25 Aribert Reimann, "Zwischen Machismo und Coolness: Männlichkeit und Emotion in der westdeutschen 'Kulturrevolution' der 1960er- und 1970er Jahre," in *Die Präsenz der Gefühle: Männlichkeit und Emotion in der Moderne*, ed. Manuel Borutta and Nina Verheyen (Bielefeld: transcript Verlag, 2010), 229–53, here 229; 230.

26 Pilzweger, *Männlichkeit zwischen Gefühl und Revolution*, 300.

In the introduction to *Die 68erinnen* (The Women '68ers), a book published in 2002 that—for the first time—centered the experience of women '68ers in the (West) German context, editor Ute Kätzel draws attention to the lack of positive models of woman's revolutionary agency: "Ein positives weibliches Rollenmodell existierte damals noch nicht. Daher identifizierten sich viele Aktivistinnen nicht als Frauen, sondern— vermeintlich geschlechtsneutral—als Menschen" (At that time a positive female role model did not yet exist. For that reason many women activists did not identify as women, but rather—in an ostensibly gender-neutral way—as people).[27] On that first point, Kätzel is not entirely correct. Several women '68ers mention RAF founder member Ulrike Meinhof in their interviews, albeit in ambivalent terms, as well as cross-referencing each other, while the front matter of the book includes a photograph of Angela Davis about to embrace East German '68er Erika Berthold before a crowd in East Berlin. Kätzel's women '68ers also mention Clara Zetkin and Rosa Luxemburg as inspiring figures: two of the few revolutionary women from the (German) past whom the antiauthoritarian movement genuinely celebrated, occasional women in the pantheon of "'great men' of the revolutionary socialist tradition."[28] In April 1970, furthermore, a group calling themselves the Frauenbefreiungsfront (Women's Liberation Front)—part of Berlin's militant underground scene, of which Viett herself was a member before going "underground"—were drawing attention to anarchist Emma Goldman, to PFLP-member Leila Khaled, to Valerie Solanas, and to Vietnamese women fighters as inspiration in a double-page spread in the radical leftist publication *Agit 883*.[29]

But these examples of women's revolutionary agency with the capacity to inspire women activists were few and far between. Overwhelmingly, representations of revolutionary women—be they German or from elsewhere, mainstream or sub/countercultural—were misogynistic, sexualized, and crucially disavowed women's revolutionary political agency, meaning that they presumably held little identificatory potential for the radical female subject.[30]

---

27 Ute Kätzel, "Vorwort," in *Die 1968erinnen: Porträt einer rebellischen Frauengeneration*, ed. Kätzel (Berlin: Rowohlt, 2002), 9–18, here 16.

28 Brown, *West Germany and the Global Sixties*, 83.

29 *Agit 883* (April 16, 1970): 6–7, http://www.agit883.infopartisan.net/. On Solanas as inspiring yet ambivalent figure, see Cristina Perincioli, *Berlin wird feministisch: Das Beste, was von der 68er Bewegung blieb* (Berlin: Querverlag, 2015), 49, 178, 182.

30 On the misogynistic nature of sub/countercultural representations of revolutionary women, see Brown, *West Germany and the Global Sixties*, 317. On the representation of terrorist women in the West German press, see Clare Bielby, *Violent Women in Print: Representations in the West German Print Media of the 1960s and 1970s* (Rochester, NY: Camden House, 2012).

Here we start to observe the male bias of Brown's emphasis on "the importance of popular culture in the formation of radical political identities in the 1960s," a point he makes with reference to Louis Malle's *Viva Maria!* (1965) and its significance for activists Rudi Dutschke and Dieter Kunzelmann in particular. "Dutschke and Kunzelmann saw in the movie what they wanted to see," he elaborates, "taking from it what was useful in their particular situation."[31] While Mererid Puw Davies outlines scope for a feminist interpretation, albeit equivocal, of the film's two women protagonists in her chapter in the present volume, *Viva Maria!* is more frequently understood as disempowering for women, and not least by Brown himself.[32] As Davies details, feminist filmmaker Helke Sander makes prominent but ambiguous use of the film's poster in her filmic account of the antiauthoritarian movement and the beginnings of West Germany's new women's movement: *Der subjektive Faktor* (The Subjective Factor, 1981).[33] Sander uses it alongside a second iconic image of women's revolutionary agency elsewhere in circulation in West Germany from the late 1960s: a Vietnamese guerrilla mother who sits with a gun in one hand, a baby on her other arm, with the words "We will fight and fight from this generation to the next" pointing to heteronormative generational models of time.[34] We first see the image propped against protagonist Anni's bedroom wall. Anni, herself a mother, attempts to mimic the woman's pose using domestic props before eventually giving up, suggesting, as Davies has argued elsewhere, "that her identification with [the woman] fails." We later see the image, among other contexts, upside down in Anni's home, "suggesting a desire to overturn the era's fraught images of fighting women," which, according to Sander herself, were "merely a male fantasy."[35]

---

31 Brown, "'1968' East and West," 78.

32 Brown, *West Germany and the Global Sixties*, 195.

33 See also Clare Bielby, "Bewaffnete Terroristinnen: Linksterrorismus, Gender und die Waffe in der Bundesrepublik Deutschland von den 1970er Jahren bis heute," *WerkstattGeschichte* 64 (2014): 88–89.

34 On feminist use of this image, see Slobodian, "Guerilla Mothers and Distant Doubles."

35 Davies, "West German Representations," 229, 245, 229. As Davies points out, Vietnamese women were heavily involved in the conflict in Vietnam and visually represented in prominent German left-wing journals such as *konkret*, notorious for its combination of left-wing politics and the objectification of women (231; 246n6). "While fighting women in Vietnam could be looked at, to write about them was nearly impossible," Davies observes further with reference to West German protest writing about Vietnam (231). In that context it is interesting to note that while revolutionary women visually dominate the Frauenbefreiungsfront's double-page spread in *Agit 883*, it is Mao and Fidel Castro whose words are cited (at length) in the main body of the text.

Violence Elsewhere, Violence Here: Transnational, Transhistorical (and Transhuman) Forms of Violent Belonging

Chapter 4 of Viett's text opens with an account of a trip to North Africa and the politicizing effects of seeing firsthand the destruction wrought by the Western world and the "slow violence" done to Third World subjects there (80–81).[36] After a page and a half description of her impressions, Viett turns to what were for her inspirational constructions of violent agency elsewhere via one of the theoretical heavyweights of the antiauthoritarian movement, the postcolonial theorist Fanon: "Als ich später Fanon las, habe ich sofort verstanden. Unsere Zuneigung und Solidarität zur 'Dritten Welt' war damals gewiß auch sehr romantisch, aber sie war gerecht, notwendig, beispielgebend und hoffnungsvoll" (81; When I read Fanon later on, I understood immediately. Our sympathy and solidarity for the "Third World" back then was certainly very romantic, but it was fair, necessary, exemplary, and hopeful). Viett is certainly referring to Fanon's *The Wretched of the Earth* (1961), excerpts of which were first published in German in the vanguard leftist journal *Kursbuch* in 1965.[37] In that text, Fanon drew on his experiences as a psychiatrist working in an Algerian hospital during the uprising against the French, notoriously describing violence as a humanizing, therapeutic force for the "native" of Algeria, whom he genders male throughout, at times suggesting the constitutive power of violence to colonized masculinity.[38]

Viett continues, now establishing her own (and other German militants') affective investment in violent agency elsewhere, and how that is bound up with her sense of self: "Mit leidenschaftlicher Anteilnahme haben wir uns *Die Schlacht um Algier* angesehen; der Sieg des Vietcong,

---

36 On "slow violence," see Rob Nixon, *Slow Violence and the Environmentalism of the Poor* (Cambridge, MA: Harvard University Press, 2011). This is one of the few occasions in the text where Viett accords narrative space to the victims of violence elsewhere, whom she anonymizes and presents as a collective mass, using collective nouns such as "Bettler" (beggars) and "Krüppelheere" (armies of "cripples") (81).

37 "Von der Gewalt," *Kursbuch* 2 (1965): 1–55. See Frantz Fanon, *The Wretched of the Earth*, trans. Constance Farrington (London: Penguin, 2001 [1965]).

38 According to Jean-Paul Sartre's preface, the Algerian man's "irrepressible violence" is "man re-creating himself." Jean-Paul Sartre, "Preface," in Fanon, *The Wretched of the Earth*, 7–26, here 18. In an earlier, lesser-known text, and one I have found no discussion of in West German New Left discourse, Fanon wrote about Algerian women involved in the uprising. Frantz Fanon, "Algeria Unveiled," in *A Dying Colonialism*, trans. Haakon Chevalier (New York: Grove Press, 1994), 35–67.

der Fall von Saigon und der Sieg der Sandinisten waren Höhepunkte in meinem Guerilla-Dasein" (81; With passionate sympathies we watched *The Battle of Algiers*; the victory of the Vietcong, the fall of Saigon, and the victory of the Sandinistas were high points in my guerrilla existence). This quotation (and particularly reference to her "Guerrilla-Dasein") gestures toward what Jamie Trnka has described as West German militant groups' "affective identifications with" and "appropriation of Third World liberation struggles," where "a radical physical identification in struggle . . . supersedes moral or political identifications."[39] It also reveals the significance of filmic examples of revolutionary agency elsewhere for West German militant identities, here in the case of Gillo Pontecorvo's *The Battle of Algiers* (1966).

Accounts suggest that *The Battle of Algiers* was RAF founder member Andreas Baader's favorite film and that he identified with and strove to imitate Ali La Pointe, the charismatic Front de Libération Nationale revolutionary, played by Brahim Haggiag.[40] While Viett recounts a strong affective response to the film, she only mentions it in passing, and there is no suggestion of identification with any of its protagonists. Certainly the film's representation of women leaves a great deal to be desired from a feminist perspective. Though it may have been hailed for representing women as active revolutionary agents, Mani Sharpe rightly argues that "Pontecorvo . . . associates the male heroes of the Revolution with subjectivity and 'the people,' whilst the mudjahida emerge rather as warped Hollywood stars, stripped of their agency through an obsessive and singular emphasis upon their physical appearances."[41] There is no definitive meaning to any text. And as Kaja Silverman and Jackie Stacey have shown, it is possible to read even sexist texts against the grain, finding pleasure and identification in such works.[42] Perhaps in at least represent-

---

39 Trnka, "The West German Red Army Faction," 316, 317. Trnka posits "a theoretical shift around the '68 movement from a political concern for Third World liberation struggles to the radical identifications with the Third World performed by the RAF and other armed groups" (317).

40 Jan Henschen, "Baader, Belmondo, Brando: Eine Mediengenealogie der jungen RAF-Terroristen," in *Der Linksterrorismus der 1970er-Jahre und die Ordnung der Geschlechter*, ed. Irene Bandhauer-Schöffmann and Dirk van Laak (Trier: Wissenschaftlicher Verlag Trier, 2013), 33–47, here 38–39.

41 Mani Sharpe, "Gender, Myth, Nationalism: Gillo Pontecorvo's *The Battle of Algiers*," in *Open Democracy*, December 18, 2012, https://www.opendemocracy.net/en/gender-myth-nationalism-gillo-pontecorvos-battle-of-algiers/.

42 Kaja Silverman, *The Threshold of the Visible World* (London: Routledge, 1996); Jackie Stacey, *Star Gazing: Hollywood Cinema and Female Spectatorship* (London: Routledge, 1994). See also Rhian E. Jones and Eli Davies, eds., *Under My Thumb: Songs That Hate Women and the Women Who Love Them* (London: Repeater, 2017).

ing women revolutionaries, in however compromised a form, this film offered a flickering of something for the militant woman to pick up.

Viett goes on to describe early acts of militant violence, narrating a sense of exhilaration in, for example, the throwing of Molotov cocktails, before situating such acts in the context of an "imagined community" of violence:[43] "Jeder Steinwurf in die Glasfronten der Bankhäuser verbindet uns mit den Revolutionären in der ganzen Welt, mit dem Vietcong im Dschungel, mit dem ermordeten Che Guevara, mit den Tupamaros in Uruguay, mit den kämpfenden afrikanischen Revolutionären in Angola, Mosambik, Guinea-Bissau, Namibia und Südafrika, mit den großen Schlachten der Arbeiterbewegung, die in den Straßen Berlins geführt wurden" (87; Every stone thrown into the glass fronts of banks connects us to revolutionaries the world over, to the Vietcong in the jungle, to the murdered Che Guevara, to Tupamaros in Uruguay, to fighting African revolutionaries in Angola, Mozambique, Guinea-Bissau, Namibia and South Africa, to the great battles of the workers' movement fought on the streets of Berlin). With the exception of Guevara, a "brash, guntoting, self-confident image of the masculine rebel," according to Sara M. Evans,[44] Viett's description of Third World revolutionary agents here is ostensibly gender neutral. Consistent with the gendered bias implicit in the default masculine plural "Revolutionäre," however, the wider cultural resonances of such constructions of revolutionary agency are masculine-connoted.[45]

Viett's imagined community of violence is not only transnational but also transhistorical: it includes the workers' movement and the legendary street battles fought between Communists and fascists in interwar Berlin. She makes reference to the battles themselves, rather than to any concrete historical agents, reflecting the shadowy nature of the left-wing German past, as it could appear to New Leftists on account of the National Socialist "erasure" of the "German revolutionary tradition" (Brown). While imagining one's fight as part of an ongoing struggle has been important for diverse left-wing movements, as the phrase "Lotta Continua" demonstrates, Brown highlights the particular significance of the revolutionary past for the West German New Left. A "desire to recover this lost revolutionary past . . . became a central component of the West German 1968," making that movement unique: "[it] was marked, in a way that no other radical movement in history had been or has been

---

43 Benedict Anderson, *Imagined Communities: Reflections on the Origin and Spread of Nationalism* (London: Verso, 1991 [1983]).
44 Sara M. Evans, "Sons, Daughters, and Patriarchy: Gender and the 1968 Generation," *American Historical Review* 114, no. 2 (2009): 331–47, here 337.
45 Viett does make use of the gender-neutral plural form on occasion: see reference to "GenossInnen und FreundInnen" (111).

since, by the attempt to historicize and theorize itself in real time."[46] Viett's autobiography exemplifies this historicizing tendency more broadly.[47] Her desire to write herself into history is no doubt also bound up with a need, as both post-terrorist and prison writer, to construct meaning and purpose for her life.[48] Meanwhile, Viett's failure here to imagine concrete revolutionary agents in the German twentieth-century past may point to the difficulty of finding a gendered position and any gendered agency to identify with in that particular context.[49] Though she may strive to insert herself (and comrades) in a radical German antifascist past, this is seemingly not possible; hence she inserts herself into a global radical contemporary history.[50]

At times, Viett constructs herself in more personal terms in relation to transnational, trans/historical revolutionary violence, where that violence transcends the human. Viett first uses the pronoun "wir" (we) to denote a sense of collective political identity and belonging in chapter 3, where that identity/belonging is transnational in scope (73). The pronoun "wir" is then used repeatedly in chapter 4 (see particularly 86–87), suggesting a strong sense of collective (transnational) identity or at least a desire to convey that impression. Then in chapter 5, "wir" has become "ich" (I) when Viett declares bombastically, "Ich war ein Teil des ewigen Kampfes, der überall dort, wo die Unterdrückung nicht mehr ertragen wird, seine revolutionäre Spur hinterläßt. Die Spur der Gegengeschichte. An sie hatte ich mein Leben mit Haut und Haar angekoppelt, nur ihr war ich verpflichtet und verantwortlich" (120; I was part of the eternal struggle that leaves its revolutionary trace wherever oppression will no longer be tolerated. The trace of counterhistory. I had connected my life to it neck and crop, only to that counterhistory was I obligated and answerable). In a passage that is striking for its existential qualities, but also for the sense of exhilaration that she narrates, Viett's sense of self dissolves into an abstract notion of disembodied transnational/transhistorical struggle.

According to certain contemporary West German feminists, women terrorists exhibited self-sacrificing, selfless tendencies that were indicative of a particularly feminine sensibility. In an editorial, "Terroristinnen" (Women Terrorists), in the feminist magazine *Emma* of October 1977,

46   Brown, *West Germany and the Global Sixties*, 13; 105.
47   See in particular the prologue.
48   See also Karcher, "'Ich bin parteilich."
49   On two occasions, Viett cites examples of revolutionary male agency from the distant Germanic past in the form of Thomas Müntzer (10, 89).
50   In her account of Paris later in the text, Viett is able to insert herself and comrades into a radical (French/European) history (conceived as family) with French revolutionaries Maximilien Robespierre and Louis Blanqui as great-grandfather and grandfather, respectively (227).

Alice Schwarzer asserted, "Frauen haben Übung in Selbstaufgabe. Haben sie sich bisher für Menschen aufgeopfert, so tun sie es in diesem Falle für eine Sache—die oft so abstrakt ist, daß sie mit ihrer Person kaum noch zu tun hat: ihre Identität tritt bis zur Selbstleugnung zurück" (Women are well practiced in self-sacrifice. While until now they have been sacrificing themselves for other people, here they are doing it for something that is often so abstract that it has barely anything to do with themselves: their identities withdraw to the point of self-denial).[51] Edelgart Quensel, meanwhile, suggested that feminine traits such as selflessness and loyalty made women ideal candidates for terrorism ("besonders geeignet" [particularly suitable]).[52] This is an extraordinary, counterintuitive claim. Though women terrorists such as Viett might have been tapping into key aspects of women's gendered subjectivity at the time, this does not mean that they were merely living out their normative gendered script, as was the implication. Choosing to direct that self-sacrificing sensibility in a different, nonheteronormative direction, particularly at this historical moment, is the result of a strong degree of agency. Understandings of terrorist women as typically feminine are not only the result of a huge logical strain, then (these are surely extraordinary women), they also reveal the limited ways in which women's politically violent agency could be conceptualized at the time.[53]

A self-sacrificing, passionate sensibility is frequently in evidence in Viett's text. As she declares one page earlier, again assertively locating herself in a grand sweep of history, "Ich genoß mein neues Leben im Untergrund. Ich hatte ein stolzes, starkes Gefühl der totalen Hingabe an eine Sache, für die seit Jahrhunderten die besten Menschen ihre Kraft und ihr Leben hingegeben hatten" (119; I enjoyed my new life in the underground. I had a proud, strong feeling of total devotion to something that the best of humanity had been devoting their power and life to for centuries [see also 10, 90]). According to both Pilzweger and Reimann, a heroic, self-sacrificing model of masculinity functioned as ideal for the antiauthoritarian movement, with the murdered Guevara seen as the embodiment of those qualities.[54] Postterrorist life writing by

51 Alice Schwarzer, "Terroristinnen," *Emma* (October 1977): 5.
52 Edelgart Quensel, "Auf der Suche nach Identität," in *Frauen und Terror: Versuche, die Beteiligung von Frauen an Gewalttaten zu erklären*, ed. Susanne von Paczensky (Reinbek bei Hamburg: Rowohlt, 1978), 69–78, here 72.
53 A different perspective was put forward by RAF founding member Gudrun Ensslin. As Patricia Melzer points out, Ensslin claimed that women, on account of their alienating cultural role within the family, were predisposed to be "radical thinkers and ultimately to become under-ground guerrillas if they ever want to achieve an authentic self." Melzer, *Death in the Shape of a Young Girl*, 92.
54 Pilzweger, *Männlichkeit zwischen Gefühl und Revolution*, 179; Reimann, "Zwischen Machismo und Coolness," 235–36.

West German male militants such as Michael Baumann and Till Meyer, however, shows no evidence of such a sensibility.[55]

Viett is seemingly able to identify, then, with a masculine-connoted and at times masculinist "imagined community of global revolt" (Simon Prince). But her construction of it has German and gendered particularities. While a need to locate one's own struggle historically has been identified as a particularly German phenomenon, Viett's representation of a transnational, trans/historical community of violence goes further. Her apparent identification with an implicitly masculine history has strikingly feminine dimensions as Viett imagines herself, in self-sacrificing terms, as part of a transcendent revolutionary struggle, indicative perhaps of the unavailability for her of this masculine history/global "imagined community."

Encountering (Male) Violent Agency Elsewhere

I now turn to Viett's construction in the text of the few embodied examples of violent agency elsewhere: the Palestinian guerrilla fighters whom she encountered in the Middle East. The Middle East as locale and the Palestinian Liberation Movement in particular played a crucial role for West German militant groups from the late 1960s onward. Jeremy Varon has suggested that Palestinians and their cause were a stronger source of identification than the Vietcong for West German activists and militants, among other reasons because of the proximity of the Middle East, as well as "existential source[s] of affinity," such as a shared sense of being "politically and spiritually homeless."[56] For Thomas Skelton-Robinson, it is "praktisch unmöglich" (practically impossible) to tell the story of West German left-wing terrorism without discussion of the Middle East and the Palestinian movement.[57] It was the experience of guerrilla military training in Jordan that catalyzed the formation of the first urban guerrilla group in the Federal Republic: the Tupamaros West Berlin, who perpetrated the earliest urban guerrilla attacks in November 1969.[58] In contrast to Vietnamese fighters and those of many other Third World

---

55 Michael Baumann, *Wie alles anfing* (1975; Berlin: Rotbuch Verlag, 2007); Till Meyer, *Staatsfeind* (1996; Berlin: Rotbuch Verlag, 2008).

56 Varon, *Bringing the War Home*, 69. Further reasons cited for this claim include a possible "thinly veiled anti-Semitism," as well as "the self-serving sense that they, as the post-Nazi generation, were utterly free of anti-Semitism and therefore had license to condemn Israel without qualification or apology" (70).

57 Skelton-Robinson, "Im Netz verheddert," 903.

58 See Wolfgang Kraushaar, *Die Bombe im jüdischen Gemeindehaus* (Hamburg: Hamburger Edition, 2005).

revolutionary groups, West German militants came into at times sustained close contact with Palestinian fighters. These encounters took place in the Middle East; for example, when they were undertaking guerrilla military training in Jordan, Lebanon, and Yemen,[59] and later when they were planning collaborative actions such as the Landshut plane hijack during the notorious "German Autumn" of 1977, regarded as the violent climax of West Germany's terrorist period. Such encounters also took place in Europe.[60]

Viett narrates six visits to the Middle East, including two experiences of guerrilla military training. Though Palestinian and other Third World women were active as fighters in conflicts in the Middle East, and women from diverse trans/national revolutionary groups undertook guerrilla military training there,[61] Viett only mentions encounters with male Palestinian fighters in that context. In her text, those fighters serve as a sort of guerrilla ideal whose revolutionary masculinity eclipses that of her German male comrades. The first training Viett undertook was in Lebanon in 1975, together with Ralf Reinders ("Bär" in her text)[62] and Hans, a member of Bewegung 2. Juni who was not operating "underground"[63] and whose revolutionary commitment the group wanted to test.

In her account Viett juxtaposes Palestinian military trainer Chalil's revolutionary masculinity with the unstable masculinity of Hans. Her description of Hans as he practices throwing a hand grenade, "wie so oft etwas unschlüssig und unsicher" (155; as so often somewhat indecisive and uncertain), establishes him as the polar opposite of the masculine urban guerrilla ideal elaborated by Brazilian revolutionary Marighella in his influential *Minimanual of the Urban Guerrilla* of 1969, where decisiveness, bravery, and competence with weapons are of central

---

59 It is also likely that they encountered guerrilla fighters of other groups while in the Middle East. See Skelton-Robinson, "Im Netz verheddert."

60 See Christopher Daase, "Die RAF und der internationale Terrorismus: Zur transnationalen Kooperation klandestiner Organisationen," in Kraushaar, *Die RAF und der linke Terrorismus*, 2:905–29.

61 On the participation of women fighters who were active particularly in the earliest phase of the Lebanese civil war (1975–90), see Jennifer Philippa Eggert, "'The Mood Was an Explosion of Freedom': The 1968 Movement and the Participation of Women Fighters during the Lebanese Civil War," in Colvin and Karcher, *Women, Global Protest Movements*, 151–67, here 163.

62 Viett uses a combination of aliases, first names, and nicknames to refer to group members (including herself) in her accounts of actions/operations that have not yet been investigated (341).

63 On the different levels of membership in Bewegung 2. Juni, see Meyer, *Staatsfeind*, 299, 306.

importance.[64] Viett narrates how Hans drops the hand grenade on the floor behind himself and becomes rooted to the spot. He is saved by Chalil, whose body Viett likens to a (phallic) weapon: "Noch im Fallen sehe ich den Körper von Chalil wie einen abgeschossenen Pfeil auf Hans zufliegen" (Falling to the floor I see the body of Chalil flying toward Hans like an arrow). Viett continues, emphasizing Chalil's revolutionary discipline, self-sacrifice, and bravery: "Chalil war schwer verletzt. Er hatte die Splitterladung mit seinem Körper abgefangen, unter dem er Hans geborgen hatte. Ganz ruhig lag er da, bei klarem Bewußtsein, und befahl Bassem [a second military trainer], sich zuerst um Hans zu kümmern, dem nur zwei kleine Splitter ins Bein gedrungen waren. Chalil hatte ihm zweifellos das Leben gerettet, unter Nichtachtung seines eigenen" (155; Chalil was seriously injured. He had intercepted the bulk of the fragments with his body under which he had saved Hans. He lay there completely still, fully conscious, and commanded Bassem to first take care of Hans, whose leg had been penetrated only by two small fragments. Chalil had without doubt saved his life without so much as a thought for his own). After Hans has recovered in the hospital, Viett comments drily, "Hans beendete seinen Flirt mit dem Guerillakampf. Wir brachten einen wehleidigen Genossen zurück nach Berlin" (156; Hans ended his flirtation with the guerrilla struggle. We brought a sniveling comrade back to Berlin). Hans's masculinity is undercut by the idea that he merely "flirts" with the armed struggle, and by the attribution to him of inappropriate emotions ("wehleidig" [sniveling]), particularly for the male revolutionary.

In Viett's depiction, Chalil's self-sacrificing qualities are tied in a much more tangible sense to his violent agency and body than they are in her account of her own, more abstract (feminine) self-sacrifice, discussed above. Her construction of Chalil approximates the heroic, self-sacrificing masculine ideal for West German male New Leftists put forward by Pilzweger and Reimann that, evidence suggests, German militant men struggled to embody in reality.[65] Viett's representation is furthermore indicative of the "fetishization of [Third World] physical bodies engaged

64 Carlos Marighella, *Minimanual of the Urban Guerrilla*, accessed April 28, 2022, https://www.marxists.org/archive/marighella-carlos/1969/06/minimanual-urban-guerrilla/index.htm. Marighella's *Minimanual*, first translated into German in 1970, was a key theoretical text for the RAF. On the text's masculinist underpinnings, see Stefanie Pilzweger, "Terroristische Selbstinszenierung und massenmediale Fremddarstellung der Männlichkeiten in der Roten Armee Fraktion," in Bandhauer-Schöffmann and von Laak, *Der Linksterrorismus der 1970er-Jahre*, 49–73.

65 See Baumann, *Wie alles anfing*; Meyer, *Staatsfeind*. Note also how neither Pilzweger nor Reimann provide quotations from (former) New Leftists that exemplify this sensibility. Pilzweger, *Männlichkeit zwischen Gefühl und Revolution*, 179; Reimann, "Zwischen Machismo und Coolness," 235–36.

in struggle" that Trnka has critiqued in the writings and speeches of student leaders Dutschke and Hans-Jürgen Krahl and later in the communicative strategies of West German armed groups.[66] Trnka does not discuss West German militants' actual encounters with Third World subjects, nor what Slobodian terms "the tension between abstract identification and embodied collaboration"[67] that is in evidence in Viett's text, as discussed below. Viett's construction also recalls the "radical orientalism" conceptualized by Judy Tzu-Chun Wu to capture "how some American activists romanticized and identified with revolutionary Asian nations and political figures" in the 1960s and early 1970s. That sensibility, Wu asserts, "followed an orientalist tradition of perceiving a dichotomy between the East and the West," where "the radicalness of [American activists'] orientalism stemmed from how they inverted and subverted previous hierarchies: American travelers idealized the East and denigrated the West."[68]

In Viett's text, the revolutionary agency of Chalil, but also of other Palestinian men,[69] contrasts starkly with that of the majority of West German male comrades in ways that echo Wu's analysis, though in Viett's case that "denigration" is concentrated in the figure of the West German *male* revolutionary. With the exception of Reinders, Viett persistently undermines her West German male comrades, not least through that same strategy of undercutting their masculinity. She comments of Baumann's and Hans-Peter Knolle's decisions to leave Bewegung 2. Juni as the conflict with the state escalated in 1972 as follows: "Eine Auseinandersetzung mit dem Staat auf Leben und Tod hatten sie sich nicht vorgestellt. Sie hatten Räuber und Gendarm gespielt, wollten high und frei sein, umgeben von ihren Fans" (112; A life-and-death conflict with the state was not something they'd imagined. They had played at cops and robbers, they wanted to be high and free, surrounded by their fans). The two men's militancy is represented as a children's game/pop-cultural performance, which serves to depoliticize, emasculate, and infantilize them.[70] Elsewhere Viett shows little patience for male posturing, where these empty performances of bravado are revealed for the bluster that they are. When Viett (alias Anna)[71] storms into Meyer's prison cell to free him, during an action in 1978 carried out exclusively by Bewegung 2. Juni women, her own decisive and swift movement, recalling Marighella's, contrasts with Meyer's immobility as he is turned

66 Trnka, "The West German Red Army Faction," 320.
67 Slobodian, *Foreign Front*, 13.
68 Wu, *Radicals on the Road*, 5.
69 See also her description of Abdelatif (173).
70 While Bewegung 2. Juni is often associated with playfulness, Viett's construction of that organization is characterized more by its revolutionary discipline.
71 As with reference to other group members in her account of this operation, Viett uses an alias here.

to stone by a Medusa-like Anna/Viett: "Anna . . . stürmt auf Tills Zelle zu. Sie reißt die Tür auf, und da sitzt er. Wie versteinert, regt sich nicht und sagt kein Wort. . . . Da reagiert er endlich, und sie denkt, über diese Situation wird noch zu reden sein" (206; Anna . . . storms into Till's prison cell. She flings open the door, and he is sitting there. As if petrified, he doesn't move nor say a word. . . . Finally he responds, and she thinks, this will need to be discussed later). She continues, "Jahre später liest Anna in einer Zeitung, daß er von dieser Befreiungsaktion als von 'seinem Ausbruch' sprach. Das machte sein ganzes Maulheldentum deutlich, mit dem Anna ihre Probleme hatte, seit sie zusammen in der Bewegung waren" (206; Years later Anna reads in a newspaper that he spoke of this armed liberation as "his jailbreak." That demonstrates his whole loudmouth showing off that Anna had had problems with ever since they'd been in the movement together).

Viett's representation of the majority of her German male comrades contrasts not only with that of Palestinian male revolutionaries but also with that of herself and of the female revolutionary ideal of the "unbeugsame Kämpferin" (uncompromising woman fighter) that she constructs in the text.[72] The construction is particularly prominent in chapter 11, in which Viett narrates Meyer's armed prison liberation in considerable detail, representing the Bewegung 2. Juni women undertaking this operation as disciplined, resolute, and highly skilled. While Viett's construction of Palestinian male fighters is juxtaposed with that of West German male militants, it functions in many ways as a template for the paradigm of the woman revolutionary, who is self-sacrificing, disciplined, and committed, that Viett sketches in her text.

Also instructive is Viett's description of the tensions experienced when idealized projections or "radical orientalist" fantasies of Third World revolutionary struggle and a sense of belonging to an "imagined community of global revolt" come up against actual, embodied examples of Third World actors. During her account of how Chalil saved Hans's life, Viett draws attention to how Chalil's example of self-sacrificing, revolutionary agency gave her and Reinders pause for thought: "Der bedingungslose Einsatz der palästinensischen Genossen, wie ein Reflex für das Leben eines anderen Genossen einzustehen, hatte uns schlagartig empfinden lassen, wie weit wir von der Realität des Krieges, den wir in der BRD dem Staat erklärt hatten, entfernt waren" (155; The unquestioning

---

72 She refers admiringly to RAF member Monika Berberich as an "unbeugsame Kämpferin" (167). "Unbeugsamkeit" appears to have been a trope within Bewegung 2. Juni: the title of an interview with Reinders and others references the idea. See *Die Unbeugsamen von der Spree: Interview mit Ronald Fritsch, Gerald Klöpper, Ralf Reinders und Fritz Teufel* (Osnabrück: Packpapierverlag, 1978).

commitment of Palestinian comrades to sacrifice their life for another comrade as a reflex response, suddenly made us grasp how far removed we were from the reality of the war that we had declared on the state in the Federal Republic). She continues, "Für die palästinensischen Fedajin war er [der Krieg] tägliche Wirklichkeit. Für uns war das militärische Training eine romantische Ausnahmesituation" (155; For the Palestinian fedajeen it [war] was a daily reality. For us military training was a romantic state of exceptional circumstances). Observing Chalil, it would seem, led both Viett and Reinders to question their own self-perception and any facile equivalences between West German and Third World contexts. While she may fetishize Third World fighting bodies and regard herself as part of a global "imagined community" of revolutionary struggle, then, Viett is at times self-critical, cognizant of the uneven interconnections between the global and the local.[73]

Viett's construction of embodied examples of violent agency elsewhere is interesting and ambivalent. While the Palestinian male fighter (unlike West German male militants) stands in many ways for ideal guerrilla agency, the template for her emerging paradigm of the woman revolutionary, her construction evinces a fetishizing, "radically orientalizing" sensibility. Viett's accounts of encounters with Palestinian comrades furthermore reveal that those encounters could induce moments of critical reflexivity.

Women's Violent Agency Elsewhere

As discussed above, examples of women's violent agency elsewhere that held identificatory potential for the revolutionary woman, however limited, were known in West Germany. But with the exception of a passing reference to Tamara Bunke,[74] and at least in regard to the geographical "elsewhere," Viett mentions none of these, though she would have been aware of the likes of Angela Davis, Leila Khaled, and women of the Weather Underground; and she may even have encountered women militants from "elsewhere" during her time in the Middle East. Interestingly, too, Viett barely makes reference to iconic West German women militants

---

73 See also her account of a euphoric sense of belonging upon arrival in Beirut, which is swiftly undercut when she realizes she is being taken for an American imperialist (151–52).

74 Viett mentions Bunke, an East-German revolutionary, born in Argentina, who fought alongside Guevara in the Bolivian insurgency of 1966–1967, in her discussion of time spent in the GDR (287). She also makes passing reference to posters of a women's brigade of the socialist Yemeni army that she sees at Aden airport (260).

Ulrike Meinhof and Gudrun Ensslin;[75] her discussion of militant women is, for the most part, limited to those with whom she worked closely. On the face of it, then, and at least with reference to constructions of violent agency elsewhere, Viett's text would seem to support Kätzel's suggestion that "many [women '68ers] did not identify as women, but rather—in an ostensibly gender-neutral way—as people."[76] As well as evincing a profoundly gendered and, at times, feminist sensibility, however,[77] Viett's text demonstrates a desire to plot herself into a history of women's revolutionary agency, even though she does not identify as a feminist in the text and has distanced herself and women comrades from the feminist movement in public statements.[78] This desire is indicated by her occasional construction of and seeming identification with—primarily historical—examples of women's violent agency elsewhere. As with her self-representation as "Teil des ewigen Kampfes," discussed above, this construction is personal: Viett uses "ich" rather than "wir."

Recounting her childhood in chapter 1, Viett explains that since her birthday was ignored when she was a child, she decided years later to set the date as January 15 because—strikingly—it was the date of Rosa Luxemburg's death (14).[79] Clearly, Luxemburg was a significant figure for Viett:[80] not only was she a revolutionary woman and from the

---

75 Ensslin is not mentioned at all; Meinhof is mentioned with reference to violent prison conditions (98–99) and later in passing (107).

76 Gisela Diewald-Kerkmann makes a similar point about RAF and Bewegung 2. Juni militant women, arguing "dass sie sich nicht in erster Linie als Frauen, sondern als 'Revolutionäre' und als 'Kämpfer' im bewaffneten Kampf verstanden' (that they didn't understand themselves first and foremost as women, but rather as "revolutionaries" and as "fighters" [Diewald-Kerkmann uses the default masculine collective noun here] in the armed struggle). Gisela Diewald-Kerkmann, "'. . . es gab Tausende mit einer ähnlichen Biografie, die sich nicht so entschieden haben'—Frauen und Rote Armee Fraktion," in *Terroristinnen—Bagdad '77: Die Frauen der RAF*, ed. Katrin Hentschel and Traute Hensch (Berlin: der Freitag, 2009), 107–39, here 115.

77 On that sensibility see Melzer, *Death in the Shape of a Young Girl*, 198–209; Gerhardt, *Screening the Red Army Faction*, 221–27; Bielby, "Narrating the Revolutionary Self."

78 See Gisela Diewald-Kerkmann, "Bewaffnete Frauen im Untergrund: Zum Anteil von Frauen in der RAF und der *Bewegung 2. Juni*," in Kraushaar, *Die RAF und der linke Terrorismus*, 1:657–75, here 674. On RAF/Bewegung 2. Juni women constituting a feminist practice (rather than as feminist subjects), see Melzer, *Death in the Shape of a Young Girl*.

79 This was part of Viett's invented life story in the context of her new identity in the GDR. Karcher, "'Ich bin parteilich,'" 97.

80 Viett mentions Luxemburg a second time in the text, in the context of a discussion of revolutionary role models (only one of whom is a woman) of the

German past; she also wrote powerful prison letters.⁸¹ And it is interesting that Viett takes the anniversary of Luxemburg's violent death, rather than of her birth, as her birthday. No doubt also indicating the significance of January 15 in the GDR,⁸² this choice reflects the importance—for Viett and more broadly—of Luxemburg as martyr figure, and how it tends to be "over their dead bodies" that women have most cultural impact⁸³—a masculine/masculinist perspective that Viett seems to have internalized here. This invocation of Luxemburg can be read more subversively, however, as indicative of Viett's desire, conscious or otherwise, to situate herself as picking up where Luxemburg left off, though not in any straightforward temporal sense. Viett does not position herself as Luxemburg's daughter or granddaughter, suggesting a desire for alternative constructions of history that are not based on heterosexual reproductivity and the generational paradigm that is so central to German conceptualizations of history.⁸⁴

A second example of women's violent agency elsewhere features in chapter 5, where Viett recounts how she learned to shoot her gun—and here she does posit a genealogical connection of sorts:

> Im Tegeler Forst und im Grunewald hatte ich das Schießen gelernt. Eine kleine, handliche 9-mm-Beretta mit Geschichte lag nachts unter meinem Kopfkissen und steckte, wenn ich die Straße betrat, in meinem Gürtel. Sie war einst silberglänzend gewesen. Die Zeit hatte Rostnarben in die Oberfläche des Stahls gegraben, ganz so wie die Spuren des Lebens in die Haut eines reifen Menschen. Mir gefiel die alte tadellos funktionierende Waffe. Ihr war der Partisanenkampf in naßkalten Wäldern und Bergen anzusehen, und sie vermittelte eine geschichtliche Kontinuität von den Kämpfen der jugoslawischen Widerstandsbewegung gegen die deutschen Faschisten zu meinem Kampf gegen dieselben Grundübel, denselben Geist, der dreißig

---

anarchist group Schwarze Hilfe, to which Viett belonged prior to joining Bewegung 2. Juni (89).

81 In what is likely the first letter that Viett wrote from prison after her arrest in 1990, addressed to her female partner, Viett requests two volumes of Rosa Luxemburg's writing. Inge Viett, *Einsprüche! Briefe aus dem Gefängnis* (Hamburg: Edition Nautilus, 1996), 9.

82 January 15 was commemorated each year in East Berlin.

83 Colvin, "'Wir Frauen haben kein Vaterland,'" 121. See also Elisabeth Bronfen, *Over Her Dead Body: Death, Femininity and the Aesthetic* (Manchester: Manchester University Press, 1992).

84 According to Heinz Bude, Germany can be understood as "das Land der Generationen" (the country of generations). Heinz Bude, "'Generation' im Kontext: Von den Kriegs- zu den Wohlfahrtsstaats-generationen," in *Generationen: Zur Relevanz eines wissenschaftlichen Grundbegriffs*, ed. Ulrike Jureit and Michael Wildt (Hamburg: Hamburger Edition, 2005), 28–44, here 31.

Jahre zuvor schrankenlos und entfesselt über die Völker hergefallen war. Vielleicht hätte sie bereits einer Partisanin Schutz gegeben. Sie war für eine Frauenhand vortrefflich geeignet. Ich pflegte sie wie ein kostbares Erbstück. (124)

[I had learned to shoot in Tegel Forest and in Grunewald. A small, handy Beretta M9 with its own history lay under my pillow at night and was tucked into my belt when out on the street. At one time it had been silvery. Time had scarred the surface of the steel with rust, much like the traces of life in the skin of a mature person. I liked this old, flawlessly functioning weapon. You could see the partisan struggle in cold, damp woods and mountains that it had experienced, and it conveyed a historical continuity from the battles of the Yugoslavian resistance movement against German fascists to my battle against that same fundamental evil, that same spirit that thirty years earlier had boundlessly and limitlessly savaged the people. Perhaps it had already offered protection to a woman partisan. It was particularly suitable for a woman's hand. I looked after it like a precious heirloom.]

Viett's focus is clearly on the weapon, which she humanizes and feminizes (note the feminine gender of "Beretta" and "Waffe" [weapon] and repeated use of the pronoun "sie" [she]), fleshing the object out with a history of antifascism and depicting it as a protective older woman bearing marks and scars of experience. By means of the weapon Viett connects herself to the Yugoslavian resistance movement and its battles against National Socialism, though crucially the weapon provides protection ("Schutz") rather than aggression. She therefore conveniently distances herself and her own violence from National Socialist violence. At the end of the passage and in tentative terms, Viett imagines that she has inherited the weapon from a female partisan, thus writing herself into a more explicitly gendered history of antifascist resistance, and again putting forward an alternative, perhaps even queering model of inheritance/genealogy that, unlike the Vietnamese guerrilla mother discussed above, is not reliant on heterosexual reproductivity or the figure of the child but rather on the (feminized) weapon.[85] Though not obscured, like the Communist fighters of Weimar Berlin, Viett's *Partisanin* is a hazy figure whose representation is heavily overshadowed by an inanimate object. The image is a rather lonely one, devoid of tangible (female) community and solidarity,

---

85 See Lee Edelman, *No Future: Queer Theory and the Death Drive* (Durham, NC: Duke University Press, 2004). For Judith/Jack Halberstam, queer is "inherently linked to a temporality of disruption." Jack Halberstam, *Gaga Feminism: Sex, Gender, and the End of Normal* (Boston: Beacon Press, 2012), 11.

as a solitary Viett imagines an imaginary woman in a cold, dark forest; a context that contrasts comically with Berlin's Grunewald.

Aside from mention of Bunke, these are the only two instances of women's violent agency elsewhere in the text. When considered alongside her representations of male or ostensibly gender-neutral violent agency elsewhere, discussed in the previous two sections of this chapter, Viett's constructions of women's violent agency elsewhere are more rooted in the past with a connection that is more personal. They also gesture toward Viett's desire to plot herself into an alternative history or genealogy of women's violent agency. The fact, however, that this is done on the basis of a historical revolutionary woman whose violent death is emphasized, and an imagined *Partisanin* who is overshadowed by an inanimate object, serves as an indictment of how little subjective room for maneuver Viett has.

Conclusion

As this chapter has demonstrated, violent agency elsewhere, be that in a geographical or temporal sense, offered Viett significant points of identification in the re/construction of her militant subjectivity, safely distanced from the National Socialist violent past. But her representation of it is contradictory and ambivalent, suggestive of how she is searching for and trying out different models in a context in which there was little discursive space to imagine women's revolutionary agency, and in the further context of her urgent need to construct meaning for her postterrorist life while imprisoned.

Though Viett narrates her identification with an "imagined community of global revolt," its (implicitly) masculine/masculinist discourses, icons, and affects seemingly no barrier to her own identification, her construction of it is idiosyncratic and, at times, strikingly feminine. Not only does she construct that imagined community as transhistorical; it has transhuman dimensions, indicative of Viett's gendered subjectivity and perhaps unconsciously pointing to the unavailability of this masculine history/global "imagined community" for her as a woman. Meanwhile Viett's construction of embodied examples of violent agency elsewhere that she encountered, in the form of male Palestinian guerrilla fighters, suggests that these provided a strong model for Viett's own militant subjectivity and for her emerging paradigm of the woman revolutionary. As disciplined revolutionary fighter, selflessly devoted to the political cause, Chalil provides an ideal point of identification for Viett as West German militant woman, whose gendered socialization meant that embodying those same qualities may have come more easily to her than it did to German male militants whose ego, bravado, and bluster, evidence suggests, could get in the way. At the same time, identification with (male) violent agency elsewhere, and disidentification with German male violent agency, meant that Viett was able to distance herself and her violence from the Nazi associations of German violent masculinity and therefore—in part at least—from National Socialist violence. Finally, Viett's identification with Luxemburg and the imagined figure of the *Partisanin*, as two striking examples of *women*'s revolutionary agency elsewhere, point to Viett's desire to position herself in a gendered history of violent agency, and to the seeming limitations of her identification with the (implicitly) masculine/masculinist global community/history of revolt. The fact that these figures are overshadowed by their violent death (in the case of Luxemburg) and by an inanimate object (in the case of the *Partisanin*), however, reveal the lack of usable female models available to Viett.

Though the models of violent agency elsewhere in circulation were overwhelmingly masculine/masculinist, then, they were able to offer Viett important points of identification—in however contradictory a manner. And they seemingly offered her far more than the models available at "home" in the contemporary Federal Republic of Germany in which she was most active. What might all this tell us about West German constructions of violent agency elsewhere and gender more broadly? And how representative is Viett's text of West German women revolutionaries in this regard?

What is particular to Viett's text is its sense of existential urgency, not least as a work of prison writing. The text conveys Viett's palpable need to re/construct a historically meaningful life, as she identifies, for instance, with transhuman notions of history and with historical figures such as Luxemburg, who had also spent time in prison and written powerful accounts of that experience. By contrast, a tendency to identify with and idealize Third World and Black male revolutionaries, not least on account of perceived commonalities, was discernible more widely among New Left revolutionary women.[86] At the same time, and beyond the "fraught" nature of contemporary representations of revolutionary women as discussed above, the fact that Viett will certainly have known and possibly encountered further examples of women's violent agency elsewhere during her militant career, but does not mention these, may be indicative of a more widespread tendency among women at the time to disidentify with the feminine.[87] A form of internalized misogyny that women had to unlearn through the women's liberation movement, this tendency was particularly

---

86 See, for example, feminist activist and filmmaker Cristina Perincioli's account of identifying with the Black Panthers and the "electrifying" experience of seeing images of them. Perincioli, *Berlin wird feministisch*, 43; 51.

87 On that tendency in the Italian context, see Luisa Passerini, *Autobiography of a Generation*, trans. Lisa Erdberg (1988; Middletown, CT.: Wesleyan University Press, 1996), 32–36.

pronounced at a time at which women were striving to break out of their normative femininity. Yet Viett does valorize (German) woman militants in her text, as can be seen in her paradigm of the *unbeugsame Kämpferin*. And this circumstance serves as a further example of the contradiction and ambivalence that characterize her autobiography.

Though ultimately found wanting in Viett's case, it may be that violent agency elsewhere was particularly generative and necessary for the woman militant in a context in which the ability to look outward, be open to, and identify with the elsewhere was more characteristic of a (stereotypically feminine) fissured, fragile subjectivity, as is evident with Viett. At the same time, the sense of searching that characterizes Viett's representation of violent agency elsewhere bespeaks a potentially gendered need for workable models of revolutionary agency with which to identify; something that may be less important for the male militant, whose revolutionary identity is more self-evident and who therefore has less of a need to look beyond himself and his own bounded ego.

8: Problematizing Political Violence in the Federal Republic of Germany: A Hauntological Analysis of the NSU Terror and a Hyper-Exceptionalized "9/11"

Katharina Karcher and Evelien Geerts[1]

Manchmal rütteln uns Berichte über skrupellose rechtsextremistische Gewalttäter auf. Für einige Tage bestimmen sie die Schlagzeilen der Nachrichten. Manchmal bleibt auch der Name einer Stadt als Tatort im Gedächtnis. Doch oft genug nehmen wir solche Vorfälle eher nur als Randnotiz wahr. Wir vergessen zu schnell—viel zu schnell. Wir verdrängen, was mitten unter uns geschieht; vielleicht, weil wir zu beschäftigt sind mit anderem; vielleicht auch, weil wir uns ohnmächtig fühlen gegenüber dem, was um uns geschieht.[2]

[Sometimes reports about the violence of unscrupulous right-wing extremists shake us up. For a few days, they make headlines. Occasionally, the name of the city where the crime took place becomes a lasting memory. Most of the time, however, we consider such events only marginally. We forget too quickly—far too quickly. We repress what happens right here in our midst; maybe because we are too busy with other things; maybe also because we feel a sense of powerlessness when it comes to what happens around us.]

THIS CHAPTER DISCUSSES the lives and deaths of some of the forgotten victims of far-right violence in the Federal Republic of Germany

---

1   This research was funded by the European Research Council and is part of the project "Urban Terrorism in Europe (2004–19): Remembering, Imagining, and Anticipating Violence" at the University of Birmingham (851329)

2   Chancellor Angela Merkel in a speech about the NSU terror on February 23, 2012. "Die Hintergründe der Taten lagen im Dunkeln—viel zu lange," *Sueddeutsche.de*, February 23, 2012, https://www.sueddeutsche.de/politik/merkels-gedenkrede-fuer-neonazi-opfer-im-wortlaut-die-hintergruende-der-taten-lagen-im-dunkeln-viel-zu-lange-1.1291733. Unless otherwise stated, translations are the authors' own.

(FRG; West Germany).³ Specific focus will be on three brutal killings committed by the German neo-Nazi terror group Nationalsozialistischer Untergrund (National Socialist Underground; NSU) in 2000 and 2001,[4] which were overshadowed by the violent events in the US in 2001 that made global headlines as "9/11."[5] The September 11 attacks are often described as a caesura or turning point in the history of terrorism and political violence. As we will show, however, in the FRG they reinforced a preexisting tendency among the white German majority to forget about victims of far-right violence. While the September 11 attacks were conceptualized as a hyper-exceptional event—as "9/11"—supposedly changing the course of history forever,[6] the NSU killings were wrongly classified as ordinary crimes committed by foreigners. As we shall see, they were labeled "Bosphorus murders" by investigating authorities and derogatively referred to as "kebab murders" in the German press. While the police response, media reaction, and NSU trial (re)traumatized the victims, they gave the (white) majority a sense of closure.

In what follows, we analyze the affect-laden "lingering trouble"[7] that the NSU killings and their problematic reception history provoke through a critical (new) materialist hauntological perspective.[8] Such trouble

---

3   Anna Brausam, "Todesopfer rechter Gewalt seit 1990," *Antonio Amadeo Stiftung*, December 10, 2012, https://www.amadeu-antonio-stiftung.de/rassismus/todesopfer-rechter-gewalt/.

4   The NSU was a far-right terrorist organization responsible for numerous crimes including ten murders, two bombings, and more than ten armed robberies between 2000 and 2007. The only person who stood trial for membership in the NSU is Beate Zschäpe.

5   The September 11 attacks will be referred to as "9/11" in this piece only when the hyper-exceptionalization process and the citational value of 9/11 as "9/11" are underlined.

6   "Hyper-exceptional" is used here as by Jacques Derrida in Giovanna Borradori, *Philosophy in a Time of Terror: Dialogues with Jurgen Habermas and Jacques Derrida* (Chicago: University of Chicago Press, 2003) as part of the "Derrida-Habermas" dialogues on September 11. Taking place in New York not too long after said attacks, these dialogues give readers an insight into 9/11's impact on the sociopolitical and philosophical landscape. Also see Evelien Geerts, *Materialist Philosophies Grounded in the Here and Now: Critical New Materialist Constellations & Interventions in Times of Terror(ism)* (Santa Cruz: University of California Press, 2019), for more contextualization.

7   Avery F. Gordon, *Ghostly Matters: Haunting and the Sociological Imagination* (Minneapolis: University of Minnesota Press, 2008), xix.

8   New materialist thought is a type of post-poststructuralist philosophy that emphasizes the subject's worldly embedment and material embodiment, as well as the agency of the more-than-human. See Rick Dolphijn and Iris van der Tuin, *New Materialism: Interviews & Cartographies* (Ann Arbor, MI: Open Humanities Press, 2012); Rosi Braidotti, *The Posthuman* (Cambridge: Polity Press, 2013). Critical new materialist thought stands for those new materialist theories that

requires a hauntological perspective, we would like to argue, as hauntology not only captures the immaterial characteristics of that trouble as they unsettle spatiotemporality, but, in addition, it captures the material events that provoked said trouble and allows us to show how some of the most horrific home-grown terrorist acts in the postwar Federal Republic have been prescribed an "exotic violence [from] elsewhere" status. As a space-time–crossing perspective, hauntology sheds a different light on the hyper-exceptionalized September 11 attacks vis-à-vis NSU's exoticized terror, as it disturbs the narrative of linear temporal progression that supports the construction of 9/11 as "9/11"; that is, as the most important caesura in the contemporary history of terrorism and political violence. It does so by zooming in on moments pre-, during, and post-NSU murders in nonlinear, diffracted ways, showing that there was a tendency to link crime and terrorism to imagined and real violence in other parts of the world. To unpack and problematize this "exoticizing elsewhere" dynamic and its many haunting materializations across space-time, we therefore rely on the materialist methodology of diffraction, that, because of its particular philosophical roots and queering nature, neatly complements such a hauntological point of view.[9] By diffractively weaving together crit-

---

incorporate a strong power analytic and build onto the critical materialist tradition of thinkers such as Theodor W. Adorno, Max Horkheimer, and Walter Benjamin. Also see Evelien Geerts, "Nieuw Materialisme: Een Kritische Cartografie," *Wijsgerig Perspectief* 61, no. 2 (2021): 34–41. The conceptual-methodological perspective that is explored in this piece is in line with the following critical materialist and new materialist authors' works: Benjamin, "Critique of Violence," in *Reflections: Essays, Aphorisms, Autobiographical Writings* (New York: Schocken Books, 1978), 277–300, and "Theses on the Philosophy of History," in *Illuminations: Essays and Reflections* (New York: Schocken Books, 2007), 253–64; Derrida, "Force of Law: The Mystical Foundation of Authority," in *Deconstruction and the Possibility of Justice* (New York: Routledge, 1992), 3–67, and *Specters of Marx: The State of the Debt, the Work of Mourning and the New International* (New York: Routledge, 1994); Gordon, *Ghostly Matters*; Karen Barad, *Meeting the Universe Halfway: Quantum Physics and the Entanglement of Matter and Meaning* (Durham, NC: Duke University Press, 2007), and "Nature's Queer Performativity," *Qui Parle: Critical Humanities and Social Sciences* 19, no. 2 (2011): 121–58. By combining historical materialist (Benjamin and Gordon), deconstructivist-with-Marxist-tendencies (Derrida), and critical new materialist (Barad) authors, philosophical room is made for linking critical new materialist work to previous materialist thought, while giving hauntological research—most often seen as a part of "affect studies"—more material(ist) grounding.

9   See Donna J. Haraway, *Modest_Witness@Second_Millenium: FemaleMan©_Meets_Oncomouse™: Feminism and Technoscience* (New York: Routledge, 1997); Barad, *Meeting the Universe Halfway*. Also see Evelien Geerts and Iris van der Tuin, "Almanac: Diffraction & Reading Diffractively," *Matter: Journal of New Materialist Research* 2, no. 1 (2021): 173–77. As will be noted later, diffraction,

ical theoretical snippets on the troubling powers of hauntology and the September 11 attacks' presumed hyper-exceptionalism and caesura status (9/11 as "9/11"); vignettes and other affect-laden phenomena that paint a fuller picture of the NSU terror; and some of the Federal Republic of Germany's Annual Security Reports, we piece together how this "exoticizing elsewhere" dynamic is constituted.

December 7, 1993 (Buchholz, Germany): A Racist Killing, Definitions of Violence, and the Violence of Definitions

Bakary Singateh, also known as Kolong Jamba, entered the first-class compartment of a train from Hamburg to Bremen. The only other passenger in this part of the train was Wilfried Schubert, a white German engineer traveling home from work. After a short argument about an open window, Schubert stabbed Singateh in the abdomen with a 12 cm knife.[10]

In court, Schubert successfully claimed that he had acted in "Notwehr" (self-defense) against the young Gambian asylum seeker and was acquitted.[11] The victim's brother found it hard to accept the judgment. He commented, "Wenn man in diesem Land einen Hund tötet, kommt man ins Gefängnis. Wenn man einen Menschen tötet, nicht" (If you kill a dog in this country you end up in prison. If you kill a human, you don't).[12] After a successful appeal, the court revised the decision in the case in 1997, and Schubert received a two-year prison sentence. Although colleagues

---

like hauntology, is embedded in materialist, and specifically *new* materialist, thought as well, and is characterized by a similar spatiotemporality-disrupting—here thought of as queering—nature. Because of its space-time–queering character, a diffractive reading and writing methodology is said to transcend the more traditional (and distancing) method of comparison. Meant to produce situated knowledges (also see Donna J. Haraway, "Situated Knowledges: The Science Question in Feminism and the Privilege of Partial Perspective," *Feminist Studies* 14, no. 3 [1988]: 575–99), diffraction focuses on the potential of weaving new threads of understanding that alter the examined phenomena and take into account the affective responses provoked (with)in the researcher(s).

10 "Kampf in der 1. Klasse," *Der Spiegel*, March 9, 1997, https://www.spiegel.de/politik/kampf-in-der-1-klasse-a-1e2d4a25-0002-0001-0000-000008674540?context=issue.

11 "Bakary Singateh alias Kolong Jamba," December 7, 1993, *Antonio Amadeo Stiftung*, https://www.amadeu-antonio-stiftung.de/todesopfer-rechter-gewalt/bakary-singateh-alias-kolong-jamba/.

12 "Kampf in der 1. Klasse."

reported that he had repeatedly made derogatory remarks about Black people, the court ruled out racist motives. Instead, the judges attributed the attack against Singateh to the victim's irritating behavior and the perpetrator's undiagnosed personality disorder.

Bakary Singateh is not among the 109 people officially recognized as having been killed by right-wing extremists in the FRG since 1990, but journalists and activists have identified him as one of more than 100 "vergessene Tote" (forgotten dead).[13] The court's failure to recognize the political nature of the attack against Bakary Singateh reflects a broader pattern. Often, violence linked to far-right ideologies appears to be spontaneous and targeted against marginalized groups. Although this violence can create an atmosphere of terror and intimidation among significant parts of the population, many violent attacks that contribute to this atmosphere of terror do not meet the definition of violent political extremism in the FRG. Schubert, for example, was clearly no (neo-)Nazi, and his attack was not "political" in the sense that it did not constitute a premeditated act of violence with the clear objective of undermining or overthrowing the democratically elected government. To understand the evolution and impact of this narrow concept of political extremism in the FRG, we need both to go back to the postwar years and to move forward to the twenty-first century.

After the end of World War II, the Allied powers introduced a range of "denazification" measures with the aim of destroying the political and cultural power of Nazism. In the following decades, political authorities in the FRG were keen to move on. Trying to establish a "wehrhafte Demokratie" (democratic state that could defend itself), West German authorities created a range of institutions to monitor and control what was held to be political extremism. In this context, *extremism* is an umbrella term for all efforts to undermine the FRG's constitutional democracy. As part of this effort, the Federal Republic's domestic intelligence agency, the Bundesamt für Verfassungsschutz (Federal Office for the Protection of the Constitution) releases an annual report on potential threats to the German state and its citizens. The first report was published in 1969 and focused on the turbulent year 1968.

In the 1970 national security report, threats to the state and its citizens were divided into four categories: "Bestrebungen" (efforts) by the radical right, "Bestrebungen" by the radical left, espionage, and "sicherheitsgefährdende Bestrebungen von Ausländern" (safety-endangering efforts by foreigners). Over the years, some new categories were added, but the classification has remained more or less the same.[14] Right- and

---

13 Brausam, "Todesopfer rechter Gewalt seit 1990."

14 The 1997 report included the new category "Scientology Organisation"; the 2005 report introduced "Islamistische/islamistisch-terroristische

left-wing extremism were seen as domestic problems if they were linked to white German nationals. By contrast, until 2005 all political activity linked to non-German subjects or immigrants fell into the catchall category "foreign extremism." Like espionage, the political activity of foreigners in Germany was seen as a major threat to the state because it was believed to have the potential to bring the problems associated with violence elsewhere to the FRG. As we will show, this classification and the ways in which it has been applied can be seen as both cause and result of institutional racism.

Nazism and neo-Nazism did not fit into the (self-)image of the supposedly denazified, democratic FRG. This may explain in part why the far right was underestimated for decades. Another reason is that federal authorities defined right-wing extremism in such narrow terms that violence only fell into this category if it had the clear aim to undermine the rights and values enshrined in the German constitution. In 2001, German authorities decided to broaden the focus somewhat by introducing the new category of "politisch motivierte Kriminalität" (politically motivated crime/criminality). This category included political violence motivated by racism, sexism, homophobia, and other forms of prejudice. In order to fall into this category, however, such prejudice had to be formally identified as the main motive for an attack. This did not apply to Singateh's death. As we shall see, in the case of the NSU murders, the investigating authorities did not even consider racism as a motive—casting institutional racism into a type of lingering trouble, in need of a hauntological analysis.

Affective Musings: Political Violence and the "Troubling" Powers of Hauntology

> The way of the ghost is haunting, and haunting is a very particular way of knowing what has happened or is happening. Being haunted draws us affectively, sometimes against our will and always a bit magically, into the structure of feeling of a reality we come to experience, not as cold knowledge, but as a transformative recognition.[15]

Hauntology;[16] spectral hauntings; being haunted ... taken together, these notions point to radical disruptive troublings. Be it the troubling

---

Bestrebungen und Verdachtsfälle" (Islamist and Islamist-terrorist efforts and suspected cases) as a separate category, which meant that it was no longer a subcategory of "safety-endangering efforts by foreigners."

15 Gordon, *Ghostly Matters*, 8.
16 "Hauntology," coined by Derrida (1994), is a play on the French pronunciation of "ontology" (*ontologie*). In *Specters of Marx*, Derrida employs a

caused by critical theorist Walter Benjamin's historical materialist unpacking of how "Gewalt" lies at the heart of the Western nation-state;[17] the deconstruction of Western philosophy's presence/absence dynamics by philosopher Jacques Derrida;[18] or even, as sociologist Avery F. Gordon describes it so beautifully in the above epigraph, the self-reflexive researcher's realization that submission to the research "object" haunting them could lead to a different, more embodied type of knowledge. A type of embodied knowledge that recognizes past sociopolitical transgressions, while making space for that which exceeds the purely representational. . . .

As critical theorists working on all matters of political violence and terrorism, we find that such a "hauntology-as-troubling" perspective strongly resonates with us. This particular perspective and style of writing, in this essay fully embedded in critical (new) materialisms, undoes the traditional epistemological relationship between the researcher, the research "object," and the knowledge produced as strictly separated and "distanced" from one another. In this sense, hauntology makes much-needed space for the agential capacities of research phenomena, such as their ability to provoke something affectively within the researcher in question. This forces the researcher to reflect upon their situated positionality vis-à-vis what haunts, troubles, and, basically, *touches* them. "Hauntology-as-troubling," moreover, highlights the limits of conceptual representationalism that researchers theorizing violence and the traumatic know all too well:[19] the animated state that trauma-laden spectral hauntings often engender in researchers when "repressed or unresolved social violence"[20] announces itself again—through, for instance, the narrating of lived experiences, objects, or artifacts—suggests that concepts and theories at times fall short.

The limits of the conceptual-theoretical certainly become clear when doing research on acts and events of political violence, and especially so when they are terrorism-driven: these acts and events are almost always hauntological in nature, coming back to us as lingering trouble with an added dimension of perceived senselessness; something emotional-affective exceeding the representational. Think of emotions that are often

---

hauntological analysis to disrupt Western philosophy's oppositional absence/presence logics, while writing deconstructionism into the Marxist materialist tradition to show Marxism in fact had never left us.

17 Benjamin, "Critique of Violence." The term *Gewalt*, as will be demonstrated later in the main text, has multiple, interconnected meanings: "violence," "illegitimately used force," and "institutionally legitimated power."

18 Derrida, "Force of Law"; Derrida, *Specters of Marx*.

19 Representationalism and an overreliance on the discursive are critically inspected in new materialist discussions (on the hauntological). See Barad, *Meeting the Universe Halfway*.

20 Gordon, *Ghostly Matters*, xvi.

expressed by those impacted by terrorist violence—in this particular case the families of the NSU victims, as we will shortly see—such as fear, anger, sadness, . . . and particularly of bodily-animating affects, which are harder to pin down, such as sudden tensions filling the interview, courtroom, or testimonial space, bewilderment, disgust. . . . It is the affective[21]—characterized by what affect theorists Melissa Gregg and Gregory J. Seighworth label as "visceral forces" located in between entities and entities and their representations and found in "those intensities that pass body to body (human, non-human, part-body, and otherwise)"[22]—that encapsulates this space-time–crossing trouble. A kind of bodily felt trouble that, furthermore, long after terrorist acts, events, and attacks have left their marks and markings, keeps remanifesting itself through sociopolitical, bodily, psychological, and other wounds inflicted. Such rematerializing lingering trouble is quite hard to catch, unless spotlighted through a hauntological perspective capturing its triple "inbetweenness": bridging research phenomena and researcher (*through their affectivity*); present and past (*being space-time–crossing from within the here and now*); and immateriality and materiality (*through its rematerializations*).

Working with the grief-filled lived experiences of NSU victims, we soon realized that there was no other option than to let that which unnerves us in this case study take the lead; that is, Germany's troubled relationship with far-right violence. As we will show, the NSU terror materialized itself not only against the backdrop of Germany's troubled relationship with the Nazi past but also in relation to a hyper-exceptionalized "9/11."

Hauntings Diffracted: The NSU-*Mordserie* (series of murders) and a Hyper-Exceptionalized "9/11"

The year 2021 marked the twentieth anniversary of the September 11 attacks in the United States and of three brutal murders committed by

---

21 The affective, affects, and affectivity are all focused on in "affect theory" (Melissa Gregg and Gregory J. Seighworth, eds., *The Affect Theory Reader* [Durham, NC: Duke University Press, 2010]), a humanism-troubling paradigm within literary studies that has a lot in common with new materialist and posthumanist thought. For Deleuzoguattarian thinker Brian Massumi (*Parables for the Virtual: Movement, Affect, Sensation* [Durham, NC: Duke University Press, 2002], 28 and 260n3), affects differ strongly from emotions, as affects, being agency-possessing intensities, do not require a human subject. Affects basically *affect* in their own agential ways and are hence referred to here as separate from more consciously formed emotions.

22 Gregg and Seighworth, *The Affect Theory Reader*, 1.

the NSU. The attacks in the two countries were, however, inscribed into Germany's sociocultural imaginary very differently.

Reflecting on the September 11 attacks, Derrida starts with the act of "recalling."[23] Critical of how the attacks were mediatized—and in particular broadcast live—as the event-of-all-events, Derrida points at hyper-exceptionalization through date-giving and reciting praxes. While all "'major'" events tend to be marked,[24] Derrida claims that the attacks instantly received a citational value that has been reiterated globally by the mass media ever since. Eternally linked to a date, the more the attacks are cited as "9/11" (i.e., as a linear temporality-disturbing hyper-exceptional event), the stronger their reference, or renewed presence in the here and now, becomes. The constant reciting—and rematerialization—of 9/11 as "9/11" thus disrupts and queers space-time. The "matter" that "9/11" is supposed to be referring to in this rematerialization process, however, complicates things, giving everything an extra spectral touch: the fact that a concrete date is used to refer to the event in question shows that we "have no concept and no meaning available" to fully capture and explain the horror brought about by the September 11 attacks.[25] A great deal of the affectivity attached to this event thus escapes our conceptual understanding of it, remaining with us as lingering trouble. . . .

The intricate ways in which the September 11 attacks have been constructed to mean something in Germany stands out when compared to the portrayal of the NSU terror. Three 2021 newspaper articles about "9/11," taken from the *Frankfurter Allgemeine Zeitung*, *Die Welt*, and *Die Zeit*, underscore the contrast between the reception of the home-grown NSU terror and the September 11 attacks:[26] The first article zooms in on terror-capturing pictures that haunted the globe via mass media, perfectly underwriting Derrida's critique of the attacks being constructed as hyper-exceptional. The second one narrates the life and career of a German journalist who was in New York on the day the attacks took place. The final piece is a tribute to one of the German victims who worked at the offices of Deutsche Bank in the World Trade Center.

23 Derrida in Borradori, *Philosophy in a Time of Terror*, 85.
24 Derrida in Borradori, *Philosophy in a Time of Terror*, 90.
25 Derrida in Borradori, *Philosophy in a Time of Terror*, 90.
26 See Alfons Kaiser, "20 Jahre nach 9/11: Die Erinnerungen verblassen nicht," *Frankfurter Allgemeine Zeitung*, September 11, 2021, https://www.faz.net/aktuell/gesellschaft/20-jahre-nach-9-11-die-erinnerungen-verblassen-nicht-17531250.html; Jan P. Burgard, "Und dann denkt man: Ja, da ist er jetzt. In dem ganzen Gewirr und Feuer," *Die Welt*, September 11, 2021, https://www.welt.de/politik/ausland/article233725800/9-11-Hinterbliebene-Und-dann-denkt-man-Ja-da-ist-er-jetzt-In-dem-ganzen-Gewirr-und-Feuer.html; Andrea Böhm, "Der lange Schatten," *Zeit Online*, September 10, 2021, https://www.zeit.de/2021/37/11-september-terror-anschlag-krieg-al-kaida-militaer.

Through annual reciting practices all over the world, 9/11 as "9/11" seems only to have become more important.

To tease out the "exoticizing elsewhere" dynamic in relation to the NSU vis-à-vis the hyper-exceptionalization of 9/11 as "9/11," we utilize a diffractive strategy. Briefly put, diffraction is a physical phenomenon—revealing itself as colorful diffraction patterns when, for example, sunrays hit the surface of a CD-ROM—and a metaphor for more embodied ways of situated theorizing. Put on the map by feminist theorists Donna J. Haraway and Karen Barad, it can be best understood as a critical new materialist methodology or "critical consciousness."[27] Unlike the distancing methodology of scientific reflection, which separates researcher and research phenomena, this critical new materialist methodology looks at how differences materialize in the world and what effects these differences have on knowledge production, subjects, and life. Barad in *Meeting the Universe Halfway* theorizes diffraction through their agential realist philosophy as something that "attends to the relational nature of difference" and therefore can be used as a way of philosophizing.[28] Diffraction "does not fix what is the object and subject in advance, and so . . . diffraction involves reading insights through one another in ways that help illuminate differences as they emerge."[29] A diffractive methodology in our regard is therefore characterized by a certain openness to the hauntological's troubling powers that often assert themselves in (im)material ways.

September 11, 2000 (Nuremberg, Germany): The First NSU Murder, Institutional Racism, and the "Exoticizing Elsewhere" Dynamic

> Semiya Şimşek will never forget the shock and grief she felt at the hospital bed of her dying father. On September 9, NSU members shot her father Enver Şimşek in broad daylight at his flower stall near Nuremberg in Bavaria, Germany. Enver Şimşek was still alive when police officers found him later in the afternoon, but his gun wounds were so serious that he passed away a few days after being rushed to hospital. At the time of the horrific attack, his daughter Semiya was fourteen years old. She and her brother had been born in Germany and had grown up there. Their father was from Salur, a small farming village in the Isparta province, Turkey. He had moved to Germany to work and build a better future for his family. Through decades of hard work, Enver Şimşek had built a successful flower business. He loved the smell of roses, jasmine, olive trees, and pines because it

---

27 Haraway, *Modest_Witness@Second_Millenium*, 273.
28 Barad, *Meeting the Universe Halfway*, 72.
29 Barad, *Meeting the Universe Halfway*, 30.

reminded him of home. Now that their children were almost grown up, he and his wife Adile were planning their return to Salur.

Enver Şimşek's family knew that he wanted his final resting place to be in Salur. A few days after the funeral in Turkey, his wife and children returned to Germany. Instead of experiencing empathy and compassion, they were treated like suspects. The whole family, including children, had to give DNA samples and pose for police photographs. Mobile phones, photo albums, jewelry, notes, buttons, documents, bills, and other personal possessions were confiscated without explanation. Semiya's mother, Adile Şimşek, and other family members were interrogated multiple times.

The murder investigation that began in 2000 followed a pattern that reflects the institutional racism of German authorities.[30] Although there are different definitions, *institutional racism* generally refers to a range of (im)material practices and structures that create and maintain racial inequalities in society on macro and micro levels. Many analyses of institutional racism focus on the macro level and are based on "hard" empirical evidence. Hauntology offers a different—yet complementary—approach to institutional racism. It spotlights the micropolitical or, more precisely, the affective-disruptive power of particular moments and certain phenomena—which for us include objects and human-made artifacts. The lingering trouble that these phenomena and moments provoke can serve as a starting point for an analysis of broader patterns of racist oppression that extend across space-time.

The police investigations into the murder of Enver Şimşek and other NSU victims were fraught with moments that touch upon the affective, the present and past, and the (im)material while underscoring the "exoticizing elsewhere" dynamic addressed above. Investigating authorities labeled the racist NSU murder series in ways that strongly suggested a link to the Turkish Mafia by dubbing them the "Halbmond" (crescent)

---

30 In the UK, the term "institutional racism" received wide attention in 1999 when a public inquiry into the investigation of brutal murder of Stephen Lawrence concluded that the failure to solve this case was linked to institutional racism in the police force (See Sir William MacPherson of Cluny, "The Stephen Lawrence Inquiry: Report of an Inquiry," February 1999, https://assets.publishing.service.gov.uk/government/uploads/system/uploads/attachment_data/file/277111/4262.pdf). In February 2014, the NSU victims' lawyers called for a similar inquiry in Germany to analyze and tackle "the crosscutting theme of institutional racism." Serkan Alkan et al., "Offener Brief," *MIGAZIN*, February 19, 2014, https://www.migazin.de/2014/02/19/nsu-anwaelte-beklagen-das-grosse-abhaken/.

and "Bosporus" (Bosphorus) crimes.³¹ Determined to find evidence for Enver Şimşek's suspected connections to foreign criminal networks, officers used ethically questionable means. Among other things, they tried to provoke his wife, Adile Şimşek, by claiming that her husband had secret affairs and made his money not with flowers but with heroin. Although there was no factual basis to these claims, they were picked up enthusiastically by journalists. The loss of her husband in addition to these unfounded accusations drove Adile Şimşek into a severe depression and traumatized her two children. Semiya Şimşek describes the period between 2000 and 2011 as her father's "second murder" because of the aggressive campaign against him and everything for which he stood.

In the summer of 2012, Semiya Şimşek left Germany and began a new life in Turkey. In her book *Schmerzliche Heimat* (The Painful Homeland, 2013), she notes that she found it difficult to leave Germany, but after the move she felt even closer to her father. She regularly visits her father's grave in Salur and celebrated her wedding in the house he built there for his retirement. While the event still haunts them, she and her family are trying to feel joy again, or as she has put it, "Wir trauern gemeinsam, wir feiern gemeinsam" (We mourn together, we celebrate together).³² In one of her rare public appearances since the publication of her book in October 2021, Semiya Şimşek explained that she feels no longer at home in Germany, but she doesn't feel a sense of belonging in Turkey either: "Es ist jetzt fast zehn Jahre her, dass der NSU aufgeflogen ist, seit 21 Jahren ist mein Vater tot: Ich weiß nicht, wohin ich wirklich gehöre. Ich kann keine Wurzeln mehr setzen" (Almost ten years have passed since the NSU was exposed, my father has been dead for 21 years: I don't know where I belong. I can't put down roots anywhere).³³

---

31 This exoticized-racialized labeling is also discussed in critical new materialist Jasbir K. Puar's *Terrorist Assemblages: Homonationalism in Queer Times* (Durham, NC: Duke University Press, 2007), 4, when the author analyzes "the transnational production of terrorist corporealities" in relation to the Global War on Terrorism post-9/11. By furthermore zooming in on the—rather perverse—exploitation of homonationalist discourse by the global far right, Puar underscores the immense geopolitical impact of the September 11 attacks and "9/11" narrative. Although it would be an overstatement to say that said attacks and "9/11" created a far-right resurgence in Europe, they did offer the global—and specifically German—far right the opportunity to criticize the post-9/11 political order.

32 Semiya Şimşek, *Schmerzliche Heimat: Deutschland und der Mord an meinem Vater* (Berlin: Rowohlt, 2013), 255.

33 Elke Graßer-Reitzner and Stanislaus Kossakowski, "Semiya Simsek: 'Ich kann keine Wurzeln mehr setzen!'" *Nordbayern.de*, October 29, 2021, https://www.nordbayern.de/region/semiya-simsek-ich-kann-keine-wurzeln-mehr-setzen-1.11482558.

The brutal murder of her father by the NSU and his second murder as an effect of institutional racism forced Semiya Şimşek to seek refuge in rural Turkey. This illustrates the perverse logic of the "exoticizing elsewhere" dynamic: the (im)material practices and concepts associated with institutional racism create the illusion that a place whose main characteristic is that it is *not* Germany (in this case, Turkey) is both the origin of and explanation for a violent event in Germany. Since the affective burden of this process is carried solely by the victims of the racism enacted by and through the German state, the (white) majority of the population has the luxury of not having to feel affected by said violence and its lingering trouble. The racist assumptions and microaggressions underpinning the interrogations of Adile Şimşek and other NSU victims, for example, have caused them enormous suffering but were portrayed as "business as usual" by investigating officers. Faced with this multilayered, prolonged violence, many victims were left with no other choice than to start a life elsewhere without being able to leave the painful past behind.

In her speech in February 2012, Angela Merkel promised Enver Şimşek's family and other victims that the German authorities would do everything in their power to solve the murders and to ensure that such violence must never happen again. While Merkel's apology might have been sincere, she and other political leaders failed to clearly identify and tackle the institutional racism that had (re)traumatized the NSU victims and enabled the (white) majority in Germany to forget so quickly. As we shall see, this institutional racism—as a type of lingering trouble—is not limited to Germany's police force. Rather it manifests itself in a range of public spheres, including the courtroom and the media.

Historical Materialism—Deconstructivism—Critical New Materialism: Materialist Spectral Hauntings from Benjamin to Derrida to Barad, and Back

> In urgent times, many of us are tempted to address trouble in terms of making an imagined future safe . . . of clearing away the present and the past in order to make futures for coming generations. Staying with the trouble does not require such a relationship to times called the future. In fact, staying with the trouble requires learning to be truly present.[34]

At first sight, the type of affirmative troubling described by Donna J. Haraway here differs from Avery F. Gordon's take on the hauntological: "staying with the trouble" starts from a "being-troubled," but it is

---

34 Donna J. Haraway, *Staying with the Trouble: Making Kin in the Chthulucene* (Durham, NC: Duke University Press, 2016), 1.

also rooted in a critical new materialist praxis of hope, similar to Barad's "ethics of entanglement"[35] or feminist philosopher Rosi Braidotti's posthumanist philosophy that trusts "the untapped possibilities opened"[36] by engaging with the here and now. Both configurations of the hauntological—Gordon's backward-looking, Barad's and Braidotti's more affirmatively forward-looking—nonetheless disrupt the present in favor of recognizing past injustices and working toward a better future, queering space-time. Gordon and Barad and Braidotti, in tandem with Haraway, are invested in creating a new critical new materialist imaginary and reality, in which material conditions would be improved for all and ghosts of the past reckoned with. And this imaginary-reality is built upon the same materialist roots of hauntology diffractively explored in the critical theoretical snippet presented in this section: Benjamin's historical materialist and Derrida's deconstructivist-materialist perspectives.

Two of Benjamin's best-known pieces of writing are about reckoning with (re)materializations of violence-driven trouble and could thus be seen as anticipating the concept of hauntology. Benjamin's "Critique of Violence," written in the early 1920s and uncannily anticipating what was about to come in Germany, underscores these (re)materializations and the problem with Merkel's apology. Engaging with "Gewalt"—which means at once "violence," "illegitimately used force," and "institutionally legitimated power"—the essay examines the troubled relationship between "Gewalt," "Recht" (law), and "Gerechtigkeit" (justice), and how politico-legal interventions on the part of the nation-state, or its representatives, do not always bring justice. The crux of Benjamin's analysis is that violence has two functions: a "law-making function" and a "law-preserving"[37] one, connecting violence to the law and the state. The nation-state's violent origins—as the social contract is enforced through the threat of violent outbursts—are covered up by the installation of regulative laws, so that the violence from pre-social contract times never rears its head again. This original violence, however, is that which forever haunts the state. Whether manifesting itself as excessive unlawful violence used by the nation-state's police or military forces, or by the state apparatus's deep-seated institutional racism that amplifies the injustice already done to victims and their relatives, there is "something rotten in law"[38] or at the heart of the law-based nation-state.

Derrida's "Force of Law" pushes this analysis even further by offering us a deconstruction of the entanglements between violence, the state, and justice in praxis. Building on Benjamin's argument that law is always

---

35   Barad, "Nature's Queer Performativity," 150.
36   Braidotti, *The Posthuman*, 194.
37   Benjamin, "Critique of Violence," 284.
38   Benjamin, "Critique of Violence," 286.

accompanied by foundational violence, Derrida envisions justice as a "gift without exchange,"[39] a regulative ideal transcending the politico-legal domain. Zooming in on "'democracy to come'"[40]—which is connected to the future actualization of justice-as-a-gift—Derrida claims that a democratic nation-state in its most perfect form "will never exist in the present."[41] It actually even carries the seeds of its own destruction, because "the state is both self-protecting and self-destroying, at once remedy and poison."[42] Derrida's Benjaminian take on violence and justice makes us wonder whether "real" justice can ever truly be achieved through litigation and trials alone—and this is underlined by Merkel's speech that, albeit well-intentioned, in the end underlines how hard it is to arrive at a fully realized justice-to-come.

There is thus more to be done than retroactively acting on a macropolitical level to put things right. Traversing space-time, one could argue that Benjamin hints at this in his "Theses on the Philosophy of History." In this work, composed in the first part of 1940 and consisting of a critique of linear history written by and for the victorious, Benjamin addresses the advance of political fascism in Germany—a phenomenon that in his view will keep making its presence felt throughout history. Representing the critical theorist who chooses to "stay with the trouble," the Angelus Novus or the "angel of history" has their back turned to the future, hauntologically engaging with past destruction and despair while simultaneously urged forward by a storm, labeled "progress."[43] Seen through a Benjaminian hauntological perspective, the angel and critical theorist need to first look at the past and "the spark of hope" it carries.[44] Present injustices must be connected to past wrongdoings, thereby queering space-time, so that the same mistakes would not be repeated in the future, and the threat of political fascism would be understood as perennially present. Or as Benjamin puts it, "the 'state of emergency' in which we live is not the exception but the rule."[45] The core of a better future, however, also lies in the past, its many injustices, and the lessons that can be learned from them. Trying to grasp that particular spark of hope is a tough exercise, as the angel and critical theorist tend to be seduced by the future promised by said storm (standing for the Enlightenment; scientific positivism; orthodox revolutionary Marxism . . .). Both thus need to resist the urge to jump too hastily into the future-in-becoming.

39 Derrida, "Force of Law," 25.
40 Derrida in Borradori, *Philosophy in a Time of Terror*, 120.
41 Derrida in Borradori, *Philosophy in a Time of Terror*, 120.
42 Derrida in Borradori, *Philosophy in a Time of Terror*, 124.
43 Benjamin, "Theses on the Philosophy of History," 257.
44 Benjamin, "Theses on the Philosophy of History," 255.
45 Benjamin, "Theses on the Philosophy of History," 257.

This line of thought is taken up by Derrida and Barad in *Specters of Marx* and *Meeting the Universe Halfway*, respectively. Focusing on the absence/presence-disrupting and time-bending specter—or the wronged Other—Derrida again touches upon justice as something interruptive and always to-yet-be-attained. Justice-to-come not only includes corrections of wrongdoings but implies a learning to live "*with* ghosts" as well.[46] The specters of the past, together with their material markings—or, in many cases, *missing* markings—thus need to be incessantly tracked. The need to track specters of the past, together with their (non)markings, is echoed by Barad, when they, diffracting Benjamin through Derrida, state that "matter carries within itself the sedimented historialities of the practices through which it is produced as part of its ongoing becoming."[47] Seen through a hauntological Baradian agential realist viewpoint that emphasizes the constant queering of space-time, the wounds of injustice are all around us, as the past constantly shining through the present. Yet it isn't enough to honor the NSU victims and bring the perpetrators to justice; the institutional racism-filled system itself that made the NSU crimes possible and retraumatized the families of the victims needs to be tackled. For Barad—and for all the materialist thinkers mentioned in this extract— the world carries such ethical potential from within: "each moment is alive with different possibilities for the world's becoming and different reconfigurings of what may yet be possible."[48] In the case of the NSU terror, a first step toward future justice is a collective commitment to (re)visit the past materializations of institutional violence and to take responsibility for their traumatizing impact on the families of the NSU victims.

November 11, 2011 (Hamburg, Germany): The Exposure of the NSU and the Haunting Power of Images

> Ten years after Süleyman Taşköprü's brutal murder in summer 2001, officers finally returned some of his personal possessions to his sister. When Aysen Taşköprü asked why investigating authorities had kept these items for so long, she was told that they had simply forgotten about them. The officers said that there were no new developments in the murder case.
>
> On November 11, 2011, a work colleague called Aysen Taşköprü and told her that her brother's murder was being discussed in a news report. On that day, her phone didn't stop ringing. Suddenly, there was a huge media interest in Süleyman Taşköprü's death, and his sister received numerous interview requests. However, few journalists seem to have considered how traumatic it was for her and other

---

46 Derrida, *Specters of Marx*, xvii–xviii.
47 Barad, *Meeting the Universe Halfway*, 182.
48 Barad, *Meeting the Universe Halfway*, 182.

NSU victims to see graphic images of their murdered relatives on TV. Aysen Taşköprü remembers November 11, 2011, as the day on which her brother died again.[49]

In November 2011, a failed bank robbery in Zwickau led to the suicide of leading NSU members Uwe Mundlos and Uwe Böhnhardt. In response to these events, their accomplice Beate Zschäpe tried to destroy evidence in a flat in Zwickau by setting it on fire. Then she surrendered to the police. Before her arrest, Zschäpe disseminated a DVD with a video in which the group claimed responsibility for the racially motivated killings of Taşköprü and eight other people. All these victims were men killed during broad daylight while working in small businesses. Eight had Turkish roots; one was originally from Greece. The tenth NSU murder does not appear to have racist motives: the victim was a white German woman police officer.

The NSU video combined footage featuring the American cartoon character "The Pink Panther" with graphic images of the NSU victims and news coverage about the attacks. In the burned-out flat in Zwickau, police found an external hard drive with multiple files used in the making of the fifteen-minute film. A police analysis of the material revealed that work on the video began in 2006. The Pink Panther footage was added at a later stage, probably because Mundlos was a fan of the American cartoon series.[50] The filing system and the film itself leave no doubt about the profoundly racist worldview of the NSU.[51] To this day, it is not known how many people were involved in the making of this video.

The NSU video can be seen as performing various hauntological spatiotemporal disruptions: although Mundlos and Böhnhardt were dead by the time it was released, the video tells the story of the ten murders and other NSU attacks from their perspective, forcing us to jump between different space-times. Featuring graphic photographs of dying NSU victims and crime scenes, the video haunts in bodily-affecting ways. Most people find such images disturbing. In addition, however, those images were (re)traumatizing victims of racist violence, as Aysen Taşköprü's account illustrates, giving the lingering trouble of institutional racism an extra lived and eerie dimension. Like Semiya Şimşek, Taşköprü felt like a stranger

---

49   Aysen Taşköprü, "Sehr geehrter Herr Gauck...," *taz.de*, February 15, 2013, https://taz.de/Absage-an-den-Bundespraesidenten/!5073130/. Paraphrased by the authors.

50   Tanjev Schultz, "'Ali9' und 'Ali9 aktuell': Die Video-Arbeit des NSU," *Sueddeutsche Zeitung*, March 15, 2016, https://www.sueddeutsche.de/politik/nsu-prozess-ali9-und-ali9-aktuell-die-video-arbeit-des-nsu-1.2908458-0#seite-2.

51   Out of respect for the victims, we decided to avoid including details in this essay that would force us to repeat the racist language used by the NSU and its supporters where possible.

in her home country, and this can be understood as a direct result of the "exoticizing elsewhere" dynamic described above. In an open letter to FRG president Joachim Gauck, Taşköprü said, "I don't have a home country anymore, because home is where you feel safe."[52]

Even more troubling is that the NSU video was not only shared by far-right activists (as one might expect). Unlike the testimonies and concerns of the victims in the pre-2011 era, the NSU video received a huge amount of media attention. It was even shown during the NSU trial.[53] We believe that a critical analysis of the NSU video and other perpetrator testimonies is important in order to paint a fuller picture of the violent events in question. It is, however, a painful truth that they often dominate public narratives about violent events. Against this background, it is an ethico-political imperative that an analysis of such material is characterized by respect for the victims and therefore avoids reinforcing the racist stereotypes and structural inequality it seeks to challenge. As we shall see, the NSU trial failed to do this. And this failure is completely in line with the spectral hauntings described by Benjamin and Derrida earlier.

July 11, 2013 (Munich, Germany): The NSU Trial and the Haunted Notion of Terrorism

> Pinar Kiliç used to run a small grocery shop in Munich. The shop was very popular among locals, including officers from the police station across the road. Occasionally, her husband Habil would help out in the shop after returning from his other job in a wholesale store. On August 29, 2001, he was shot while working there.
>
> Almost twelve years later, Pinar Kiliç found the courage to face Zschäpe in court. While Zschäpe made use of her right to remain silent, however, Kiliç was urged by the judge to tell him what kind of man her husband was. When she refused, the judge told her that he expected "polite answers" from her. To this, she replied: "For years I was treated like a suspect. There was a pool of blood in the shop; we had to clean that up ourselves."[54]

Habil Kiliç was killed with the same weapon as Enver Şimşek. The Česká 83 pistol was also used to kill Abdurrahim Özüdoğru and Süleyman Taşköprü in June 2001. All but one of the NSU murders followed a clear

---

52 Taşköprü, "Sehr geehrter Herr Gauck."
53 For a discussion of the two viewings during the NSU trial, see Tom Sundermann, "Der schmerzhafte Schrecken des NSU-Videos," *Zeit Online*, November 19, 2014, https://blog.zeit.de/nsu-prozess-blog/2014/11/19/medienlog-nsu-bekennervideo-zschaepe-boehnhardt/.
54 Annette Ramelsberger et al., eds., *Der NSU-Prozess: Das Protokoll* (Munich: Verlag Antje Kunstmann, 2018), 84.

pattern: the victims were shot during broad daylight while working in small shops. For example, Abdurrahim Özüdoğru was killed in his clothing alterations and repair shop in Nuremberg; Süleyman Taşköprü was shot while helping out in his father's greengrocer's shop in Hamburg. In all cases, investigating authorities suspected that the victims had been involved in organized crime and had links to the Turkish Mafia. These speculations were completely groundless. When investigating Habil Kiliç's murder, police did not even consider the possibility of a racist attack. Instead, they focused exclusively on suspected links with foreign criminal networks. Forty of the fifty witnesses questioned in the case were Turkish citizens. As if to defend himself against potential allegations of racism, one of the investigating officers stated during the NSU trial in 2013,

> Alle Hinweise, die kamen, gingen in Richtung organisierte Kriminalität, PKK, Graue Wölfe. Niemand vermutete Rechtsradikale. Der Modus entsprach auch nicht dem, was man sonst von Neonazis kannte, also Ausländer durch die Straße jagen, zu Tode prügeln. Und jetzt soll man mal nicht so tun, als ob es keine türkische Drogenmafia gibt. Im Fall Kiliç haben wir allerdings überhaupt keine Hinweise auf so was gefunden. Der Herr Kiliç war ein kreuzbraver, fleißiger, humorvoller Mensch.[55]

> [All evidence we received pointed to organized crime, PKK, Grey Wolves. Nobody suspected far-right radicals. The modus operandi did not correspond to what we know from neo-Nazis, i.e., chasing foreigners in the street, beating them to death. And let's not pretend that there is no Turkish drug Mafia. Having said that, in the case of Kiliç, we didn't find any evidence for anything like that. Mr Kiliç was as decent as anything, hardworking, humorous.]

The problematic conceptualization of (neo-)Nazism underpinning this statement is widespread among German authorities and reflects the FRG's troubled relationship with the far right.

What makes the NSU terror so haunting is not only that it brought back uncomfortable memories of the so-called Third Reich and the ongoing relevance of its ideological foundations but also that it exposed the political limitations of the legal definition of terrorism in German law—reminding us of the ambiguous relationships between violence, the law, and the state noted by Benjamin and Derrida. To understand these limitations, we have to go back to the early 1970s when the founding members of the Rote Armee Fraktion (Red Army Faction, RAF) and other leftist groups took up arms to fight for a revolution in the FRG. At the peak of the Cold War, the threat posed by the far left was seen as

---

55 Rammelsberger et al., *Der NSU-Prozess*, 83.

far more significant than the threat posed by the far right. To combat this kind of threat more effectively, the state introduced a series of legal measures that became known as "Lex RAF."[56] Probably the most significant among these was Section 129a, which was added to the German Criminal Code in 1976 and made it a crime to be a member of a "terrorist organization." The law became the subject of controversial debate because it also made it an offense to support terrorist organizations in any way, shape, or form.[57]

Between 1976 and 2014, 236 people were charged with terror offenses on the basis of Section 129a of the Criminal Code.[58] One of the few individuals associated with the far right who faced charges of this kind was Zschäpe. This is not because there was no violence that could have been classified as right-wing terrorism. According to a survey from 2014, there were at least 2,173 arson attacks, 174 armed robberies, 12 abductions, and 229 murders by right-wing extremists since 1971.[59] Many of these attacks did not follow the same pattern as the RAF terror (for example, targeting business leaders, state prosecutors, and other public figures, and releasing claims of responsibility after each attack). This is because the NSU founders and others on the far right took inspiration from right-wing terror manuals from the US promoting a leaderless "race war."[60]

In one of the most detailed studies of far-right terrorism in Germany to date, Daniel Koehler shows that the "emerging academic interest" in this topic "was halted by the September 11 events in 2001."[61] According to Koehler, "Islamist terrorism" continued to dominate public debates

---

56 Jeremy Varon, *Bringing the War Home: The Weather Underground, the Red Army Faction, and Revolutionary Violence in the Sixties and Seventies* (Berkeley: University of California Press, 2004), 228.

57 One of the most controversial applications of the Lex RAF was the so-called Mescalero affair. In 1977, the author of an article in a student magazine faced terrorism charges after expressing "clandestine joy" about the assassination of the attorney general of the FRG, Siegfried Buback, by the RAF.

58 "1976: Anti-Terror-Paragraf wird eingeführt," *bpb.de*, August 16, 2016, https://www.bpb.de/politik/hintergrund-aktuell/232718/1976-anti-terror-paragraf-16-08-2016/.

59 Daniel Koehler, "German Right-Wing Terrorism in Historical Perspective: A First Quantitative Overview of the 'Database on Terrorism in Germany (Right-Wing Extremism)'—DTGrwx' Project," *Perspectives on Terrorism* 8, no. 5 (2014): 48–58.

60 Of particular importance in this context was the concept of "leaderless resistance" by neo-Nazi Louis Beam; the *Turner Diaries* and the *Practical Guide to the Strategy and Tactics of Revolution* by David Myatt; and *The Way Forward* by Max Hammer, as Daniel Koehler shows in *Right-Wing Terrorism in the 21st Century: The "National Socialist Underground" and the History of Terror from the Far-Right in Germany* (London: Routledge, 2016), 57.

61 Koehler, *Right-Wing Terrorism in the 21st Century*, 3.

about political extremism and violence in Germany until 2011. Against this background, it is not surprising that the first extensive changes to the German terrorism legislation in 2002 were a direct response to the September 11 attacks and part of the Global War on Terrorism. The newly introduced Section 129b enabled German authorities to extend the definition of terrorism to organizations outside of Germany. These measures reinforced the status of the attacks as a hyper-exceptional event—as "9/11"—and violence from within Germany as coming from an "exotic elsewhere."

After the September 11 attacks, the headlines in Germany and many other countries were dominated by global Islamist terror networks. While security agencies were trying to respond to the emergence of this supposedly new international terrorism, the NSU murder series continued unimpeded. After the killing of Mehmet Turgut in Hamburg in February 2004 and of İsmail Yaşar in Nuremberg in June 2005 with the same weapon, journalists and police officers began to refer to the killings as "Döner Morde" (kebab murders)—a conceptual pairing that sparked international outrage.[62] Six years after it was first used, a jury of linguists declared the term "Unwort" (nonword) of the year because of its highly discriminatory nature.[63] These and other critical interventions in the post-2011 period could not, however, undo the damage caused by a decade of wild speculations and discriminatory treatment.

Conclusion: German Identity, Right-Wing Extremism, and Less Violent Futures

One of the key objectives of political authorities in the FRG in the post–World War II era was to show the world that the German people had come to terms with the past. Right-wing extremism and violence did not fit into the (self-)image of the "denazified" democratic FRG. There have, however, been thousands of violent attacks with a right-wing extremist background over the last decades. Many of these attacks received little attention by journalists and researchers and have effectively disappeared from public consciousness. The German reaction to the September 11 attacks in the US and the Global War on (Islamist) Terrorism further reinforced this tendency. Viewed from this perspective, it would be wrong to claim that "9/11" marked a turning point or caesura in Germany.

62 See, e.g., Thomas Meaney and Saskia Schäfer, "The Neo-Nazi Murder Trial Revealing Germany's Darkest Secrets," *Guardian*, December 15, 2016, https://www.theguardian.com/world/2016/dec/15/neo-nazi-murders-revealing-germanys-darkest-secrets.

63 Christian Fuchs, "Wie der Begriff 'Döner-Morde' entstand," *Der Spiegel*, July 4, 2012.

In this essay, we have drawn on a critical (new) materialist hauntological perspective to challenge the collective forgetting of victims of far-right violence in the FRG. Specific focus was on three racist murders by the neo-Nazi-terror group NSU in early 2000 and 2001. In addition to the racist ideology of the perpetrators, the families of the victims were confronted with a less visible but equally traumatizing form of violence in the form of institutional racism. We have described this process as an "exoticizing elsewhere" dynamic: the (im)material practices and concepts associated with institutional racism create the illusion that a place whose main characteristic is that it is *not* Germany (in this case, Turkey) is both the origin of and explanation for a violent event in Germany. Since the affective burden of this process is carried solely by the victims of racist violence, the (white) majority of the population has the luxury of being able to forget.

Against this background, remembering can be an act of resistance. Bakary Singateh and other victims of far-right violence were never forgotten by their families and friends, but their lives and deaths have not received the public attention they deserve. In the early 2000s this began to change owing to the campaigning efforts of victims, journalists, artists, and political activists. But, as we have shown, it is not enough to honor the NSU victims and bring the perpetrators to justice; the institutionally racist system itself that made the NSU crimes possible and retraumatized the families of the victims must be tackled. Seen through a hauntological viewpoint, the wounds of injustice are all around us, but each moment offers manifold opportunities for less violent futures. After a far-right extremist carried out a series of racist killings in Hanau in February 2020, families, friends, and supporters bravely and persistently challenged institutional racism and the "exoticizing elsewhere" dynamic. Rallying around the hashtag #saytheirnames, they made sure that all of us know and remember Sedat Gürbüz, Ferhat Unvar, Hamza Kurtović, Gökhan Gültekin, Mercedes Kierpacz, Vili Viorel Păun, Said Nesra Hashemi, Fatih Saraçoğlu, and Kaloyan Velkov.

Selected Bibliography

Alison, Miranda. *Women and Political Violence: Female Combatants in Ethno-National Conflict.* London: Routledge, 2009.
Alter, Nora M. "Excessive Pre/Requisites: Vietnam through the East German Lens." *Cultural Critique*, no. 35 (Winter 1996–97): 39–79.
———. *Projecting History: German Nonfiction Cinema, 1967–2000.* Ann Arbor: University of Michigan Press, 2002.
Ascher, Abraham. *The Revolution of 1905: A Short History.* Stanford, CA: Stanford University Press, 2004.
Asendorf, Christoph. *Super Constellation: Flugzeug und Raumrevolution.* Vienna: Springer, 1997.
Bal, Mieke. *Double Exposures: The Practice of Cultural Analysis.* New York: Routledge, 1996.
Balsen, Werner, and Karl Rössel. *Hoch die internationale Solidarität: Zur Geschichte der Dritte Welt-Bewegung in der Bundesrepublik.* Cologne: Kölner Volksblatt, 1985.
Barad, Karen. *Meeting the Universe Halfway: Quantum Physics and the Entanglement of Matter and Meaning.* Durham, NC: Duke University Press, 2007.
———. "Nature's Queer Performativity." *Qui Parle: Critical Humanities and Social Sciences* 19, no. 2 (2011): 121–58.
Barkawi, Tarak. "Decolonizing War." *European Journal of International Security* 1, part 2 (2016): 199–214.
Barthes, Roland. *Mythologies*, translated by Annette Lavers. London: Vintage, 1993.
Bauman, Zygmunt. *Modernity and the Holocaust.* Cambridge: Polity, 1989.
Benjamin, Walter. "Der Autor als Produzent." In *Gesammelte Schriften*, volume 2, part 2, edited by Rolf Tiedemann and Hermann Schweppenhäuser, 683–701. Frankfurt am Main: Suhrkamp, 1977. Translated by Edmund Jephcott as "The Author as Producer." In *Walter Benjamin: Selected Writings*, vol. 2, part 2: *1931–1934*, edited by Michael W. Jennings, Howard Eiland, and Gary Smith, 768–82. Cambridge, MA: Belknap Press of Harvard University Press, 2005.
———. "Critique of Violence." In *Reflections: Essays, Aphorisms, Autobiographical Writings*, translated by Edmund Jephcott, edited by Peter Demetz, 277–300. New York: Schocken Books, 1978.
———. "Über den Begriff der Geschichte." In *Gesammelte Schriften*, volume 1, part 2, edited by Rolf Tiedemann and Hermann Schweppenhäuser, 691–704. Frankfurt am Main: Suhrkamp, 1977. Translated by Harry

Zohn as "Theses on the Philosophy of History." In *Illuminations: Essays and Reflections*, edited with an introduction by Hannah Arendt, 253–64. New York: Schocken, 2007.

———. "Zur Kritik der Gewalt." In *Gesammelte Schriften*, volume 2, part 1, edited by Rolf Tiedemann and Hermann Schweppenhäuser, 179–204. Frankfurt am Main: Suhrkamp, 1977.

Bergman, Arlene Eisen. *Women of Vietnam*, 2nd ed. San Francisco: People's Press, 1975.

Beutelschmidt, Thomas. "'Die Fahne von Kriwoj Rog': Materialien zur Adaptionsgeschichte eines Kanontextes der frühen DDR-Literatur." In *Realitätskonstruktion: Faschismus und Antifaschismus in Literaturverfilmungen des DDR-Fernsehens*, edited by Thomas Beutelschmidt and Rüdiger Steinlein, 53–100. Leipzig: Leipziger Universitätsverlag, 2004.

Bielby, Clare. "Bewaffnete Terroristinnen: Linksterrorismus, Gender und die Waffe in der Bundesrepublik Deutschland von den 1970er Jahren bis heute." *WerkstattGeschichte* 64 (2014): 77–101.

———. "Gendering the Perpetrator; Gendering Perpetrator Studies." In *The Routledge International Handbook of Perpetrator Studies*, edited by Susanne C. Knittel and Zachary J. Goldberg, 155–68. London: Routledge, 2020.

———. "Narrating the Revolutionary Self in German Post-Terrorist Life Writing: Gender, Identity and Historical Agency." *German Life and Letters* 76, no. 2 (2014): 219–41.

Blangy, Eugenie M. "A Reappraisal of Germany's Vietnam Policy, 1963–1966: Ludwig Erhard's Response to America's War in Vietnam." *German Studies Review* 27, no. 2 (2004): 341–60.

Blaylock, Sarah. "Bringing the War Home to the United States and East Germany: *In the Year of the Pig* and *Pilots in Pajamas*." *Cinema Journal* 56, no. 4 (2017): 26–50.

Borradori, Giovanna. *Philosophy in a Time of Terror: Dialogues with Jurgen Habermas and Jacques Derrida*. Chicago: University of Chicago Press, 2003.

Böttcher, Claudia, Julia Kretzschmar and Corinna Schier, eds. *Walter Heynowski und Gerhard Scheumann—Dokumentarfilmer im Klassenkampf: Eine kommentierte Filmographie*. Leipzig: Leipziger Universitätsverlag, 2002.

Braidotti, Rosi. *The Posthuman*. Cambridge: Polity Press, 2013.

Brandt, Marion. "Vorfassungen zu Anna Seghers' Erzählung *Steinzeit*—Beschreibung und Kommentar in bezug auf eine mögliche Interpretation." *Zeitschrift für Germanistik* 2, no. 1 (1992): 138–48.

Braun, Rebecca, and Benedict Schofield, eds. *Transnational German Studies*. Liverpool: Liverpool University Press, 2020.

Braun, Volker. *KriegsErklärung*. Halle an der Saale: Mitteldeutscher Verlag, 1967.

———. *Texte in zeitlicher Folge*, vol. 2. Halle an der Saale: Mitteldeutscher Verlag, 1990.

Brecht, Bertolt. "Der Dreigroschenprozess: Ein soziologisches Experiment." In *Große kommentierte Berliner und Frankfurter Ausgabe*, vol. 21, edited by Werner Hecht, Jan Knopf, Werner Mittenzwei, and Klaus-Detlev Müller, 448–514. Frankfurt am Main: Suhrkamp, 1992.
———. *Kriegsfibel*. Berlin: Eulenspiegel, 1955.
———. "Über Fotografie." In *Große kommentierte Berliner und Frankfurter Ausgabe*, vol. 21, 264–65.
———. *War Primer*, translated by John Willett. London: Libris, 1998.
———. "Zum zehnjährigen Bestehen der A-I-Z." In *Große kommentierte Berliner und Frankfurter Ausgabe*, vol. 21, 515. Frankfurt am Main: Suhrkamp, 1992.
Brock, Bazon. *Ästhetik als Vermittlung: Arbeitsbiographie eines Generalisten*, edited by Karla Fohrbeck. Cologne: DuMont, 1977.
Brothers, Caroline. *War and Photography: A Cultural History*. London: Routledge, 1997.
Brown, Timothy Scott. "'1968' East and West: Divided Germany as a Case Study in Transnational History." *American Historical Review* 114, no. 1 (February 2009): 69–96.
———. *West Germany and the Global Sixties: The Antiauthoritarian Revolt, 1962–1978*. Cambridge: Cambridge University Press, 2013.
Burghard, Ciesla. "Korea als Generalprobe?" In *Korea—ein vergessener Krieg? Der militärische Konflikt auf der koreanischen Halbinsel 1950–1953 im internationalen Kontext*, edited by Bernd Bonwetsch and Matthias Uhl, 103–14. Berlin: de Gruyter, 2012.
Burrows, Larry. "One Ride with Yankee Papa 13." *Life*, April 16, 1965, 26–34D.
Busch, Peter. "'The Vietnam Legion': West German Psychological Warfare against East German Propaganda in the 1960s." *Journal of Cold War Studies* 16, no. 3 (2014): 164–89.
Carrière, Jean-Claude. *Viva Maria: Roman nach dem Originaldrehbuch von Louis Malle und Jean-Claude Carrière*, translated by Ruth Groh. Munich: Heyne, 1968.
Chamberlain, Paul Thomas. *Cold War's Killing Fields: Rethinking the Long Peace*. London: HarperCollins, 2018.
Charney, Leo, and Vanessa R. Schwartz, eds. *Cinema and the Invention of Modern Life*. Berkeley: University of California Press, 1996.
Chaussy, Ulrich. *Die drei Leben des Rudi Dutschke*. 2nd ed. Munich: Pendo, 1993.
Colvin, Sarah, and Katharina Karcher, eds. *Women, Global Protest Movements, and Political Agency: Rethinking the Legacy of 1968*. London: Routledge, 2019.
Crowdus, Gary, and Richard Porton. "Coming to Terms with the German Past: An Interview with Volker Schlöndorff." *Cinéaste* 26, no. 2 (2001): 18–23.

Cuthbert, Lauren. "'Ich hatte Befehle': Multidirectional Memory and the Vietnam War in Heynowski and Scheumann's *Piloten im Pyjama* (1968)." *German Life and Letters* 75 (2022): 521–39.
Daase, Christopher. "Die RAF und der internationale Terrorismus: Zur transnationalen Kooperation klandestiner Organisationen." In Kraushaar, *Die RAF und der linke Terrorismus*, 905–29.
Dahlke, Birgit. "'Frau komm': Vergewaltigungen 1945; Zur Geschichte eines Diskurses." In *LiteraturGesellschaft DDR: Kanonkämpfe und ihre Geschichte(n)*, edited by Birgit Dahlke, Martina Langermann, and Thomas Taterka, 275–311. Stuttgart: Metzler, 2000.
Daum, Andreas, Lloyd Gardner, and Wilfried Mausbach, eds. *America, the Vietnam War, and the World: Comparative and International Perspectives*. Cambridge: Cambridge University Press, 2003.
Davies, Mererid Puw. *Poetic Writing and the Vietnam War in West Germany: On Fire*. London: UCL Press, 2023.
———. "West German Representations of Women and Resistance in Vietnam, 1966–73." In *Women and Death 2: Warlike Women in the German Literary and Cultural Imagination since 1500*, edited by Sarah Colvin and Helen Watanabe-O'Kelly, 229–49. Rochester, NY: Camden House, 2009.
———. *Writing and the West German Protest Movements: The Textual Revolution*. London: imlr books, 2016.
Derrida, Jacques. "Force of Law: The Mystical Foundation of Authority," translated by Mary Quaintance, in *Deconstruction and the Possibility of Justice*, edited by Drucilla Cornell, Michel Rosenfeld, and David Gray Carlson, 3–67. New York: Routledge, 1992.
———. *Specters of Marx: The State of the Debt, the Work of Mourning and the New International*, translated by Peggy Kamuf. New York: Routledge, 1994.
Dolle-Weinkauff, Bernd. "Pop, Protest und Politik: Die Comics der 68er." *Forschung Frankfurt* 2 (2008): 38–45.
Dölling, Irene. "Frauen in der ehemaligen DDR." *Women in German Yearbook* 7 (1991): 121–36.
Dolphijn, Rick, and Iris van der Tuin. *New Materialism: Interviews & Cartographies*. Ann Arbor, MI: Open Humanities Press, 2012.
Douma, Eva. "Die Entwicklung des Familiengesetzbuches der DDR 1945–1966: Frauen und Familienpolitik im Spannungsfeld zwischen theoretischer Grundlage und realexistenter wirtschaftlicher Situation." *Zeitschrift der Savigny-Stiftung für Rechtsgeschichte: Germanistische Abteilung* 111 (1994): 592–620.
Dussel, Konrad. "Rundfunk in der Bundesrepublik und in der DDR: Überlegungen zum systematischen Vergleich." In *Zwischen Pop und Propaganda: Radio in der DDR*, edited by Christoph Classen and Klaus Arnold, 301–22. Berlin: C. H. Links, 2004.
Dutschke, Gretchen. *Wir hatten ein barbarisches, schönes Leben: Rudi Dutschke; Eine Biographie*. Cologne: Kiepenheuer & Witsch, 1996.

Edwards, Elizabeth. "The Colonial Archival Imaginaire at Home." *Social Anthropology* 24, no. 1 (2016): 52–66.
Engels, Friedrich. *Der Ursprung der Familie, des Privateigentums und des Staates: Im Anschluss an Lewis H. Morgans Forschungen*. In *Marx-Engels Werke*, vol. 21, edited by Institut für Marxismus-Leninismus beim ZK der SED, 25–173. Berlin: Dietz, 1973.
Enzensberger, Ulrich. *Die Jahre der Kommune I: Berlin 1967–1969*. Cologne: Kiepenheuer & Witsch, 2004.
Fehervary, Helen. *Anna Seghers: The Mythic Dimension*. Ann Arbor: University of Michigan Press, 2001.
Forlenza, Rosario. "The Politics of the Abendland: Christian Democracy and the Idea of Europe after the Second World War." *Contemporary European History* 26, no. 2 (2017): 261–86.
Garraio, Júlia. "Hordes of Rapists: The Instrumentalization of Sexual Violence in German Cold War Anti-Communist Discourses," translated by João Paulo Moreira. *RCCS Annual Review* 5 (2013): 46–63.
Gebhardt, Miriam. *Als die Soldaten kamen: Die Vergewaltigung deutscher Frauen am Ende des Zweiten Weltkriegs*. Munich: Pantheon, 2016.
Geerts, Evelien. "Materialist Philosophies Grounded in the Here and Now: Critical New Materialist Constellations & Interventions in Times of Terror(ism)." PhD diss., University of California, Santa Cruz, 2019. https://escholarship.org/uc/item/5p99j0b7.
———. "Nieuw Materialisme: Een Kritische Cartografie." *Wijsgerig Perspectief* 61, no. 2 (2021): 34–41.
Geerts, Evelien, and Iris Van der Tuin. "Almanac: Diffraction & Reading Diffractively." *Matter: Journal of New Materialist Research* 2, no. 1 (2021): 173–77.
Gerhardt, Christina. *Screening the Red Army Faction: Historical and Cultural Memory*. New York: Bloomsbury, 2018.
Gerhardt, Christina, and Marco Abel, eds. *Celluloid Revolt: German Screen Cultures and the Long 1968*. Rochester, NY: Camden House, 2019.
Glynn, Ruth. "Writing the Terrorist Self: The Unspeakable Alterity of Italy's Female Perpetrators." *Feminist Review* 92 (2009): 1–18.
Goldberg, Vicki. *The Power of Photography: How Photographs Changed Our Lives*. New York: Abbeville, 1991.
Gordon, Avery F. *Ghostly Matters: Haunting and the Sociological Imagination*. Minneapolis: University of Minnesota Press, 2008.
Gotsche, Otto. *Zwischen Nacht und Morgen*. Berlin: Kultur und Fortschritt, 1959.
Gregg, Melissa, and Gregory J. Seighworth, eds. *The Affect Theory Reader*. Durham, NC: Duke University Press, 2010.
Grossmann, Atina. *Jews, Germans, and Allies: Close Encounters in Occupied Germany*. Princeton, NJ: Princeton University Press, 2009.
Günther, Anton. "S'is Feierohmnd." Accessed January 27, 2022. http://noten.bplaced.net/weltlich/abschied/Gunther_SIsFeieromd.pdf.

Hanebrink, Paul. *A Specter Haunting Europe: The Myth of Judeo-Bolshevism*. Cambridge, MA: Harvard University Press, 2018.
Haraway, Donna J. *Modest_Witness@Second_Millenium: FemaleMan©_Meets_Oncomouse™;Feminism and Technoscience*. New York: Routledge, 1997.
———. *Staying with the Trouble: Making Kin in the Chthulucene*. Durham, NC: Duke University Press, 2016.
Hariman, Robert, and John Louis Lucaites. *No Caption Needed: Iconic Photographs, Public Culture and Liberal Democracy*. Chicago: University of Chicago Press, 2007.
Heineman, Elizabeth. "The Hour of the Woman: Memories of Germany's 'Crisis Years' and West German National Identity." *American Historical Review* 101, no. 2 (1996): 354–95.
Herminghouse, Patricia, and Magda Mueller. "Introduction: Looking for Germania." In *Gender and Germanness: Cultural Productions of Nation*, edited by Patricia Herminghouse and Magda Mueller, 1–16. Providence, RI: Berghahn, 1997.
Herzog, Dagmar. *Cold War Freud: Psychoanalysis in an Age of Catastrophes*. Cambridge: Cambridge University Press, 2017.
Heynowski, Walter. "Walter Heynowski: Einen Film macht man 1:1." In Poss, Mückenberger, and Richter, *Das Prinzip Neugier*, 59–97.
Heynowski, Walter, and Gerhard Scheumann. "Die Angkar." *Sinn und Form* 34, no. 5 (September/October 1982): 989–98.
———, dirs. *Die Angkar*. German Democratic Republic, Studio H&S. 1981.
———. *Filmen in Vietnam: Tagebuch*. Berlin: Henschelverlag, 1976.
———. *Piloten im Pyjama*. Berlin: Verlag der Nation, 1969.
———. *Die Teufelsinsel*. Berlin: Verlag der Nation, 1977.
Higgins, Lynn, and Brenda Silver. "Introduction: Rereading Rape." In *Rape and Representation*, edited by Lynn Higgins and Brenda Silver, 1–14. New York: Columbia University Press, 1991.
Hilmes, Carola, and Ilse Nagelschmidt, eds. *Anna Seghers Handbuch: Leben–Werk–Wirkung*. Stuttgart: Metzler, 2020.
hooks, bell. *Ain't I a Woman: Black Women and Feminism*. New York: Routledge, 2015.
Horten, Gerd. "Sailing in the Shadow of the Vietnam War: The GDR Government and the 'Vietnam Bonus' of the Early 1970s." *German Studies Review* 36, no. 3 (2013): 557–78.
Hosek, Jennifer Ruth. *Sun, Sex and Socialism: Cuba in the German Imaginary*. Toronto: University of Toronto Press, 2012.
Hurwitz, Harald, Ursula Böhme, and Andreas Malycha. *Die Stalinisierung der SED: Zum Verlust von Freiräumen und sozialdemokratischer Identität in den Vorständen 1946–1949*. Opladen: Westdeutscher Verlag, 1997.
James, Sarah E. *Common Ground: German Photographic Cultures across the Iron Curtain*. New Haven, CT: Yale University Press, 2013.
Janzen, Marike. *Writing to Change the World: Anna Seghers, Authorship, and International Solidarity in the Twentieth Century*. Rochester, NY: Camden House, 2018.

Juchler, Ingo. *Rebellische Subjektivität und Internationalismus.* Marburg: Arbeiterbewegung und Geschichtswissenschaft, 1989.

———. *Die Studentenbewegungen in den Vereinigten Staaten und der Bundesrepublik Deutschland der sechziger Jahre: Eine Untersuchung hinsichtlich ihrer Beeinflussung durch Befreiungsbewegungen und -theorien aus der Dritten Welt.* Berlin: Duncker & Humblot, 1996.

Karcher, Katharina. "'Ich bin parteilich, subjektiv und emotional'—*Eigen-Sinn* and the Narrative (Re)construction of Political Agency in Inge Viett's *Nie war ich furchtloser.*" In *Experiencing Postwar Germany: Everyday Life and Cultural Practice in East and West, 1960–2000,* edited by Erica Carter, Jan Palmowski, and Katrin Schreiter, 85–106. Oxford: Berghahn, 2018.

Kätzel, Ute, ed. *Die 1968erinnen: Porträt einer rebellischen Frauengeneration.* Berlin: Rowohlt, 2002.

Kelly, Liz. "Wars against Women: Sexual Violence, Sexual Politics and the Militarized State." In *States of Conflict: Gender, Violence and Resistance,* edited by Susie Jacobs, Ruth Jacobson, and Jen Marchbank, 45–65. London: Zed Books, 2000.

Kirby, Dianne. *Religion and the Cold War.* Basingstoke, UK: Palgrave Macmillan, 2003.

Klimke, Martin. *The Other Alliance: Student Protest in West Germany and the United States in the Global Sixties.* Princeton, NJ: Princeton University Press, 2010.

Klonk, Charlotte. *Terror: Wenn Bilder zu Waffen werden.* Frankfurt am Main: Fischer, 2017.

Knittel, Susanne C., and Zachary J. Goldberg, eds. *The Routledge International Handbook of Perpetrator Studies.* London: Routledge, 2020.

Koehler, Daniel. "German Right-Wing Terrorism in Historical Perspective: A First Quantitative Overview of the 'Database on Terrorism in Germany (Right-Wing Extremism)'—DTGrwx' Project." *Perspectives on Terrorism* 8, no. 5 (2014): 48–58.

———. *Right-Wing Terrorism in the 21st Century: The "National Socialist Underground" and the History of Terror from the Far-Right in Germany.* London: Routledge, 2016.

Korte, Helmut, and Stephen Lowry. *Brigitte Bardot: Materialien und Analysen.* Brunswick, NJ: IMF, 1997.

Kozol, Wendy. *Distant Wars Visible: The Ambivalence of Witnessing.* Minneapolis: University of Minnesota Press, 2010.

Kramer, Alan. "From Great War to Fascist Warfare." In *Fascist Warfare, 1922–1945: Aggression, Occupation, Annihilation,* edited by Miguel Alonso, Alan Kramer, and Javier Rodrigo, 25–50. Cham, Switzerland: Palgrave Macmillan, 2019.

Kraushaar, Wolfgang, ed. *Frankfurter Schule und Studentenbewegung: Von der Flaschenpost zum Molotowcocktail 1946 bis 1995,* 3 vols. Frankfurt am Main: Rogner bei Zweitausendeins, 1998.

———, ed. *Die RAF und der linke Terrorismus*, vol. 2. Hamburg: Hamburger Edition, 2006.

———. "Der *Vietcong* als Mythos des bewaffneten Volksaufstandes." In Kraushaar, *Die RAF und der linke Terrorismus*, 751–67.

Krimmer, Elisabeth. *German Women's Life Writing and the Holocaust: Complicity and Gender in the Second World War*. Cambridge: Cambridge University Press, 2018.

Lawlor, Ruth. "Contested Crimes: Race, Gender, and Nation in Histories of GI Sexual Violence, World War II." *Journal of Military History* 84 (2020): 541–69.

Leuenberger, Christine, "Socialist Psychotherapy and Its Dissidents." *Journal of the History of the Behavioral Sciences* 37, no. 3 (2001): 261–73.

Long, J. J. "Paratextual Profusion: Photography and Text in Brecht's *Kriegsfibel*." *Poetics Today* 29, no. 1 (2008): 197–224.

Lönnendonker, Siegward, Bernd Rabehl, and Jochen Staadt. *Die antiautoritäre Revolte: Der Sozialistische Deutsche Studentenbund nach der Trennung von der SPD; Band 1: 1960–1967*. Opladen: Westdeutscher Verlag, 2002.

Maguire, Peter. *Facing Death in Cambodia*. New York: Columbia University Press, 2005.

Malle, Louis, dir. *Viva Maria!* France/Italy, NEF-Nouvelles Éditions de Films, Cristaldifilm, Associated Artist Productions, 1965.

Markwick, Roger, and Euridice Charon Cardona. *Soviet Women on the Frontline in the Second World War*. Basingstoke: Palgrave Macmillan, 2012.

Massumi, Brian. *Parables for the Virtual: Movement, Affect, Sensation*. Durham, NC: Duke University Press, 2002.

Mausbach, Wilfried. "America's Vietnam in Germany—Germany in America's Vietnam." In *Changing the World, Changing Oneself: Political Protest and Collective Identities in West Germany and the US in the 1960s and 1970s*, edited by Belinda Davis, Wilfried Mausbach, Martin Klimke, and Carla MacDougall, 41–64. New York: Berghahn, 2010.

McLellan, Josie. *Antifascism and Memory in East Germany: Remembering the International Brigades, 1945–1989*. Oxford: Oxford University Press, 2004.

———. *Love in the Time of Communism: Intimacy and Sexuality in the GDR*. Cambridge: Cambridge University Press, 2011.

Melzer, Patricia. *Death in the Shape of a Young Girl: Women's Political Violence in the Red Army Faction*. New York: New York University Press, 2015.

Michel, Robert, ed. *Dokument und Kunst: Eine Werkstatt—Ein Thema—Elf Jahre—Dreizehn Filme—Vietnam bei H&S*. Berlin: Akademie der Künste der Deutschen Demokratischen Republik, 1977.

Mosler, Hannes. "South Korea's April Revolution through the Lens of West Germany." *Korea Journal* 60, no. 3 (2020): 118–50.

Mostov, Julie. "Sexing the Nation/Desexing the Body: Politics of National Identity in the Former Yugoslavia." In *Gender Ironies of Nationalism:*

Sexing the Nation, edited by Tamar Mayer, 89–112. London: Routledge, 2000.
Mühlhäuser, Regina. "Vergewaltigungen in Deutschland 1945: Nationaler Opferdiskurs und individuelles Erinnern betroffener Frauen." In *Nachkrieg in Deutschland*, edited by Klaus Naumann, 384–408. Hamburg: Hamburger Edition, 2001.
Naimark, Norman. *The Russians in Germany: A History of the Soviet Zone of Occupation 1945–1949*. Cambridge, MA: Belknap, 1995.
Niven, Bill. *Representations of Flight and Expulsion in East German Prose Works*. Rochester, NY: Camden House, 2014.
Nixon, Rob. *Slow Violence and the Environmentalism of the Poor*. Cambridge, MA: Harvard University Press, 2011.
Orzechowski, Marcin, Katarzyna Woniak, Maximilian Schochow, and Florian Steger. "Policy Approaches toward Combatting Venereal Diseases in the Soviet Occupation Zone in Germany (1945–1949), the German Democratic Republic (1949–1989), and the Polish People's Republic (1945–1989)." *Frontiers in Medicine* 8 (2021): 1–7.
Paul, Gerhard. *Bilder des Krieges, Krieg der Bilder: Die Visualisierung des modernen Krieges*. Munich: Schoningk/Fink, 2004.
Pilzweger, Stefanie. *Männlichkeit zwischen Gefühl und Revolution: Eine Emotionsgeschichte der bundesdeutschen 1968er Bewegung*. Bielefeld: Transcript, 2015.
Pleyer, Peter. "Neger und Weiße in dem Film Africa Addio." *Rundfunk und Fernsehen* 15, no. 3 (1967): 271–89.
Plievier, Theodor. *Berlin*. Cologne: Kiepenhauer und Witsch, 2018.
Poiger, Uta. *Jazz, Rock, and Rebels: Cold War Politics and American Culture in a Divided Germany*. Berkeley: University of California Press, 2000.
Poss, Ingrid, Christiane Mückenberger, and Anne Richter, eds. *Das Prinzip Neugier: DEFA-Dokumentarfilmer erzählen*. Berlin: Neues Leben, 2012.
Prince, Gerald. *Narrative as Theme: Studies in French Fiction*. Lincoln: University of Nebraska Press, 1992.
Prince, Simon. "The Global Revolt of 1968 and Northern Ireland." *Historical Journal* 49, no 3 (September 2006): 851–875.
Puar, Jasbir K. *Terrorist Assemblages: Homonationalism in Queer Times*. Durham, NC: Duke University Press, 2007.
Rabehl, Bernd. "Karl Marx und der SDS." *Der Spiegel* 18 (April 29, 1968): 86.
Ramelsberger, Annette, Tanjey Schultz, Rainer Stadler, and Wiebke Ramm, eds. *Der NSU-Prozess: Der Protokoll*. Munich: Antje Kunstmann, 2018.
Reimann, Aribert. "Zwischen Machismo und Coolness: Männlichkeit und Emotion in der westdeutschen 'Kulturrevolution' der 1960er- und 1970er Jahre." In *Die Präsenz der Gefühle: Männlichkeit und Emotion in der Moderne*, edited by Manuel Borutta and Nina Verheyen, 229–53. Bielefeld: Transcript, 2010.
Rezzori, Gregor von. *Die Toten auf Ihre Plätze! Ein Filmtagebuch*. Munich: Goldmann, 1990.

Riemann, Hannes. *Eine Herausforderung an jeden Kommunisten: Die Khmer Rouge, der III. Indochinakrieg und Kambodscha im Fokus von Dokumentarfilmen des Dokumentarfilmstudios H&S (1979–1983)*. Erfurt: TKG, 2011.
Robinson, Thomas Skelton. "Im Netz verheddert: Die Beziehungen des bundesdeutschen Linksterrorismus zur *Volksfront für die Befreiung Palästinas* (1969–1980)." In Kraushaar, *Die RAF und der linke Terrorismus*, 828–904.
Romero, Christiane Zehl. *Anna Seghers: Eine Biographie 1947–1983*. Berlin: Aufbau, 2003.
Rosenberg, Stanley D. "The Threshold of Thrill: Life Stories in the Skies over Southeast Asia." In *Gendering War Talk*, edited by Miriam Cooke and Angela Woollacott, 43–66. Princeton, NJ: Princeton University Press, 1993.
Rupprecht, Caroline. *Asian Fusion: New Encounters in the Asian-German Avant-Garde*. Oxford: Peter Lang, 2020.
Sander, Helke, dir. *Der subjektive Faktor*. Federal Republic of Germany, Helke Sander Filmproduktion, 1981.
Schaefer, Bernd. "Socialist Modernisation in Vietnam: The East German Approach, 1976–89." In *Comrades of Color: East Germany in the Cold War World*, edited by Quinn Slobodian, 95–113. Oxford: Berghahn, 2015.
Schele, Timothy. "Cowboy and Alien: The Bardot Westerns." *Studies in French Cinema* 19, no. 2 (2019): 103–12.
Schlöndorff, Volker. "Zauberlehrling in Mexiko: Die Geschichte des Films 'Viva Maria.'" *Die Zeit*, July 8, 1966, Literature Section: 25.
Schmackpfeffer, Petra. *Frauenbewegung und Prostitution: Über das Verhältnis der alten und neuen deutschen Frauenbewegung zur Prostitution*. Oldenburg: BIS Verlag, 1999.
Schwenkel, Christina. *Building Socialism: The Afterlife of East German Architecture in Urban Vietnam*. Durham, NC: Duke University Press, 2020.
Seghers, Anna. *Erzählungen 1967–1980: Werkausgabe*. Das erzählerische Werk II/6, edited by Helen Fehervary and Bernhard Spies. Berlin: Aufbau, 2005.
———. *Tage wie Staubsand: Briefe 1953–1983*. Berlin: Aufbau, 2010.
———. *Über Kunst und Wirklichkeit*, 4 vols., edited by Sigrid Bock. Berlin: Akademie, 1970–79.
Sharp, Ingrid. "The Sexual Unification of Germany." *Journal of the History of Sexuality* 13, no. 3 (2004): 348–65.
Simpson, Patricia A. "Allegories of Resistance: The Legacy of 1968 in GDR Visual Cultures," in *Celluloid Revolt: German Screen Cultures and the Long 1968*, edited by Christina Gerhardt and Marco Abel, 201–18. Rochester, NY: Camden House, 2019.
Şimşek, Semiya. *Schmerzliche Heimat: Deutschland und der Mord an meinem Vater*. Berlin: Rowohlt, 2013.

Sjoberg, Laura. "Conclusion: The Study of Women, Gender, and Terrorism." In *Women, Gender, and Terrorism*, edited by Laura Sjoberg and Caron E. Gentry, 227–39. Athens: University of Georgia Press, 2011.

Slobodian, Quinn. *Foreign Front: Third World Politics in Sixties West Germany*. Durham, NC: Duke University Press, 2012.

———. "Guerilla Mothers and Distant Doubles: West German Feminists Look at China and Vietnam." *Zeithistorische Forschungen* 12 (2015): 39–65.

Smith, Tom. *Comrades in Arms: Military Masculinities in East German Culture*. Oxford: Berghahn, 2020.

Soldovieri, Stefan. "Germans Suffering in Spain: Cold War Visions of the Spanish Civil War." *Cinémas* 18, no. 1 (2007): 53–69.

Solomon-Godeau, Abigail. *Photography at the Dock: Essays on Photographic History, Institutions, and Practices*. Minneapolis: University of Minnesota Press, 1991.

Southern, Nathan C., with Jacques Weissberger. *The Films of Louis Malle: A Critical Analysis*. Jefferson, NC: McFarland, 2006.

Steinmetz, Rüdiger. "Heynowski & Scheumann: The GDR's Leading Documentary Film Team." *Historical Journal of Film, Radio and Television* 24, no. 3 (2004): 365–79.

Steinmetz, Rüdiger, and Tilo Prase, eds. *Dokumentarfilm zwischen Beweis und Pamphlet: Heynowski & Scheumann und Gruppe Katins*. Leipzig: Leipziger Universitätsverlag, 2002.

Tagg, John. *The Burden of Representation: Essays on Photographies and Histories*. Basingstoke, UK: Macmillan, 1988.

Teraoka, Arlene A. *East, West, and Others: The Third World in Postwar German Literature*. Lincoln: University of Nebraska Press, 1996.

Thomaneck, J. K. A. "The Iceberg in Anna Seghers's Novel *Überfahrt*." *German Life and Letters* 28, no. 1 (1974): 36–45.

Timm, Annette. *The Politics of Fertility in Twentieth-Century Berlin*. Cambridge: Cambridge University Press, 2010.

Trnka, Jamie. "The West German Red Army Faction and Its Appropriation of Latin American Urban Guerilla Struggles." In *Counter-Cultures in Germany and Central Europe: From Sturm und Drang to Baader-Meinhof*, edited by Steve Giles and Maike Oergel, 315–32. Bern: Peter Lang, 2003.

Varon, Jeremy. *Bringing the War Home: The Weather Underground, the Red Army Faction, and Revolutionary Violence in the Sixties and Seventies*. Berkeley: University of California Press, 2004.

Viett, Inge. *Nie war ich furchtloser: Autobiographie*. Reinbek bei Hamburg: Rowohlt, 1999.

Virilio, Paul. *War and Cinema: The Logistics of Perception*, translated by Patrick Camiller. London: Verso, 1989.

Wallace, Ian. *Volker Braun: Forschungsbericht*. Amsterdam: Rodopi, 1986.

Warhol-Down, Robyn. "'What Might Have Been Is Not What Is': Dickens's Narrative Refusals." *Dickens Studies Annual* 41 (2010): 45–59.

Warner, Marina. *Alone of All Her Sex: The Myth and Cult of the Virgin Mary*. London: Weidenfeld & Nicolson, 1976.

———. *Monuments and Maidens: The Allegory of the Female Form*. London: Vintage, 1996 [1985].

Wende, Waltraud. "Beschützer kritisiert man nicht—oder vielleicht doch? Zum Bild Amerikas in der westdeutschen Publizistik der späten 40er und 50er Jahre." In *Modernisierung als Amerikanisierung? Entwicklungslinien der westdeutschen Kultur 1945–1960*, edited by Lars Koch, 63–89. Bielefeld: Transcript, 2007.

Wernicke, Günter. "The World Peace Council and the Antiwar Movement in East Germany." In *America, the Vietnam War, and the World: Comparative and International Perspectives*, edited by Andreas Daum, Lloyd Gardner, and Wilfried Mausbach, 299–320. Cambridge: Cambridge University Press, 2003.

Weßel, Daisy. *Bild und Gegenbild: Die USA in der Belletristik der SBZ und der DDR (bis 1987)*. Wiesbaden: Springer, 1989.

Wolle, Stefan. *Der Traum von der Revolte: Die DDR 1968*. Berlin: Links, 2008.

Wu, Judy Tzu-Chun. *Radicals on the Road: Internationalism, Orientalism, and Feminism during the Vietnam era*. Ithaca, NY: Cornell University Press, 2013.

Yuval-Davis, Nira. *Gender & Nation*. London: Sage Publications, 1997.

Zelizer, Barbie. *About to Die: How News Images Move the Public*. New York: Oxford University Press, 2010.

Contributors

SEÁN ALLAN is professor of German at the University of St Andrews and holds a joint research professorship in Neuere Deutsche Literaturwissenschaft at the Rheinische-Friedrich-Wilhelms-Universität Bonn. His main research areas are Heinrich von Kleist, the culture of the European Enlightenment, and the cinema of the GDR. His publications include *DEFA: East German Cinema, 1946–1992*, coedited with John Sandford (New York: Berghahn, 1996); *Unverhoffte Wirkungen: Erziehung und Gewalt im Werk Heinrich von Kleists*, coauthored with Ricarda Schmidt and Steven Howe (Würzburg: Königshausen & Neumann, 2014); *Re-Imagining DEFA: East German Cinema in Its National and Transnational Contexts*, coedited with Sebastian Heiduschke (New York: Berghahn, 2016); *Screening Art: Modernist Aesthetics and the Socialist Imaginary in East German Cinema* (New York: Berghahn, 2019), and *Inspiration Bonaparte? German Culture and Napoleonic Occupation*, coedited with Jeffrey L. High (Rochester, NY: Camden House, 2021).

CLARE BIELBY is senior lecturer in the Centre for Women's Studies, University of York. She is the author of *Violent Women in Print: Representations in the West German Media of the 1960s and 1970s* (Rochester, NY: Camden House, 2012) and coeditor with Jeffrey Murer of *Perpetrating Selves: Doing Violence, Performing Identity* (London: Palgrave, 2018) and, with Anna Richards, of *Women and Death 3: Women's Representations of Death in German Culture since 1500* (Rochester, NY: Camden House, 2010). Clare has published widely on the subject of gender, violence, and (self-)representation, with a particular focus on the postwar culture of the Federal Republic of Germany. Together with Mererid Puw Davies, she was principal investigator on the research project "Violence Elsewhere: Imagining Violence outside Germany since 1945," which was funded by the German Academic Exchange Service and out of which the present volume emerged.

MARTIN BRADY is emeritus reader in German and film studies at King's College London. He has published on European cinema (Danièle Huillet and Jean-Marie Straub), German Democratic Republic cinema, Brechtian and experimental film, documentary (Wim Wenders, Želimir Žilnik), music (Arnold Schönberg, Paul Dessau, Thomas Larcher, Krautrock), philosophy (Theodor W. Adorno), literature (Heinrich Böll, Bertolt Brecht, Peter Handke, Barbara Honigmann, Elfriede Jelinek), Jewish exile architects, the visual arts (Joseph Beuys, Anselm Kiefer), disability (thalidomide), foraging, and ordinariness. He translated Victor Klemperer's *LTI* (1947) as *The Language of the Third Reich* (London: Continuum, 2000); has interpreted for Alexander Kluge, Michael Haneke, Christian Petzold, Ulrich Seidl, and Edgar Reitz; and is also a visual and performance artist.

MERERID PUW DAVIES is professor of German studies at University College London. She has published widely on modern German-language literature, film, and culture. She has coedited two volumes of scholarly essays and is the author of three monographs. Her interests include the representation of gender and violence and the culture and literature of the 1960s protest movements in West Germany. Together with Clare Bielby, she was principal investigator on the research project "Violence Elsewhere: Imagining Violence outside Germany since 1945," which was funded by the German Academic Exchange Service and out of which the present volume emerged.

EVELIEN GEERTS (PhD, University of California, Santa Cruz; e.m.l.geerts @bham.ac.uk) is an interdisciplinary philosopher, a research fellow at the University of Birmingham, and an affiliated researcher at the Posthumanities Hub and the Eco- and Bioart Lab (Linköping University). Her work focuses on questions of identity, difference, and violence; critical posthumanist, new materialist, and Deleuzoguattarian approaches; and theorizing in (post-)Anthropocenic crisis times. She has published in *Philosophy Today*, *Women's Studies International Forum*, and *CounterText*, and recently coedited the special issues "Dis/Abling Gender" of *Tijdschrift voor Genderstudies* (2022) and "The Somatechnics of Violence" of *Somatechnics: Journal of Bodies Technologies—Power* (forthcoming 2024), publications that can be found at www.eveliengeerts.com.

KATHARINA KARCHER's research focuses on political protest and violence in the twentieth and twenty-first centuries. In this context, she is particularly interested in questions of gender, race, class, dis/ability, and political ideology. She is the author of *Sisters in Arms: Militant Feminisms in the Federal Republic of Germany since 1968* (New York: Berghahn, 2017; paperback edition, 2019; translated into German, 2018). Katharina has coedited three books on political protest and terrorism in Europe and has published numerous articles on feminist struggles, political protest, and violence. Recent articles include "The Pleasure and Pain of Passing as (Dis)Abled: Rudi Dutschke's Exile in the UK (1968–1971) and the Ableism of the West German Student Movement" in *New German Critique* (2021) and "A Threat to National Security? The Legal Dispute between 'Red Rudi' and the British Home Office, 1970–1971" in *Contemporary European History* (2022).

J. J. LONG is professor of German and visual culture at Durham University. He has published extensively on twentieth-century German literature and photography, including the monograph *W. G. Sebald: Image, Archive, Modernity* (Edinburgh: Edinburgh University Press, 2007), and on photography in the work of Bertolt Brecht, Thomas Bernhard, Ernst Jünger, Franz Kafka, and Monika Maron. He is a regular contributor to *Source: Thinking through Photography*. His current research focuses on the photographic book in the Weimar Republic.

ERNEST SCHONFIELD is Lecturer in German at the University of Glasgow. His PhD on Thomas Mann was supervised by Martin Swales and Stephanie Bird at UCL. His research is on modern German literature from Heinrich Heine to Kerstin Hensel. He has written two monographs: *Art and Its Uses in Thomas Mann's Felix Krull* (London: Maney Publishing for the Modern Humanities Research Association, 2008) and *Business Rhetoric in German Novels: From Buddenbrooks to the Global Corporation* (Rochester, NY: Camden House, 2018). His interviews with the Scottish poet (and translator of Brecht) Tom Leonard (1944–2018) are available as an open access PDF: *Tom Leonard in Conversation* (https://www.academia.edu/78312909/Tom_Leonard_in_Conversation, 2022). His most recent publication, coedited with Katya Krylova, is *Thomas Bernhard: Language, History, Subjectivity* (Leiden: Brill, 2023). He is the editor of the website www.germanlit.org.

KATHERINE STONE is associate professor of German studies at the University of Warwick. Her research focuses on the intersections between gender, memory, and contemporary German culture, with a focus on discourses surrounding motherhood and sexual violence. Her first monograph, *Women and National Socialism in Postwar German Literature: Gender, Memory, and Subjectivity* (Rochester, NY: Camden House, 2017), explored the ongoing cultural reluctance to acknowledge the full extent of women's complicity in the "Third Reich." Her next book project will analyze cultural works and media discourse to show how the cultural memory of wartime rape evolved after 1945, with a focus on the role played by emotion in the reception of difficult histories.

Index

1968 (as a signifier for the 1960s protest movements), 40–41, 151, 154–55, 159
9/11 (September 11, 2001), 4–5, 9–10, 175–95; the hyper-exceptionalism of, 9, 175–95

AAM. *See* Antifaschistische Arbeitergruppe Mitteldeutschlands
"Abendland, das" (concept), 21, 24, 34
abortion, 23
action movie (genre), 42
Adams, Eddie, 82
Adorno, Theodor W., 46, 176
Africa: in film, 51, 57; North Africa, 157; postcolonial Africa, 65. *See also* Angola; Guinea-Bissau; Mozambique; Namibia; South Africa
agency: female agency, 95–96, 101, 161; moral agency, 71, 77; revolutionary agency, 9, 155–56, 158–59, 165–66, 168, 171–73; violent agency elsewhere, 9, 149–73
Agent Orange, 105. *See also* US
Agit 883 (journal), 155
Albrecht, Susanne, 150
Albuquerque, 108
Algeria, 157
Alison, Miranda, 12
Allan, Seán, 6, 7
allegory, 6, 14, 20, 22, 25, 27, 33–34, 36–38, 52, 57
Allende, Salvador, 78
Alter, Nora, 61, 129
Amado, Jorge, 104
Amazon, the, 109, 113, 118–19, 122–23

American Psychiatric Association (APA), 109
anarchism, 6, 31, 44, 49, 56, 169
Anderson, Benedict, 159
Andes, the, 109, 111, 119
Angola, 159
antiauthoritarianism: and Frantz Fanon, 157; and Che Guevara, 44, 161; and Marxism, 6, 44, 57; in West Berlin and West Germany, 38–59, 96; and West German reception of *Viva Maria!*, 6, 38–59; and women, 41, 45, 155–56
anti-Bolshevism, 34
anti-communism, 64
antifascism, 25, 62–63, 77, 121, 160, 170
Antifaschistische Arbeitergruppe Mitteldeutschlands (AAM), 25–26, 29
anti-Nazism, 34
antisemitism, 22, 34, 56
antiwar, 13, 31, 66–67, 76, 82
APA. *See* American Psychiatric Association
Arbeiter Illustrierte Zeitung (*AIZ*) (newspaper), 84
Arlen, Michael J., 71
Asendorf, Christoph, 91
Asia, 60, 101, 103, 133, 165; "Asiatic" stereotypes in German discourse on the USSR, 22, 34; East and Southeast Asia, 8, 10, 112, 141
Auschwitz, 144–45
Austria-Hungary, 54
authoritarianism, 31, 34
autobiography, 2, 9–10, 105, 149, 160, 173

avant-garde, 47–48, 68, 73

Baader, Andreas, 39, 158
Baden-Württemberg, 24
Bal, Mieke, 37
Baldwin, James, 115–16
Baldwin, James, works by: *Giovanni's Room*, 115
Bamberg, 24
Barad, Karen, 183, 186–87, 189
Barad, Karen, works by: *Meeting the Universe Halfway*, 180, 183, 189
Bardot, Brigitte, 6, 11, 38, 40, 42, 44, 51, 58
Barkawi, Tarak, 16
Barthes, Roland, 52–53
Barthes, Roland, works by: *Mythologies*, 52
Battle of Berlin, 33
Beijing, 148. *See also* Peking
Bellag, Lothar, 62
Baumann, Michael, 162, 165
Bendandi, Poldi, 55
Benjamin, Walter, 7, 84–85, 88, 134, 180, 186, 188–89, 191–92
Benjamin, Walter, works by: "Der Autor als Produzent," 84; "Über den Begriff der Geschichte," 188
Bergen-Belsen, 140
Bergman, Arlene Eisen, 96
Berlin, 25, 35–36, 57, 124, 138, 155, 159, 164. *See also* West Berlin
Berlin crisis, 77
Berlin Wall, 77, 122–24, 152
Berliner Ensemble, 85, 135, 142
Berliner Rundfunk I (radio station), 20
Berliner Zeitung (newspaper), 23
Berthold, Erika, 155
Bewegung 2. Juni, 9, 149, 152, 163, 165, 166
Beyer, Frank, 64, 77
Beyer, Frank, works by: *Fünf Patronenhülsen*, 64, 73, 75, 77
Bielby, Clare, 9, 15, 40
Bilbao, 146
Black Panthers, 172
Blaylock, Sarah, 61

"Blut und Boden" (concept), 140
Böhnhardt, Uwe, 190
Boieldieu, François-Adrien, 48
Boieldieu, François-Adrien, and Eugène Scribe, works by: *La Dame blanche*, 48, 53
Bolshevism, 22–32
Borchert, Wolfgang, 106
Borchert, Wolfgang, works by: *Draußen vor der Tür*, 106
borders (of nation states), 45, 121, 123–24
BPRS. *See* Bund proletarisch-revolutionärer Schriftsteller
Brady, Martin, 8, 13, 72
Braidotti, Rosi, 187
Brandt, Marion, 115
Brandt, Willy, 76–77
Braun, Volker, 7, 67, 81–103, 132–33
Braun, Volker, works by: *Der ferne Krieg*, 132–33; *KriegsErklärung*, 7, 67, 81–103, 133; *Texte in zeitlicher Folge*, vol. 2, 85, 86, 88, 98–99
Brazil, 122, 123
BRD. *See* Germany
Brecht, Bertolt, 7, 10, 13, 71, 74, 83–85, 88, 119, 132–35, 142
Brecht, Bertolt, works by: *Aufstieg und Fall der Stadt Mahagonny*, 119; "Der Dreigroschenprozess," 84; *Kriegsfibel*, 7, 83, 133, 134, 135, 142; *Mann ist Mann*, 74; "Über Fotografie," 84
Bredemeyer, Reiner, 73, 139
Britain, 62; British bombing campaigns in Second World War, 19; British military, 21, 47, 50
Brown, Timothy Scott, 39–40, 44, 151, 153, 156, 159
Browning, Christopher, 12
Buchenwald, 63, 140
Buchholz (location in Germany), 177
Bund proletarisch-revolutionärer Schriftsteller (BPRS), 30
Bundesamt für Verfassungsschutz, 178
Bundesrepublik Deutschland (BRD). *See* Germany

Bundeswehr, 66
Bunke, Tamara, 167, 171
Busch, Peter, 66
bystanders, 14, 79

California, 79, 83
Cambodia, 3, 13, 128–31, 137–38, 144, 146, 147; Killing Fields, 8, 127–28, 139. *See also* Heynowski, Walter
capitalism, 23, 62, 69, 79, 83, 84, 88, 101, 133; and alienation, 61, 72, 78, 79, 83, 98; anticapitalism, 95–96, 103; capitalist socialization, 7; and colonialism, 78; and Marxist theory, 7, 67; monopoly capitalism, 135; relationship to slavery and racism, 28; and *Steinzeit*, 120; and Vietnam War, 88, 90, 93; and violence, 33, 78, 91
Carrière, Jean-Claude, 43
Carrière, Jean-Claude, works by: *Viva Maria: Roman*, 43
Castro, Fidel, 156
Catholicism, 42, 72, 108
Cayrol, Jean, 147
CBS (US television station), 79
CDU. *See* Christlich Demokratische Union
Celan, Paul, 56
Celan, Paul, works by: "Todesfuge," 56
censorship, 30, 129
Chamberlain, Paul, 81
von Chamisso, Adalbert, 54
von Chamisso, Adalbert, works by: "Peter Schlemihls wundersame Geschichte," 54
chemical weapons, 133
Chile, 78, 129–30, 137
China, 8, 34, 44, 127–29, 138–39, 140, 146; and the Cultural Revolution, 44, 128, 139–40
Chopin, Frédéric, 147
Chopin, Frédéric, works by: *Piano Sonata No. 2*, 147
Christianity, 31, 35, 72. *See also* Catholicism

Christlich Demokratische Union (CDU), 76
Christlich-Soziale Union (CSU), 76
Cimino, Michael, 79, 112
Cimino, Michael, works by: *The Deer Hunter*, 79, 112
cinematography, 7, 71–73, 79, 134
climate change, 4
Clinton, George, 111
Clinton, George, works by: "March to the Witch's Castle," 111
Clodfelter, Mark, 105
Cold War, 3, 7, 9, 11, 13, 18–37, 63, 79, 81, 82, 103, 153, 192; Cold War allies, 5, 13; Cold War anxieties, 124; Cold War memories of CRSV, 37; Cold War narratives, 5, 19; Cold War political climate, 124; Cold War tensions, 43, 72; global Cold War, 60–80, 105
Colombia, 8, 104–5, 107, 111, 113, 119, 122–23
colonialism, 50; anticolonialism, 6, 39, 62; and capitalism, 78; colonial exploitation, 140; colonial legacy, 63, 105; French colonialism, 135, 146; German colonial projects, 58
comedy, 6, 11, 38, 42, 48–49
communism: anti-communism, 31, 64, 145; and Cambodia, 138; communist fighters, 170; communist iconography, 148; communist identity, 138; communist orthodoxy, 106; communist prisoners, 63; conflict with fascists, 159; Eastern communism, 23–24; German communists, 63; Jewish communism, 104, 124; and Khmer Rouge, 137, 147; and North Korea, 24; and Pol Pot, 138, 141
Côn Sơn, 140
concentration camps, 73, 110, 111, 140, 144. *See also* Auschwitz; Bergen-Belsen; Buchenwald
Condor Legion, 60, 66, 76

conflict-related sexual violence (CRSV), 18–37. *See also* Cold War; propaganda; victims; violence
Connell, R. W., 115
Cooper, Gary, 115–16
Coppola, Francis Ford, 79, 112
Coppola, Francis Ford, works by: *Apocalypse Now*, 79, 112
cowboy, 38, 116
critical (new) materialisms, 9, 183, 186–87, 195
Critical Theory, 13, 41, 48
CRSV. *See* conflict-related sexual violence
CSU. *See* Christlich-Soziale Union
Cuautla (location in Mexico), 56, 58
Cuba, 44, 65
Cuthbert, Lauren, 61, 122
Czechoslovakia, 124
Czernowitz, 54, 55, 56

Dartmouth Medical School, 112
Davies, Mererid Puw, 6, 96, 156
Davis, Angela, 78, 155, 167
DDR. *See* Germany
DDR Magazin (newsreel), 65, 67
De Niro, Robert, 111–12
deconstruction, 75, 77, 134, 142, 176, 180, 186–87
DEFA (Deutsche Film-Aktiengesellschaft), 60–80, 129
DEFA Studio für Wochenschau und Dokumentarfilme, 65
DEFA-Gruppe Heynowski und Scheumann, 69. *See also* Heynowski, Walter; Scheumann, Gerhard; Studio H&S
Delacroix, Eugène, 51–52
Delacroix, Eugène, works by: *La Liberté guidant le peuple*, 51
Democratic Republic of Vietnam (DRV). *See* Vietnam
denazification, 178. *See also* National Socialism
Der Augenzeuge (newsreel), 65, 67
Der Kurier (newspaper), 43, 57
Der Spiegel (journal), 44, 56

Derrida, Jacques, 175, 179–80, 182, 186–89, 191–92
Derrida, Jacques, works by: *Specters of Marx*, 179, 189
Dessau, Paul, 68, 132–33
Dessau, Paul, works by: *Deutsches Miserere*, 133; "Friedenslied," 132; *Geschäftsbericht*, 133; *Fünf Melodramen*, 133; *Vietnam in dieser Stunde*, 132
Deutsche Bank, 182
Deutsche Demokratische Republik (DDR). *See* Germany
Deutscher Schriftstellerverband (DSV), later the Schriftstellerverband der DDR, 104
Diagnostic and Statistical Manual of Mental Disorders, third edition (DSM-III), 109
Die Welt (newspaper), 182
Die Zeit (newspaper), 43, 182
Dietrich, Marlene, 116
Dimitroff, Georgi, 62
Diogenes (Classical figure), 45
documentaries, 6, 8, 11, 13, 31, 60–61, 62, 65, 67–71, 127, 132, 135, 139, 142, 146–48
Döner Morde, 194
DRV. *See* Vietnam
Dubost, Paulette, 55
Dutschke, Rudi, 39, 41, 43–45, 49, 156, 165

East, the: East Berlin, 67, 77, 124, 155, 169; East/West divide, 3, 22, 84, 98, 133, 135, 165; Eastern bloc, 67, 81; Eastern Communism, 23; Eastern Europe, 70; Eastern Front, 31; Eastern territories (German, prior to 1945), 19. *See also* Germany
Eastman Kodak Company, 142
Eichmann, Adolf, 76
Emma (journal), 160
Engels, Friedrich, 28
Enlightenment, the (cultural movement), 188
Ensslin, Gudrun, 39, 168

Enzensberger, Ulrich, 48
epigram. *See* photo-epigram
Erhard, Ludwig, 66
Eulenspiegel Verlag, 134
Evans, Sara M., 159
Eve (Biblical figure), 47

fall of Berlin (1945), 31
Fanon, Frantz, 154, 157
Fanon, Frantz, works by: *The Wretched of the Earth*, 157
fascism, 34, 60, 62–64, 66, 68, 72, 76, 79, 122, 129, 133, 144–45, 159, 170, 188
feature films, 6, 40, 62, 65, 79, 148
Federal Republic of Germany (FRG). *See* Germany
Fehervary, Helen, 106, 107
femininity, 14, 172; feminine imagery, 46; feminine sensibility, 160; feminine traits, 161; feminine Uncanny, 53; normative femininity, 173
feminism: and Bewegung 2. Juni, 168; Black feminism, 28; feminist affect studies, 2; feminist identity, 168, 172; feminist interpretation of *Viva Maria!*, 6, 52, 156; feminist movement, 168; feminist scholarship on victimhood, 12; feminist scholarship on violence, 2, 14, 15, 16; feminist sensibility, 168; and filmmaking, 41, 156, 158, 172; and gender identity, 2; the personal is political, 15; and queer theory, 170; West German feminists, 160. *See also* Frauenbefreiungsfront, die; women's liberation movement
Film und Fernsehen (journal), 138
Filo, John Paul, 82
"Final Solution," the, 76, 144
First World War. *See* World War I
Fischer, Joschka, 153
Fleming, Victor, and King Vidor, works by: *The Wizard of Oz*, 111
FLN. *See* Front de Libération Nationale
Fonda, Jane, 76

France, 54, 104, 115, 135; French troops, 21
Frankfurt am Main, 39
Frankfurter Allgemeine Zeitung (newspaper), 182
Frauenbefreiungsfront, die, 155–56
Freud, Sigmund, 53, 55, 57
Freud, Sigmund, works by: "Das Unheimliche," 53
FRG. *See* Germany
Friedensrat der DDR, 67, 85
Front de Libération Nationale (Algeria) (FLN), 158
Führer, the, 142, 144
Fulbrook, Mary, 121, 126
Funkadelic, 111
Funkadelic, works by: "March to the Witch's Castle," 111

Garden of Eden, 47
Garraio, Júlia, 21
Gauck, Joachim, 191
GDR. *See* Germany
GDR psychology, 110
GDR workers' uprising, 31
Gebhardt, Miriam, 21
Geerts, Evelien, 9–10
Gehler, Fred, 138–39
Geneva Convention, 7, 70
Gerhardt, Christina, 14
German Autumn, the, 163
German Democratic Republic (GDR). *See* Germany
German soldiers, 112, 121. *See also* Bundeswehr; Nationale Volksarmee
German Studies, 2, 4, 15
Germany: Cold War Germany, 18–37; Democratic Republic of Germany (GDR), 3, 5, 6–8, 10–11, 15, 18–20, 22–25, 28–29, 60–69, 75–77, 81, 83, 85, 95, 97, 98, 101, 103–4, 106, 116, 120–24, 126–48, 150, 152, 167, 169; East Germany (*see* German Democratic Republic); Federal Republic of Germany (FRG), 3, 5, 6, 9–11, 13, 18–19, 21–24, 31, 37–59, 60, 62–67, 76–77, 80–82, 85, 94,

Germany: Federal Republic of
Germany (FRG) (*continued*)
96–97, 101, 104, 106, 129–30,
133, 151–54, 156, 158, 162–67,
171–72, 174–95; postunification
Germany, 10; postwar Germany, 1,
15, 65, 83, 121; West Germany
(*see* Federal Republic of Germany)
Gerron, Kurt, 145
Gerron, Kurt, and Karel Pečený,
works by: *Theresienstadt: Ein
Dokumentarfilm aus dem jüdischen
Siedlungsgebiet*, 145
Gestapo, 25, 140
Glenn H. Martin Aerospace
Manufacturing Company, 91
Global North, 13
Global South, 6, 13, 59, 63, 81
Godard, Jean-Luc, 135–37
Godard, Jean-Luc, works by: *Jusqu'à
la victoire*, 135; *Loin du Vietnam*
(collaboratively made film), 132
Godard, Jean-Luc, and Anne-Marie
Miéville, works by: *Ici et ailleurs*,
135–37
Goebbels, Joseph, 31
von Goethe, Johann Wolfgang, 46
von Goethe, Johann Wolfgang, works
by: *Die Leiden des jungen Werther*,
46
Goldman, Emma, 155
Gordon, Avery F., 180, 186–87
Gotsche, Otto, 5, 19–20, 25–26, 28,
30, 32, 37
Gotsche, Otto, works by: *Zwischen
Nacht und Morgen*, 5, 19–20,
25–27, 29–30, 36
Greece, 190
Gregg, Melissa, 181
Grunewald, 170–71
guerrilla fighting, 44, 69, 96, 150,
153–54, 156, 158, 162–64, 167,
170–71
Guevara, Che, 44, 132, 152, 154,
159, 161 167
Guinea-Bissau, 159
Gültekin, Gökhan, 195
Günther, Anton, 98

Günther, Anton, works by:
"Feierohmd," 98
Gürbüz, Sedat, 195

Habsburg Empire, 54
Haeberle, Ron, 82
Haggiag, Brahim, 158
Hallstein Doctrine, 65
Hamburg, 152, 189, 192, 194
Hamilton, George, 50
hammer and sickle, 8, 29, 127–48
Hanau, 195
Hanebrink, Paul, 22
Hanoi, 61, 69, 108
Haraway, Donna, J., 177, 183, 187
Hashemi, Said Nesra, 195
hauntology, 9, 174–95
Heimkehrer (literary and film genre),
106, 112, 121
Heineman, Elisabeth, 22
Hellmich, Peter, 69, 73
Herzog, Dagmar, 110, 114
Heynowski, Walter, 6, 60–61, 67–80
Heynowski, Walter, works by:
Brüder und Schwestern, 131
Heynowski, Walter, and Gerhard
Scheumann, 60, 67–72, 74–76,
78–79, 122, 127–48
Heynowski, Walter, and Gerhard
Scheumann, works by: *400 cm3*,
68–69, 131–34; *Amok*, 61, 79;
Cambodia trilogy, 129, 139, 140,
148; *Der Dschungelkrieg*, 129;
Der lachende Mann, 69; *Der
Mann an der Rampe*, 131;
Die Angkar, 8, 127–48; *Die
Teufelsinsel*, 78, 135, 140;
*Kampuchea: Sterben und
Auferstehn*, 129, 137, 139; *O.K.*,
130; *Piloten im Pyjama*, 7, 60–61,
67, 69, 71–78, 80, 122, 140;
Remington Cal 12, 78, 135
Higgins, Lynn, 27
Hitler, Adolf, 31, 55, 64, 121, 145
Ho Chi Minh, 133, 154
Ho Chi Minh, works by: "Die rot und
goldene Fahne," 133
Hölderlin, Friedrich, 68

Hölderlin, Friedrich, works by: "Der Tod für das Vaterland," 68
Hollywood, 62, 115
Holocaust, the, 22, 56, 125, 147
Homo Sovieticus, 126
Honecker, Erich, 69, 140
horror (film genre), 62
Huberty, James, 79
Humphrey, Hubert, 88

ideological elsewhere, 20, 22, 25, 30–33, 36–37
Ieng Sary, 127–28
imagined communities, 40, 159, 162, 166–67, 171
imperialism: British imperialism, 58, 62; GDR ideas about FRG imperialism, 62, 68; ideas about capitalist imperialism, 103; ideas about Chinese imperialism, 128, 139; ideas about global imperialism, 129; ideas about imperial ideology, 128, 135, 137–38; ideas about imperialist expansionism, 63; ideas about US imperialism, 24, 44, 61–62, 66, 81–82, 94, 103, 167; within *Steinzeit*, 120, 123
Indochina, 65, 76, 128
institutional racism, 179, 183–84, 186–87, 189–90, 195
International Brigades (in the Spanish Civil War), 63. *See also* Thälmann Brigade
internationalism, 6, 39, 123–24, 153
Ireland, 42, 44
Irving, Douglas, 114
Israel, 135, 162
Ivens, Joris, 132
Ivens, Joris, works by: *Loin du Vietnam* (collaboratively made film), 132

Jacopetti, Gualtiero, and Franco Prosperi, 51
Jacopetti, Gualtiero, and Franco Prosperi, works by: *Africa Addio*, 51, 57

Jamba, Kolong, 177
Janzen, Marike, 124
Japan, 105
Jeffords, Susan, 117
Jews, Jewish people, people of Jewish background, 22, 56, 104, 124, 144, 145; Jewish identity, 124, 145
Johnson, Lyndon B., 66, 88
Johnson, Michael, 78
Jordan (country), 162–63

Kafka, Franz, 35, 107
Karcher, Katharina, 9, 10
Kätzel, Ute, 155, 168
Keilson, Hans, 114
Kelly, Liz, 15
Kent State University shootings, 82
Khaled, Leila, 155, 167
Khmer Rouge, 8, 127–48
Khrushchev, Nikita, 64
Kierpacz, Mercedes, 195
Kiesinger, Kurt-Georg, 76, 77
Kılıç, Habil, 191–92
Kılıç, Pinar, 191
Killing Fields. *See* Cambodia
Kim Il Sung, 24
Klonk, Charlotte, 77–78
Knolle, Hans-Peter, 165
Kodak, 142
Koehler, Daniel, 193–94
Kohlhaase, Wolfgang, 150
Kommunistische Partei Deutschlands (KPD), 25
konkret (journal), 96, 156
Korea, 18; Korean War, 19, 24, 123; South Korea, 24
Korte, Helmut, 49
Kozol, Wendy, 95
KPD. *See* Kommunistische Partei Deutschlands
Krahl, Hans-Jürgen, 165
Kreuzberg (location in Berlin), 152
Krimmer, Elisabeth, 19
Kulturbund zur demokratischen Erneuerung Deutschlands, 31
Kunzelmann, Dieter, 156
Kursbuch (journal), 157
Kurtović, Hamza, 195

La Conquista (Spanish colonization of the Americas), 123
Landshut plane hijack, 163
Latin America, 3, 6, 13, 38, 41, 150–51
Lawrence, Stephen, 184
Lebanon, 163
"Lehrstück," 7, 71. *See also* Brecht, Bertolt
Leipzig, 103
LeMay, Curtis, 105
Lennox, Sara, 153
Leupold, Hans, 73
liberalism, 22
Liberty (allegorical figure), 51–52. *See also* Delacroix, Eugène
Life (magazine), 134
life writing, 11, 161
literature. *See* novels
Long, J. J., 7
Long Biên Bridge, 108
Lowry, Stephen, 49
Lukács, Georg, 125
Lumumba, Patrice, 69
Luxemburg, Rosa, 9, 155, 168–69, 172

MacGuire, Peter, 148
Madonna (religious figure), 95. *See also* Virgin Mary
Madrid, 63
Magdeburg, 152
Maier-Witt, Silke, 150
Mainz, 104
Malaya, 105
male fraternity and relationships, 115, 116, 117, 118–20
Malle, Louis, 6, 13–14, 38–59, 156
Malle, Louis, works by: *Viva Maria!*, 38–59
Mao Zedong, 137, 139–41, 154
Maoism, 128, 144
Marighella, Carlos, 154, 163, 165
Marighella, Carlos, works by: *Minimanual of the Urban Guerrilla*, 163
Marxism, 28, 49, 67, 83; Marx, Karl, 44, 49; Marxism-Leninism, 8, 130, 137–38, 141, 147

Marxist intellectuals, 83; Marxist theory, 7; orthodox Marxism, 6, 44, 56; orthodox revolutionary Marxism, 188; revolutionary Marxism, 32
masculinity, 8, 10, 90, 97, 115–17, 120, 154, 161, 163–65; colonized masculinity, 157; hegemonic masculinity, 115; military masculinity, 7, 95, 97–99, 101, 103, 115, 120; phallic masculinity, 91; revolutionary masculinity, 163; Soviet-style masculinity, 117; US masculinity, 29, 99, 101, 116; violent masculinity, 8, 172
McArthur, Douglas, 24
McCarthyism, 64
McDonald's Massacre, 79
Meinhof, Ulrike, 155, 168
memoir, 6, 14, 41, 43, 54, 56, 58, 70
memory, 5, 10, 15, 19–21, 30, 37, 57, 76–77, 122
Merkel, Angela, 186–88
Mexico, 6, 40–41, 51, 54–56, 59, 104–5, 124; Mexico City, 55; Mexican Revolution, 49, 56, 58
Meyer, Till, 162
Mickel, Karl, 133
Mickel, Karl, works by: "Das zerschossene Dorf," 133
Middle East, 3, 65, 151, 162–63, 167
Miéville, Anne-Marie, 135–37
Miéville, Anne-Marie, works by. *See* Godard, Jean-Luc
Ministerium für Staatssicherheit (GDR) (Stasi), 124, 152
modernism: and Bertolt Brecht, 13; and Paul Dessau, 68; and filmmaking, 71, 73, 79, 134; GDR modernism, 10, 11, 15; modernist blatancy, 72, 146
Möller, Olaf, 130
Molotov cocktails, 159
montage (aesthetic technique), 33, 71, 88, 134, 137
Mora, Dennis, 78
Moreau, Jeanne, 6, 11, 38, 40, 42, 44, 51, 58

motherhood, 87, 95–96, 102, 156, 170
Mozambique, 159
Müller, Friedrich, 69
Müller, Hans-Harald, 31
Münch, Gerhard, 73
Mundlos, Uwe, 190
Munich, 101, 191
musical (film genre), 43
musical comedy (film genre), 6, 38
My Lai massacre, 67, 82

Namibia, 159
nation state, 126, 180, 187–88
National Liberation Front (NLF) (RVN), 69. See also Vietcong
National Socialism (Nazism), 8, 12, 26, 29–30, 56, 58, 110–11, 121, 124–25, 129, 131, 138, 145, 153–54, 159, 170–72, 178–79, 181; denazification, 121, 178–79, 194; National Socialist (Nazi) Germany, 63, 76, 144; National Socialist (Nazi) Party, 31; National Socialist (Nazi) persecution, 110, 124–26; neo-Nazism, 9, 175, 178–79, 192, 195
Nationale Volksarmee (NVA), 60, 63–64
Nationalsozialistischer Untergrund (NSU), 9–10, 12, 175–95
NATO. See North Atlantic Treaty Organization
Nazism. See National Socialism
NBC (US broadcasting network), 70
Nemmersdorf (location in former East Prussia), 20
Neruda, Pablo, 104, 132
"Neuer Mensch" (concept), 126
Neues Deutschland (ND) (newspaper), 24, 66, 127–28, 148
Neukölln (location in Berlin), 132
New Left: New Leftists, 153, 159, 164; and sexuality, 45; and violence, 58; in West Berlin and the FRG, 43, 45, 56, 150–51, 157, 159, 164; and women, 154, 172
New York, 182
New York Stock Exchange, 88–90, 93

New Yorker (magazine), 71
newspapers, 23, 43, 84, 91–92, 127–28, 134, 166, 182
Nielinger-Vakil, Carola, 72
Nixon, Rob, 4, 16
North Atlantic Treaty Organisation (NATO), 63, 128
Notre Dame (cathedral in Paris), 46, 51
novella, 7–8, 104, 106
novels, 5, 13–14, 19–20, 25–29, 31–35, 43, 46, 58
Noyd, Dale, 78
NSU. See Nationalsozialistischer Untergrund
nuclear weapons, 67, 76–77, 80
Nuremberg, 183, 192, 194
Nuremberg trials, 56, 76, 140
NVA. See Nationale Volksarmee

omission technique, 8, 108, 113, 125–26
Operation Linebacker II (in Vietnam conflict), 105, 112
Operation Rolling Thunder (in Vietnam conflict), 69
orientalism, 28, 34–35, 103, 151, 165–67
Özüdoğru, Abdurrahim, 191–92

pacifism, 57, 99, 153
Palestine, 135; Palestinian fighters and militants, 150–51, 162–63, 165–67, 171; Palestinian Liberation Movement, 162
paranoia, 109, 111, 114, 121, 124–25
Paris, 45, 46, 152
Paris Peace Accords, 111
Paryla, Karl, 63
Paryla, Karl, works by: *Mich dürstet*, 63–64
Paul, Rudolf, 34–35
Păun, Vili Viorel, 195
Pavlov, Ivan, 110
peace, 16, 20, 24, 27, 61, 78, 81, 118–19, 124, 128, 132
Pečený, Karel, works by. See Gerron, Kurt

Peking, 128. *See also* Beijing
Perincioli, Christina, 155, 172
perpetrator studies, 3, 11, 12
Perpetrator Studies Network, 12
perpetrators, 12, 14, 20, 25, 36, 78, 98, 99, 110–11, 122, 125–26, 139–40, 178, 189, 191, 195
Phnom Penh, 139–40
photo-epigram, 7, 83, 86–88, 90–91, 93–101, 103
photography: Brecht's writing on, 84–85; history of, 83; moving-image photography, 142; news photography, 83; postwar photography, 83; as a truth-telling medium, 88; and victimhood, 95; and the Vietnam War, 7, 82–83
Pilzweger, Stefanie, 153–54, 161
Pink Panther, 190
Plievier, Theodor, 5, 19–20, 30–37
Plievier, Theodor, works by: *Berlin*, 5, 19–20, 30–36; *Moskau*, 20; *Stalingrad*, 20, 31
poetry, 7, 10, 56, 67–68, 83, 87–88, 90, 93, 95–101, 103, 132–34
Pol Pot, 127–28, 140–41, 144–45, 147; Pol-Potism, 138
Politburo (GDR), 127
political extremism, 178, 194
Polizeiruf 110 (TV series), 61
Pontecorvo, Gillo, 158
Pontecorvo, Gillo, works by: *The Battle of Algiers*, 158
postcolonialism: interpretation of *Steinzeit*, 124; postcolonial Africa, 65; postcolonial conflict, 39; postcolonial politics, 13, 57; postcolonial world, 81
poststructuralism, 139
post-traumatic stress disorder (PTSD), 8, 10, 106, 109–10, 112, 114, 125
Prince, Gerald, 27, 30, 162
prison writing, 152, 160, 169, 172
prisoner(s) of war (POW), 61, 70, 77
propaganda: anti-American propaganda, 73; Chinese propaganda, 138, 142–44; counterpropaganda, 29; and CRSV, 19–20, 35, 37; and the Cold War, 19, 37; and the FRG, 21; GDR propaganda, 24, 28–29, 65; military-industrial propaganda, 93; political propaganda, 19; and Studio H&S, 6, 61, 69, 71, 75, 77, 79, 130, 133, 138, 142, 144; and the "Third Reich," 20, 31, 34; and Vietnam, 82; Western propaganda, 85, 134
Prosperi, Franco. *See* Jacopetti, Gualtiero
PTSD. *See* post-traumatic stress disorder
Puar, Jasbir K., 185

queer theory, 170, 176–77, 182, 187–89
Quensel, Edelgart, 161

Rabehl, Bernd, 6, 41, 44–47, 49–50, 52, 56, 57
racism, 16, 22, 28, 51, 57, 103, 177–79, 184, 186–87, 190–92, 195
RAD. *See* Reichsarbeitsdienst
Radványi, László, 124
RAF. *See* Rote Armee Fraktion
rape, 18–24, 26–27, 32–35, 37. *See also* violence
realist fiction, 11
Red Army, 19, 21, 23, 30–35, 144
Red Brigade, 145
Reichsarbeitsdienst (RAD), 32
Reichstag, 138, 144
Reiling, Annette, 104
Reimann, Aribert, 154, 161
Reinders, Ralf, 163, 165–67
Reinl, Harald, 64
Reinl, Harald, works by: *Solange du lebst*, 64
Republic of Vietnam. *See* Vietnam
Resnais, Alain, 147
Resnais, Alain, works by: *Nuit et brouillard* (film), 147
von Rezzori, Gregor, 6, 41–43, 51, 54–56, 58

von Rezzori, Gregor, works by: *Die Toten auf Ihre Plätze! Ein Filmtagebuch*, 41, 54, 56, 58
Riemann, Hannes, 127, 129, 148
right-wing extremism in postwar Germany, 178–79, 194. *See also* National Socialism; Nationalsozialistischer Untergrund
Ringsdorf, H. B., 75–77, 140
Risner, Robinson, 70
Robeson, Paul, 78
Rodriguez, Pio Olmos, 51, 54–55, 58
Röhl, Klaus-Rainer, 39
Romania, 54–55
romantic comedy (film genre), 42
Romanticism, 106
Romero, Christiane Zehl, 120, 126
Rosenberg, Stanley D., 112–13
Rote Armee Fraktion (RAF), 9, 39, 77, 149, 152, 155, 158, 192, 193
Rothberg, Michael, 122
Russell, Bertrand, 133
Russian Revolution (1905), 32; Russian Revolution (1917), 21
RVN. *See* Vietnam

Sahara Desert, 116
Said, Edward, 3
Saigon, 69, 99, 158
Salazar, Emiliano Zapata, 56
Salur (location in Turkey), 183–85
San Sebastián (location in Colombia), 108
San Ysidro (location in California), 79
Sander, Helke, 40–41, 51–52, 156
Sander, Helke, works by: *Der Subjective Faktor*, 40, 51–52, 156
Sandinistas, 158
Saraçoğlu, Fatih, 195
Sartre, Jean-Paul, 157
Savage, John, 112
Saxony-Anhalt, 25
Schenk, Ralf, 147
Scheumann, Gerhard, 6, 61, 67–72, 74–76, 78–79, 122, 127–48
Scheumann, Gerhard, works by: "Dokumentarfilm im Spannungsfeld von Strategie und Taktik (Gedanken zur Selbstverständigung und zur Diskussion," 145. *See also* Walter Heynowski
Schleyer, Hanns Martin, 77–78
Schlöndorff, Volker, 40, 43, 150
Schlöndorff, Volker, works by: *Die Stille nach dem Schuss*, 150
Schneider, Peter, 153
Schonfield, Ernest, 7–8
Schriftstellerverband der DDR. *See* Deutscher Schriftstellerverband
Schubert, Wilfried, 177
Schutzstaffel (SS), 121
Schwarzer, Alice, 161
Scorsese, Martin, 111
Scorsese, Martin, works by: *Taxi Driver*, 111
scientific positivism, 188
"scorched earth," 29, 30, 115
Scribe, Eugène, 48
Scribe, Eugène, works by. *See* Boieldieu, François-Adrien
SDS. *See* Sozialistischer Deutscher Studentenbund
Second World War. *See* World War II
Section 129a (in FRG Criminal Code), 193, 194
SED. *See* Sozialistische Einheitspartei Deutschlands
Seghers, Anna, 7–8, 11–12, 104–26
Seghers, Anna, works by: "Das Ende," 111; *Der Mann und sein Name*, 121; *Steinzeit*, 7, 8, 104–26; *Wiederbegegnung*, 104–5
Seighworth, Gregory J., 181
September 11, 2001. *See* 9/11
sexual assault, 24. *See also* rape; violence
sexual harassment, 28–29
sexual objectification, 28–29, 33
Shanghai, 35
Sharpe, Mani, 158
SI. *See* Situationist International
Silver, Brenda, 27
Silverman, Kaja, 158
Simpson, Patricia, 61
Şimşek, Adile, 184–86

Şimşek, Enver, 183–86, 191
Şimşek, Semiya, 183–86, 190
Şimşek, Semiya, works by:
    Schmerzliche Heimat, 185
Singateh, Bakary, 177–79, 195
Sinn und Form (journal), 104, 131
situated knowledges, 177
Situationist International (SI), 47, 49
Sjoberg, Laura, 15
Skelton-Robinson, Thomas, 162
Slánský, Rudolph, 124
slapstick, 42
Slobodian, Quinn, 3, 16–17, 153–54, 165
Smith, Tom, 97, 120
socialism, 21–23, 26, 29, 30–31, 61, 72, 76–77, 81, 97, 101, 121, 145, 155, 166
Socialist Realism, 26, 106
soft power and the GDR, 65
Solanas, Valerie, 155
Soldovieri, Stefan, 63
Solomon-Godeau, Abigail, 87–88
South Africa, 159
Southern, Nathan C., 50, 52
Soviet Union, 5, 18, 24, 31, 32, 35, 64, 65, 81, 137, 138, 148; and the GDR, 19; Soviet attitudes towards women, 33; Soviet brutality, 19, 21, 30; Soviet expansionism, 22, 26; Soviet historians, 64; Soviet soldiers, 5, 20–22, 31–32, 33, 64; Soviet zone of occupation, 22, 31, 34, 68; Soviet-German relations, 23, 29;
Sozialdemokratische Partei Deutschlands (SPD), 76
Sozialistische Einheitspartei Deutschlands (SED), 35, 64–66, 73, 76, 78, 81–82, 127, 139, 148
Sozialistischer Deutscher Studentenbund (SDS), 39–40, 44
Spain, 105
Spanish Civil War, 6, 60, 63–64, 66, 79
Spanish Republicanism, 63–64
SPD. *See* Sozialdemokratische Partei Deutschlands

Spree (river), 34
St. Petersburg, 32
Stacey, Jackie, 158
Stalin, Joseph, 64
Stalinism, 31, 124, 147
Stasi. *See* Ministerium für Staatssicherheit
Steinmetz, Rüdiger, 129, 146
Stern (journal), 135
von Sternberg, Josef, 116
von Sternberg, Josef, works by:
    Morocco, 116
Stone, Katherine, 5, 12, 14, 15
Stott, Rosemary, 62
Strauß, Franz-Joseph, 76–77
Studio H&S, 60–80; in the 1980s, 8, 69; aesthetic, 8, 134; Cambodia trilogy, 129; demise of, 8, 145, 148; and Khmer Rouge, 8, 145; and propaganda, 6, 73, 144; Vietnam films, 7, 60, 78–79, 131; and violence, 8, 79, 130. *See also* Heynowski, Walter, and Gerhard Scheumann
subjective factors of politics, 6, 41
subjectivity; militant subjectivity, 149, 151, 171; revolutionary subjectivity, 9, 45, 151
Süddeutsche Zeitung (newspaper), 43
Summers, David, 78
Sundvor, Pål, 111
Sundvor, Pål, works by: *Dschungel und Soldat*, 110–11
surrealism, 11, 42, 49, 54, 57
surveillance, 83, 109, 124, 126
survivors, 12, 14, 22, 25, 37, 56, 110, 125
Sweden, 83

Taiping Rebellion, 34
Taşköprü, Aysen, 189–91
Taşköprü, Süleyman, 189, 191–92
television: in the FRG, 62; in the GDR, 6, 61–62, 68–69, 79, 129, 145–46, 148; and Vietnam, 71
Teraoka, Arlene A., 1, 124, 153
terrorism, 3, 9, 10, 15, 175, 176, 180, 191, 192, 194; Global War

on Terrorism, 185, 194; international terrorism, 194; Islamist terrorism, 193; leftist terrorism, 150, 162; right-wing terrorism, 193; West German terrorism, 50, 149–73
Thai Nguyen (location in the DRV), 94
Thälmann Brigade, 60, 63
Theresienstadt, 144–45
"Third Reich," the, 11, 20, 34, 121, 124, 192
Third World, 3, 9, 13, 44, 50–51, 58, 123, 152, 154, 157–59, 162–67, 172
Thomaneck, Jürgen, 108
Thuringia, 31, 34
Tieck, Ludwig, 106
Tieck, Ludwig, works by: *Der blonde Eckbert*, 106
Tower of Nanjing, 34
transnationalism: and 1968, 40, 151; historiographical perspective, 150, 151; transnational motherhood, 95; transnational movements, 4, 39; transnational solidarity, 57; and Inge Viett, 160, 162; and violence, 4, 159; and *Viva Maria!*, 45, 57
trauma, 35, 110–11, 117, 126. *See also* post-traumatic stress disorder
Trnka, Jamie, 158, 165
Truman, Harry S., 24
Truman Doctrine, 24
Tuol Sleng, 140–41
Tupamaros, Uruguay, 159
Tupamaros West Berlin, 162
Turgut, Mehmet, 194
Turkey, 186, 190, 195
Turkish Mafia, 184, 192
Tzu-Chun Wu, Judy, 165

Ulbricht, Walter, 25
UN. *See* United Nations
Uncanny, the, 53–58
United Nations (UN), 24, 77
Unvar, Ferhat, 195
Uruguay, 159

US, 3, 5, 7, 9, 19, 24, 25, 30, 54, 66, 81, 82, 103, 119, 175, 193, 194; and Central America, 42, 45, 50, 57; US bombings of Germany, 19; US bombings of Vietnam, 75, 105; US culture and media, 8, 24, 28, 79, 111–12, 116–17; US involvement in Vietnam, 66–67, 96, 103, 105; US military, 26, 35, 75, 76–77, 91–94, 98–101, 105, 107–8; US occupation of Germany, 18, 26, 29, 30; US personnel and soldiers, 5, 21, 23–24, 27–29, 67, 98–99, 111, 134, 149; US pilots, 7, 61, 76–77; US zone of postwar Germany, 35
USSR. *See* Soviet Union
Ut, Nick, 82
Ut, Nick, works by: *Accidental Napalm Attack*, 82

Varon, Jeremy, 162
Väterliteratur (literary genre), 106
Velkov, Kaloyan, 195
Verband der Film- und Fernsehschaffenden der DDR, 145, 147
VFF. *See* Volksbund für Frieden und Freiheit
Via, Sandra, 11
victimhood, 14, 95–96, 99, 103
victims: of capitalism, 78; of CRSV, 12, 14, 32, 34, 37; of far-right violence, 9–10, 12, 174–75, 177–78, 181, 184, 186, 187, 189–92, 195; gendering of, 14, 93, 95–96, 99, 103; of the Holocaust, 124–25, 144; relationship to perpetrators, 98, 110–11, 126, 140; of trauma, 110–11, 126; of Vietnam conflict, 72, 93, 95, 96, 99, 103, 120, 139, 140, 147; within novels, 12, 14, 20, 27, 32–35, 37
Vidor, King, works by. *See* Fleming, Victor
Vietcong, 82, 112, 132, 150, 152, 158–59, 162. *See also* National Liberation Front

Vietnam: anti-Vietnam-war protest, 81, 94, 101; Democratic Republic of Vietnam (DRV), 7, 61, 65, 67, 69, 70, 72, 75–77, 81, 85, 90, 92–94, 96, 101, 103, 105, 111; National Liberation Front (NLF) in the RVN, 81 (*see also* Vietcong); North Vietnam (*see* Democratic Republic of Vietnam); Republic of Vietnam (RVN), 66, 72, 78, 81–82, 99, 100–101; South Vietnam (*see* Republic of Vietnam); Vietnam Committee of the Friedensrat der DDR, 67, 85; Vietnam conflict (*see* Vietnam War); Vietnam films, 7, 60–61, 131, 135, 140; Vietnam pilots, 112; Vietnam veterans, 7–8, 79, 104–26; Vietnam War, 7–8, 13, 60, 65–69, 71–72, 75–79, 81–83, 88, 90–95, 99–101, 103, 105, 107–9, 111, 113–14, 117–18, 122, 125, 135. *See also* Agent Orange; Operation Linebacker II; Operation Rolling Thunder

Viett, Inge, 9, 11, 14, 149–73

Viett, Inge, works by: *Nie war ich furchtloser*, 9, 149–73

violence: conflict-related sexual violence (CRSV), 3, 5, 10, 12, 14, 18–37; direct violence, 6, 11; discursive violence, 2, 16; domestic violence, 15–16; environmental violence, 16; epistemological violence, 16; extreme violence, 1, 7, 12, 62; far-right violence, 10, 174–75, 181, 195; gendered understandings of, 14; militant violence, 159; National Socialist violence, 170–72; normative violence, 2; on-screen violence, 62; patriarchal violence, 53; political violence, 3, 9, 11, 15, 39, 49, 57, 174–95; psychological violence, 16; revolutionary violence, 160; sexual violence, 5, 14–16, 18–20, 23, 27, 32–33, 36, 37; slow violence, 2, 4, 16, 157; Soviet violence, 30; state violence, 3; structural violence, 2; violence against women, 26

Virgin Mary (religious figure), 46, 5. *See also* Madonna

Viva Maria Group, West Berlin, 39, 43

Volksbund für Frieden und Freiheit (VFF), 21–22

Walken, Christopher, 112
Warhol, Robyn, 27, 30
Warsaw Pact, 65
Weather Underground, 132, 167
Wehrmacht, 20, 31, 69
Weigel, Sigrid, 152
Weill, Kurt, 119
Weill, Kurt, works by: *Aufstieg und Fall der Stadt Mahagonny*, 119
Weimar Republic, 30, 63, 83–84, 88, 170
Weltkongress der Intellektuellen zur Verteidigung des Friedens, 104
West, the: capitalist West, 133; cinematic depiction of, 36; (post-) Christian West, 95; relationship with FRG, 19; West/East divide, 3, 22, 84, 98, 133, 135, 165; Western Allies, 21; Western Europe, 22, 60, 62, 66, 69–70, 81, 135; Western military, 97–98; Western philosophy, 180; Western press, 95; Western TV, 65; Western values, 24; Western world, 157
West Berlin, 6, 23, 34–35, 39–40, 43, 48, 51, 59, 66, 77, 128, 132, 152, 162
Western (film genre), 42, 52, 57, 116
Wiesbaden, 152
women's liberation movement, 58, 156, 172. *See also* feminism; Frauenbefreiungsfront, die
World Peace Council, 104
World Trade Centre, 182
World War I, 11, 21, 114
World War II, 5, 9, 11, 13–15, 18–19, 54–55, 62, 64, 83, 105, 120, 122, 130, 178, 194
Wrocław, 104

Yalta Agreements, 26
Yangtze (river), 34
Yaşar, İsmail, 194
Yemen, 163
Yugoslavia, 9
Yugoslavian wartime resistance movement, 170

Zetkin, Clara, 155
Zinnemann, Fred, 116
Zinnemann, Fred, works by:
   High Noon, 116
Zschäpe, Beate, 190–91, 193
Zwickau, 190

www.ingramcontent.com/pod-product-compliance
Lightning Source LLC
Chambersburg PA
CBHW070802230426
43665CB00017B/2455